THE BUSINESS OF OPERA

ASHGATE INTERDISCIPLINARY STUDIES IN OPERA

The *Ashgate Interdisciplinary Studies in Opera* series provides a centralized and prominent forum for the presentation of cutting-edge scholarship that draws on numerous disciplinary approaches to a wide range of subjects associated with the creation, performance, and reception of opera (and related genres) in various historical and social contexts. There is great need for a broader approach to scholarship about opera. In recent years, the course of study has developed significantly, going beyond traditional musicological approaches to reflect new perspectives from literary criticism and comparative literature, cultural history, philosophy, art history, theatre history, gender studies, film studies, political science, philology, psycho-analysis, and medicine. The new brands of scholarship have allowed a more comprehensive interrogation of the complex nexus of means of artistic expression operative in opera, one that has meaningfully challenged prevalent historicist and formalist musical approaches. The *Ashgate Interdisciplinary Studies in Opera* series continues to move this important trend forward by including essay collections and monographs that reflect the ever-increasing interest in opera in non-musical contexts. Books in the series are linked by their emphasis on the study of a single genre—opera—yet are distinguished by their individualized and novel approaches by scholars from various disciplines/ fields of inquiry. The remit of the series welcomes studies of seventeenth century to contemporary opera from all geographical locations, including non-Western topics.

The Business of Opera

Edited by

ANASTASIA BELINA-JOHNSON
Royal College of Music, UK

and

DEREK B. SCOTT
University of Leeds, UK

Routledge
Taylor & Francis Group

LONDON AND NEW YORK

First published 2015 by Ashgate Publishing

2 Park Square, Milton Park, Abingdon, Oxfordshire OX14 4RN
52 Vanderbilt Avenue, New York, NY 10017

Routledge is an imprint of the Taylor & Francis Group, an informa business

First issued in paperback 2020

British Library Cataloguing in Publication Data
A catalogue record for this book is available from the British Library

The Library of Congress has cataloged the printed edition as follows:
The business of opera / edited by Anastasia Belina-Johnson and Derek B. Scott.
    pages cm. – (Ashgate interdisciplinary studies in opera)
 Includes bibliographical references and index.
 ISBN 978-1-4724-2945-2 (hardcover : alk. paper)
1. Opera—Economic aspects. I. Belina-Johnson,
Anastasia. II. Scott, Derek B.
 ML1700.B98 2015
 792.5–dc23

2015014777

ISBN 978-1-4724-2945-2 (hbk)
ISBN 978-0-367-59712-2 (pbk)

Contents

List of Figures

List of Tables and Music Examples

Tables

Music Examples

Notes on Contributors

Paul Alan Barker is a composer of 15 operas and various other stage works that have been televised, recorded, and performed at major international festivals and venues. He has also written many orchestral, chamber, and choral works, the book *Composing for Voice* (2004), and works as a stage director. He is currently Professor of Music Theatre and course leader of MA Music Theatre at the Central School of Speech and Drama.

Anastasia Belina-Johnson is a music historian, writer, and opera director. She is Deputy Head of Programmes at the Royal College of Music, and a Senior Research Fellow at the School of Music, University of Leeds, where she is working on a European Research Council-funded project *German Operetta in London and New York in 1907–37: Cultural Transfer and Transformation* with Derek Scott. Her research interests include Russian and British opera, nineteenth-century opera, Wagner, and Greek and Roman myth in Russian opera. Recent publications include *A Musician Divided: André Tchaikowsky in His Own Words* (2013), *Die tägliche Mühe ein Mensch zu sein* (2013), and *Wagner in Russia, Poland and the Czech Lands: Musical, Literary, and Cultural Perspectives* (2013, co-edited edition). She has appeared in a documentary about André Tchaikowsky *Rebel of the Keys* (entertaining: tv), and several radio programmes on BBC Radio 3. Her current research examines performances and reception of Silver Age operetta in Poland.

Cordelia Chenault is currently an advanced PhD candidate in musicology at Stony Brook University in New York. Since 2009 she has lived in Frankfurt am Main, Germany, where she has directly observed and worked first hand with members of the Frankfurt Opera in order to prepare her dissertation, 'Behind a Flourishing Avant-Garde: A Recent History of Opera Production in Germany', a project which provides a backstage view of that company as it discusses a handful of the most noteworthy productions brought to stage at that house during the last quarter-century. In addition to her work in musicology, she is also a classical soprano who has worked for over a decade as an opera and concert singer in the United States; she holds both a Bachelor of Music degree in Voice and a Masters of Arts degree in Opera Performance from the University of North Carolina at Chapel Hill and the New England Conservatory of Music, respectively.

Jennifer Daniel is an AHRC Collaborative Doctoral Award holder, working between the School of Performance and Cultural Industries and the School of Music at Leeds University, and also at Opera North. She teaches in both

The Business of Opera

departments and spent the previous 10 years teaching and managing music in secondary education. Her PhD thesis examines the role of Opera North and how this role is communicated to the public via the work of the company.

Christine Fischer, musicologist, earned her PhD at University of Berne with a thesis on the compositions of Maria Antonia Walpurgis, Electress of Saxony, after having completed her studies in Munich and Los Angeles. Since 2007 she holds an assistant professorship of the Swiss National Science Foundation at Schola Cantorum Basiliensis, Hochschule für Alte Musik, Musik Akademie Basel. She leads an interdisciplinary team in a research project dealing with performance practice of Italian opera at German courts. As part of her research she is responsible for the scientific conception and dramaturgy of the opera performances at Schola Cantorum Basiliensis.

Jason E. Geistweidt is a sonic artist working in the fields of interactivity and live performance. He is currently a post-doctoral researcher with the VERDIONE Project in Tromsø, Norway, developing a distributed staging system for the presentation of interactive theatre, dance, and music across high-bandwidth networks. In 2006 he was awarded a Camargo Fellowship to develop an improvisatory sonic environment for solo performer and game pad. His recent works include *Cubes 2009*, an interactive sound installation (with Gary Kupczak and Laura Thompson), and, in May 2010, *Algorhythm*, an interactive score for dancers of the Columbia College Dance Center.

Liisamaija Hautsalo is a musicologist who was awarded her PhD at the University of Helsinki in 2008 for a thesis on the first opera of Kaija Saariaho (b. 1952). Since then she has been working at the Sibelius Academy on several projects. Her own research project in 2011–14, 'Articulation of Identity in Finnish Opera', was funded by the Academy of Finland. Currently, she works as a Senior Researcher at the University of Turku on the project 'Finnish Music in the 21st Century: The Socio-Cultural Significance of Art Music in the Postmodern World'. Besides contemporary opera analysis and expertise in musical semantics, she has recently published articles on the connections between the early Finnish-language opera and Fennomania, the Finnish nationalist movement.

George Kennaway is Director of Music and Performance Coordinator at the University of Hull, and visiting research fellow at the Universities of Leeds and Huddersfield. He is a cellist, conductor, and musicologist specializing in historical performance and in the music of the Baltic States. Born in Edinburgh, he studied at the universities of Newcastle and Oxford, the Salzburg Mozarteum, the Guildhall School of Music, and the University of Leeds. From 1980 until 2008 he was principal cello no. 2 in the Orchestra of Opera North. He has conducted orchestras in Russia, Kazakhstan, Uzbekistan, Italy, and Lithuania. In 2008 he took up a post-doctoral research post at Leeds working on nineteenth-century editions of string music. Recent publications include *Playing The Cello 1780–1930* (2014), and articles on nineteenth-century editions of Haydn cello concertos, aspects of octatonic composition, and the discourse of musical performance. However, his most read article compares IKEA flat-pack assembly instructions, recipes for fish pie, and nineteenth-century annotated musical scores. He is the leading UK specialist in the work of the Lithuanian composer-artist M. K. Čiurlionis, and is a regular visitor to Lithuania. He currently performs as a soloist and chamber music player on period and modern instruments, and conducts the Harrogate Philharmonic, the Sheffield Chamber orchestra, the Pennine Sinfonia, and the University of Hull Symphony Orchestra.

Niels Windfeld Lund was the first employee and full professor in Documentation Studies at the Department of Documentation Studies, University of Tromsø, Norway, in 1996. In 2001 Professor Lund founded The Document Academy, an international network for documentation studies organizing annual DOCAM (The Document Academy) conferences in North America and summer schools in Norway at the University of Tromsø. In 2006 Professor Lund initiated the World Opera Project, aiming to create a worldwide-distributed opera stage with performers in multiple locations making one coherent opera performance all together for audiences in the multiple sites. It has resulted in a large research grant from the Norwegian Research council for the VERDIONE (Virtually Enhanced Real-life synchronizeD Interaction – ON the Edge) project in collaboration with Norwegian partners in Oslo and Tromsø as well as in North America.

Christopher Newell has 25 years of experience of directing opera. As an assistant director he assisted Trevor Nunn at Glyndebourne and Sir Peter Hall at Glyndebourne; he has also worked at The Royal Opera House Covent Garden, The National Theatre, and in the West End, where he taught Dustin Hoffman Shakespearian verse speaking. In 1986 he set up the Modern Music Theatre Troupe with Paul Barker, specializing in the performance of new music theatre. The company produced over 20 world premieres. He has a PhD in Computer Science from the University of York with a thesis entitled 'Place, Authenticity, and Time: A Framework for Liveness in Synthetic Speech'. In 2012 he will collaborate with Professor Roger Moore (The Speech and Hearing Group University of Sheffield) on an Interdisciplinary book entitled 'Computers as Voice Actors'. Most recently he directed The Magic Flute for Co-Opera Co combining it with a research project into 'The Tingle Factor: What Makes a Winning Voice?' This was subsequently featured in the *Guardian* newspaper.

Nicholas Payne is the Director of Opera Europa, the leading organization for professional opera companies throughout Europe. He has worked for four different UK opera companies over 27 consecutive years: as Financial Controller of Welsh National Opera, General Administrator of Opera North, Director of the Royal Opera Covent Garden, and General Director of English National Opera.

Derek B. Scott is Professor of Critical Musicology at the University of Leeds. He researches into music, culture, and ideology, and is the author of *The Singing Bourgeois: Songs of the Victorian Drawing Room and Parlour* (1989, R/2001), *From the Erotic to the Demonic: On Critical Musicology* (2003), *Sounds of the Metropolis: The 19th-Century Popular Music Revolution in London, New York, Paris, and Vienna* (2008), and *Musical Style and Social Meaning* (2010). He is the editor of *Music, Culture, and Society: A Reader* (2000), *The Ashgate Research Companion to Popular Musicology* (2009), and *Bawdy Songbooks of the Romantic Period*, vol. 4 (2011). He was a founder member of the UK Critical Musicology Group in 1993, and at the forefront in identifying changes of critical perspective in the sociocultural study of music. He is the General Editor of Ashgate's Popular and Folk Music Series. His musical compositions range from music theatre to symphonies for brass band and a concerto for highland bagpipe. He has also worked professionally as a singer and pianist in radio, TV, concert hall, and theatre.

Sarah Zalfen works in the research group 'Felt Communities: Emotions in European Music Life' at the Max Planck Institute for Human Development, Berlin. In 2010, she gained a PhD with a thesis on the crises of opera and the role of the state at the end of the twentieth century. Besides her academic career, Sarah has been working as a freelance manager of several opera productions. She was a fellow of the Deutsche Bank 'Opera Today' academy, and is currently a Master of Executive Arts Management student at the University of Zurich. She worked for the New York Foundation for the Arts in New York City and as personal assistant and adviser for cultural policy to Mr Michael Roth, member of the German Bundestag.

Series Editor's Preface

Ashgate Interdisciplinary Studies in Opera provides a centralized and prominent forum for the presentation of cutting-edge scholarship that draws on numerous disciplinary approaches on a wide range of subjects associated with the creation, performance, dissemination, and reception of opera and related genres in various historical and social contexts. The series includes topics from the seventeenth century to the present and from all geographical locations, including non-Western traditions.

In recent years, the field of opera studies has not only come into its own but has developed significantly, going beyond traditional musicological approaches to reflect new perspectives from literary criticism and comparative literature, cultural history, philosophy, art history, theatre history, gender studies, film studies, political science, philology, psycho-analysis, and even medicine. The new brands of scholarship have allowed a more comprehensive and intensive interrogation of the complex nexus of means of artistic expression operative in opera, one that has meaningfully challenged prevalent historicist and formalist musical approaches. Today, interdisciplinary, or as some prefer cross-disciplinary, opera studies are receiving increasingly widespread attention, and the ways in which scholars, practitioners, and the public think about the artform known as opera continue to change and expand. *Ashgate Interdisciplinary Studies in Opera* seeks to move this important trend forward by including essay collections and monographs that reflect the ever-increasing interest in opera in non-musical contexts.

In *The Business of Opera*, Anastasia Belina-Johnson and Derek Scott have brought together essays that address the state of the opera world today in its commercial aspects – marketing and promotion, audience building, administration, and economic issues. Through case studies, the editors outline challenges that opera faces in the twenty-first century in an increasingly unstable financial environment. Authored by both academics and practitioners (directors, producers, singers, conductors, composers), the ten essays deal with a variety of topics related to opera today. Taking different critical perspectives, they are aimed at a broad readership and accessible to an interdisciplinary readership. One of the first attempts to treat opera as a business (rather than as an art form), this collection promises to become a seminal work in this field.

Roberta Montemorra Marvin

Introduction

Anastasia Belina-Johnson and Derek B. Scott

The study of the business of opera has taken on new importance in the current harsh economic climate for the arts. The purpose of this book is to present research that sheds new light on a range of different aspects concerning marketing, audience development, promotion, arts administration, and the economic issues that beset opera professionals. The aim of the editors has been to put together a collection of essays that forms a coherent whole by engaging with a single theme (business), although these essays differ in their particular choice of topic and critical perspective. The original impetus was a conference held at the University of Leeds, an institution that has, over the past few years, enjoyed a close relationship with Opera North, the largest English opera company outside of London. The University's School of Music and Opera North worked together to organize a novel kind of international opera conference in April 2012 in order to debate key themes in the theory, practice, and business of opera that would relate specifically to the twenty-first century. It included a stimulating mixture of academics and opera professionals – including directors, producers, performers, composers, and music directors. The conference consisted of papers, practice-based research, multimedia presentations, and workshops. The event lasted just three days, but it was always hoped that that the outcomes would have a long-lasting effect. One of these outcomes is the present book, although its content does not draw exclusively on presentations given at that conference. It is designed to be accessible to a wide readership, to appeal to anyone with an interest in leisure studies and business management, as well as to those studying music and arts administration. The editors hope it will also prove interesting to professionals and practitioners involved with opera, its management, its promotion, and its production.

The emphasis is on opera *today*. Opera was, of course, big business in the eighteenth and nineteenth centuries. If the actual day-to-day workings of that business have been somewhat neglected, there has been no shortage of scholarship on the careers of celebrated singers and on opera composers and their music. The world's best-known opera houses have also received scholarly attention. When it comes to the business of opera, the available literature begins to shrink. Philippe Agid and Jean-Claude Tarndeau's *The Management of Opera*[1] examines how opera companies in Europe and North America strive to make their work relevant and

---

[1] Philippe Agid and Jean-Claude Tarondeau, *The Management of Opera: An International Comparative Study* (Basingstoke, 2010).

commercially viable. The authors seek to answer such questions as programming, creativity, producing new operas and/or preserving historical repertoire, and funding. One of the questions raised in the book is whether opera houses deserve both private and public funding, when only 2 or 3 per cent of the population on those continents regularly attend operatic productions. Using the statistics collected during 2005–06 and 2006–06 from 80 opera houses in Europe and North America, the authors present a thorough comparative analysis, the first of its kind in this field of study.

Prior to the publication of Agid and Tarondeau's book, studies of the business of opera have almost always concentrated on a particular historic period: the seventeenth century, for example, in Beth and Jonathan Glixon's *Inventing the Business of Opera*, or the nineteenth century, in William Crosten's *French Grand Opera*.[2] Elizabeth Silsbury's *State of Opera* does have a contemporary focus, but it is a study restricted to the business of one company, the State Opera of South Australia.[3] There are a few books that overlap at times with the content of the essays in the present volume, but their emphasis tends to fall primarily on cultural policy: for example, Ruth Bereson's *The Operatic State: Cultural Policy and the Opera House*, and David Ranan's *In Search of a Magic Flute*.[4] There is, indeed, a chapter on the economics of opera in the USA included in Rosanne Martorella's *The Sociology of Opera*;[5] but, on the whole, as its title indicates, her book is oriented towards questions of social organization rather than business matters. Significantly, the final chapter on the structure of the market amounts to no more than six pages, two of which are taken up with a call for further research to be done. Martorella's book appeared more than thirty years ago, but her call has gone largely unheeded. The business of opera is rarely the focus in academic historical studies of the social and cultural context of opera production. This is not to claim that business aspects of opera are completely ignored but, rather, that they form part of contextualization only, as, for example, in Anselm Gerhard's *Die Verstädterung der Oper: Paris und das Musiktheater des 19. Jahrhunderts*.[6]

---

[2]   Beth Glixon and Jonathan Glixon, *Inventing the Business of Opera: The Impresario and His World in Seventeenth-Century Venice* (New York, 2006); William Loran Crosten, *French Grand Opera: An Art and a Business* (New York, 1972). To these could be added: Katherine K. Preston, *Opera on the Road: Traveling Opera Troupes in the United States, 1825–60* (Urbana-Champaign, 1993); Ian Woodfield, *Opera and Drama in Eighteenth-Century London: The King's Theatre, Garrick and the Business of Performance* (Cambridge, 2004); and John Rosselli, *The Opera Industry in Italy from Cimarosa to Verdi: The Role of the Impresario* (Cambridge, 1984).

[3]   Elizabeth Silsbury, *State of Opera: An Intimate New History of the State Opera of South Australia 1957–2000* (Adelaide, 2001).

[4]   Ruth Bereson, *The Operatic State: Cultural Policy and the Opera House* (London, 2002); David Ranan, *In Search of a Magic Flute: The Public Funding of Opera* (Bern, 2003).

[5]   Rosanne Martorella, *The Sociology of Opera* (South Hadley, MA, 1982).

[6]   Gerhard Anselm, *Die Verstädterung der Oper: Paris und das Musiktheater des 19. Jahrhunderts* (Stuttgart, 1992). English translation by Mary Whittall as *The Urbanization of Opera* (Chicago, 1998).

Several books explore opera in different countries (Italy especially) and contain historical information about the business of opera. The multidisciplinary study *Opera Production and Its Resources*, edited by Lorenzo Bianconi and Giorgio Pestelli, is an exception; certainly, its investigation is confined to the Italian operatic tradition, but it includes several chapters in its second volume that are dedicated to an examination of opera production in the twentieth century.[7] Academic studies of the business side of opera have, in fact, been moving closer and closer to the present day. At one time it seemed as if only the activities of entrepreneurs, such as Alfred Bunn in early nineteenth-century London, were of interest. It is significant that at a recent British music conference in Cardiff Paul Rodmell chose to focus on the activities of Augustus Harris, who may be said to have saved opera at Covent Garden from collapse in the 1890s.[8] In achieving this success, Harris was not so much guided by knowledge of music, but by business principles and tactics (for example, working to 'choke off' competition). Rodmell presented a persuasive argument to show that Harris, rather than being a moulder of taste, was driven by his ambition to make money.

A significant change in the business of opera, compared to a hundred years ago, has been the decline of touring companies. In the early twentieth century, more than sixty touring companies existed in the UK. The British National Opera Company (1921–29), which was the first opera company in the UK to receive public funding, thrived primarily as a touring company (despite short seasons in London).[9] In contrast, Britain's oldest opera company, Carl Rosa Opera, lost its Arts Council funding and almost disappeared in the 1960s, although it managed to revive itself in 1997. It is based in Shoreditch, London, touring the UK during spring and autumn, and also undertaking international tours, specializing in lighter forms of opera.[10] Another company, English Touring Opera also has a spring and autumn season, and advertises itself with the punning motto 'opera that *moves*'.[11] In addition, Opera North and Welsh National Opera tour their productions. Together, they serve eight English and Welsh cities, bringing to them world-class opera performances. Owing to limited funding, however, even these relatively short tours are under threat, as David Pountney pointed out in November 2014.[12]

---

[7]   Lorenzo Bianconi and Giorgio Pestelli (eds), *Opera Production and Its Resources*. The History of Italian Opera, Part II: Systems, trans. Lydia G. Cochrane (Chicago, 1998).

[8]   Paul Rodmell, 'Augustus Harris: Opera's Saviour or Saboteur?' Paper given at the Ninth Biennial Conference on Music in Nineteenth-Century Britain, Cardiff University School of Music, 25 June 2013.

[9]   Steven Martin suggested that it was awarded public funding because of its relationship with the BBC; the British National Opera Company's first live broadcast was as early as 1923. Presentation at the Royal Musical Association Study Day 'Wandering Minstrels: The History of Travelling Opera in Britain', Royal Academy of Music, London, 26 October 2013.

[10]   <www.carlrosaopera.co.uk>.

[11]   http://englishtouringopera.org.uk/productions (accessed 8 June 2015).

[12]   David Pountney's response to Kate Molleson's article for *The Guardian* about English National Opera's cancellation of *Orfeo* in collaboration with Bristol Old Vic, 14 November 2014, <www.wno.org.uk/news/response-david-pountney> (accessed 8 June 2015).

Birmingham Opera Company promotes itself as 'not what you would expect from opera', and its website declares that it is 'bringing local people into the life and work of the company'.[13] The artistic director Graham Vick created an opera company that has no home base in a theatre, uses unconventional spaces for its performances, and engages local audiences not only in the process of watching, but in taking part in productions. A variety of promotional strategies range from open days and calls to action, to 'Opera while you shop!' when two singers involved in the 2014 production *Khovanskygate* performed at Springhill Tesco Superstore. Huge efforts are made by the company to show that opera does not have to be elitist or elite, and that it can be enjoyed by all audiences, not only those who have been educated to understand it. Vick's contribution to the opera business received further recognition when he was made Visiting Chair in Opera Studies at Oxford University for 2014–15. He launched his post with an appropriately titled lecture 'Opera and the Socially Responsible Artist' on 14 November 2014.

Nicholas Payne, long-serving Director of Opera Europa, offers a wide-ranging international survey of the current business of opera in the first chapter of this book. In this Introduction, therefore, the editors have chosen to consider briefly some aspects of the business of opera from the perspective they know best, that of the UK. Much of what is happening here, however, is common to other countries that are looking to the creative industries to boost a national economy that has experienced a decline in heavy industry. A policy knowledge briefing in London on 20 May 2014, organized by Government Knowledge, a group specializing in the provision of public policy conferences, had the future of the creative economies as its theme. The pre-briefing invitation declared:

> The creative industries grew by almost 10% in 2012 and are now worth £71.4 billion to the UK economy. In 2012 they accounted for 1.68 million (5.6%) of jobs in the UK. They employ over 1.5m people and account for £1 in every £10 of UK exports. It is estimated that creative industries will grow further contributing 6.8% of GDP next year.[14]

This offers a rare glimpse of fiscal optimism after the collapse of world markets in October 2008. Among the topics considered important for strengthening the role of the creative industries in boosting the UK economy were the provision of specialist training to businesses, and the equipping of students with skills for the next generation of creative industries. In addition, and perhaps unsurprisingly, there was a desire to see tax cuts and investment in order to ensure easier operation.

---

[13]   <www.birminghamopera.org.uk>.

[14]   The reader needs to be aware that no sources were given that might help to verify the accuracy of these statistics. This briefing invitation was sent out via email on 3 February 2014.

A month after this briefing, Westminster Media Forum organized a seminar in Whitehall specifically on the UK performing arts sector.[15] It was presided over, for most of the day, by Gerald Kaufman, chair of the All-Party Parliamentary Dance Group and All-Party Parliamentary Opera Group, and included presentations from a dozen people professionally involved in the theatre business, including a speaker from English National Opera (ENO). The key topics were public and private funding (and the need for stronger relationships between subsidized and commercial organizations), and digital strategy for 'live screening, marketing, and diversifying audiences'. The threat facing the performing arts in the UK in an austere economic climate is of further cuts in public funding and the damaging impact these may have on talent, creativity, research and development, and risk taking. At the time of writing, it is not yet clear what effect the theatre relief tax – planned for later in 2014 – will have, and where the benefits will be felt most. There is also the prospect of changes in the proportionality of funding in order to support the performing arts outside of London.

The subsidized sector is now seeking to learn from the commercial sector how to alleviate the effects of cuts. Some performing arts organizations are linking to higher education institutions for collaborative ventures, new creative work, and strengthening of local networking. Opera North's formal partnership with the University of Leeds has resulted in joint projects being developed and delivered since 2006. They have ranged from international opera research projects to local outreach activities, performances of new artistic work, and opportunities for both job experience and scholarly learning that have been to the benefit of each partner. If a community values its opera company, then there is a strong possibility that private donations can be increased. The money available from trusts and foundations appears to be diminishing, and most companies are concentrating on strategies for attracting sponsorship from businesses and wealthy individuals. However, the problem for company managers is to find a sustainable model for business funding. The hot topic right now is how far digital technology can help to develop more efficient business practices. Digital marketing is demonstrating that it can play an effective role in audience development strategy, but at present its beneficial effects are most evident in the case of large opera companies.

The Opera Audience

Developing and diversifying the opera audience have become of particular concern in the UK, because the British media is inclined to portray opera as an expensive entertainment for the upper classes and snobbish intellectuals, funded by excessive demands on the ordinary taxpayer. Politicians add to these criticisms. Harriet Harman, in her former role as the Culture Secretary for the Labour Party,

---

[15] 'Supporting the UK performing arts sector – talent, funding, partnerships and marketing'. 61 Whitehall, London, 5 June 2014.

criticized the Royal Opera House (ROH) for having an audience that is 'white, metropolitan and middle class', and announced that, if Labour were to come to power, subsidy would be tied to 'public' support.

> Public funding is only sustainable to the extent that the public supports it. So the public have got to see what they are getting out of it.[16]

The ROH received subsidy of £25 million in 2013 (the largest amount given to any arts organization), and opera as a whole accounts for 11 per cent of Arts Council England's total budget.[17]

In September 2014, an academic conference 'Beyond Black Tie and Bubbly: Rescuing Opera from Stereotypes' was held at Oxford Brookes University's OBERTO research unit, examining critically the idea that opera is a socially exclusive and intellectually forbidding genre. That idea arises from many sources, which include the opera buff whose specialized knowledge, the organizers say, 'excludes or positively repels the uninitiated'.[18] The opera buff, here, may sound a little like the opera academic. The conference website describes the poor image of opera in the British media, and suggests that the UK may have a particular opera problem with complex historical roots:

> The media, in an online economy, are hungry for hits and comments and happily fan the flames of controversy; and the accessibility agenda in the arts creates an environment where, in the UK in particular, opera companies have to demonstrate their openness and their efforts to reach out to new audiences of 'ordinary people'. Concerns about the squandering of public funds are never far from the surface of the debate.[19]

A concern about excessive demands on the taxpayer easily translates into demands for cuts in subsidy. The conference investigated the historic roots of operatic 'elitism', interrogated the negative perception of elite achievement in an operatic context, and compared attitudes in continental Europe. Questions of accessibility and outreach were also addressed, and opera's audiences were given a reassessment.[20] Accessibility is a matter of concern in the cultural policy of other

---

16   Quoted in Patrick Wintour, 'State-backed arts must reach out to public – Harman', *The Guardian*, 6 June 2014, p. 5.

17   Charlotte Higgins, 'Arts Council considers opera shakeup', *The Guardian*, 16 January 2013 <www.theguardian.com/music/2013/jan/16/arts-council-opera-eno-loss> (accessed 8 June 2015).

18   'Beyond Black Tie and Bubbly: Rescuing Opera from Stereotypes'. OBERTO Conference <http://obertobrookes.com/conference-2014> (no longer available).

19   Ibid.

20   A conference report can be found here: <http://obertobrookes.com/2014/09/23/oberto-2014-beyond-black-tie-and-bubbly-rescuing-opera-from-stereotypes> (accessed 8 June 2015).

countries, but as Sarah Zalfen reveals in Chapter 3, the 'primacy of accessibility' developed most strongly in the UK's opera policy.

Michael Volpe, who grew up in disadvantageous social conditions on a London estate, runs Opera Holland Park, established in 1996 as a non-state company committed to the idea of opera for all. He gave a talk at the OBERTO conference entitled 'Reassessing audiences and the "not for us debate"'.[21] It is this egalitarian belief in the appeal of opera that underpins the summer festival in Holland Park (London). Volpe comments:

> [A]t Opera Holland Park we will continue to present our work for its own sake, to hope we can encourage the banker, the builder, the nurse and everybody in between to try something purely because it will enrich them emotionally. A season that features Puccini, Bellini and Rossini is in the very least suffused with gorgeous music, but the drama, the extraordinary human feats that emerge on stage before our eyes, in real time – well, those are things that, so heartbreakingly, many have yet to usher into their lives. These are often the same people who cry watching *EastEnders* or blub like babes at videos of Chelsea winning the Champions League.[22]

This raises the question of repertoire. Does opera, for Holland Park, mean canonic nineteenth-century Italian operas? No, because some rarities have been performed there, such as Italo Montemezzi's *L'amore dei tre re* (1913).[23] In 2013, a 'family opera' was commissioned (Will Todd's *Alice in Wonderland*), Britten's *The Turn of the Screw* features in the 2014 season, and Jonathan Dove's *Flight* and Cilea's *Adriana Lecouvreur* have been announced in the 2015 season. Nevertheless, there is a sense in which opera is a heritage genre rather than a living contemporary art form at this festival.

Making operetta and musical theatre a regular part of a company's repertoire, as has happened, for example, at Opera North and ENO, is another means by which audience diversification may be achieved. Indeed, a blurring of distinctions between stage genres may be thought to help in attracting new audiences. Opera North's poster for a production of *La Bohème* in April 2014 contained this advice: 'If you only see one musical this year, make it this opera.' Impresario Cameron Macintosh, speaking about his revival of the Alain Boublil and Claude-Michel Schönberg musical *Miss Saigon* in May 2014, identifies a change in audiences since this musical's hugely successful run in the 1990s:

---

[21]   Volpe's paper can be read at <http://volpeversion.blogspot.co.uk/2014/09/oberto-conference-paper.html> (accessed 8 June 2015).

[22]   Michael Volpe, 'Why opera really isn't just for toffs', *The Sunday Times*, *Culture* supplement, 1 June 2014, pp. 6–7 (p. 7).

[23]   Rather than a 'discovery' of a neglected work, this was a revival of an opera whose international popularity waned in the 1940s.

> The big thing that's changed is that the audience coming to shows is young. [...]
> I've found that 60% of the people coming to see *Les Mis[érables]* on Broadway
> are under 30. It's a complete culture switch.[24]

There is no evidence yet to show that there has been any such change in the audience for opera, but it does seem likely that an opera company that puts on the occasional operetta or musical may find this helps to draw in a younger audience.

There is always, however, the possibility that moves towards a musical theatre ethos may backfire. The opera critic of *The Sunday Times*, Hugh Canning, castigates ENO's *Così fan tutte* (May 2014) as a 'downmarket, end-of-the-pier production', describing the staging as 'an insult to the core opera audience that is deserting the ENO in droves', and he wonders if it is 'a foretaste of ENO's promised foray into West End popular theatre'.[25] It is not absolutely clear how he would define the 'core opera audience'. English National Opera, for a start, caters to an audience that wishes to hear opera sung in English, so it is unlikely to be identical to the opera audience found at the ROH. There is also an implication in his review that ENO is betraying its audience, whereas it may be considering a return, in part, to the repertoire seen at its theatre the London Coliseum in the 1930s, when the operetta *White Horse Inn* played to a full house night after night. The Coliseum is London's largest theatre, and its seating capacity of 2,358 is rarely filled. There are pressing reasons for ENO to consider changes to repertoire. Its Arts Council grant was cut by £1.3 million in 2011–12, and at the beginning of 2013 the company posted a loss of almost £2.2 million.[26] In July 2014, as this book was being prepared for the press, *The Guardian* reported that ENO was to have its support from the public purse reduced by £5 million a year, meaning that its annual funding for 2015–18 drops from £17 million to £12 million, a cut of 29 per cent.[27] This is almost certainly the consequence of failing to achieve box office targets. The Arts Council had wanted ENO to reduce numbers of performances, but the company developed an alternative strategy that relied on an increase in productions of musical theatre, and income from its bars and cafés.

When considering the distinction between musicals and opera, it is easy to forget that it is not just about ticket prices and classifications of genre. Theatres, especially those in the West End or on Broadway tend to present just one musical

[24]   David Jays, 'Will it be unmissable?' *The Sunday Times: Culture*, 11 May 2014, pp. 6–7.

[25]   Hugh Canning, 'It's not all roses', *The Sunday Times: Culture*, 25 May 2014, pp. 22–3 (p. 23). The next month, Canning attacked ENO's production of Berlioz's *Benvenuto Cellini* on similar grounds: 'This is opera as West End show – the translation is by Charles Hart, Andrew Lloyd Webber's *Phantom* lyricist – and it looks a frantic, overpopulated mess'. 'Opera as West End show', *The Sunday Times: Culture*, 15 June 2014, p. 30.

[26]   Higgins, 'Arts Council considers opera shakeup'.

[27]   Mark Brown and Mark Tran, 'ENO forced to tighten the reins while 58 groups lose all funding from Arts Council', *The Guardian*, 2 July 2014, p. 11.

at a time. They change to another once audience figures decline, and revivals of older musicals are not often successful. An opera house announces a new season in which three or four different operas may feature, and the performance of existing work easily outnumbers new work. Operetta is now caught between the two systems, partly, no doubt, because it is nowadays regarded as something of an historic form. One theatre may be offering a single operetta night after night, and another (for instance the Volksoper in Vienna) will have an operetta season with new productions of several different operettas being performed on different nights.

The only near equivalent to the night-after-night performances of a single work found in the West End theatres producing musicals is found in the opera promotions of Raymond Gubbay (who also promotes 'classical spectacular' concerts). His opera 'in the round' at the Royal Albert Hall has been especially successful, and his presentation of *Madam Butterfly*, staged in an 'enchanting Japanese water garden', returns for 20 consecutive performances in February 2015.[28] Not everyone is attracted to Gubbay's blockbuster productions and amplified sound, but these are not the only examples of such an approach – the annual 'Opera on the Lake' at the Bregenz Festival in Austria has a similar ethos.

Digital Media and Marketing

Opera companies use a remarkable diversity of means for publicizing themselves and bringing their wares to the attention of the public. Recent developments in marketing have concentrated on an increased use of social media, such as Facebook and Twitter, to keep in touch, distribute news, and make announcements. Opera North asks people to look, additionally, at Pinterest, tumblr, Instagram, YouTube, and its own blog for updates and insights about its productions via photos, videos, audio, articles, and more. YouTube is a useful site for uploading trailers, and it is increasingly common for an opera company to have its own YouTube channel to which people can subscribe. Email also provides an effective means of promoting forthcoming attractions to existing customers, and the communication may include special offers. Opera companies, like other businesses, are careful to maintain records of those who have contacted them online. There is often an attempt to soften the commercial character of this relationship with friendly greetings: the ROH, for instance, sends Christmas e-cards. There is a section of ROH's website where the audience's reactions to productions, posted on Twitter, are collected and organised alphabetically. In this way, the company not only has a useful way of evaluating reception of each production, but ROH's audience and patrons have a handy collection of reviews all in one place. Audience reaction can now be viewed instantly—a tweet can be sent as soon as the performance is over (and, in many cases, during it). This was the case with a recent production of *Guillaume Tell*

---

[28] <www.raymondgubbay.co.uk/whatson/madam-butterfly-2015> (accessed 8 June 2015). It was first seen in 1998, and the designer was David Freeman.

(June 2015), when the viewers' comments started pouring in after a scene that proved to be rather divisive.[29]

In 1988, the ROH began a partnership with BP (formerly, the British Petroleum Company), which had been privatized by the Thatcher government following the previous year's stock market crash and was now busy establishing itself as a major multinational oil and gas company from its headquarters in London. At first, BP sponsored outreach activities by the ROH (especially in schools), but a dozen years later the first BP Big Screen broadcast was seen in Covent Garden. By 2013, the ROH was broadcasting to 22 Big Screens situated in large public spaces from Aberdeen to Plymouth. They declared it their most successful ever, with over 45,000 people watching live opera and ballet.[30] This success was also good for BP, after a series of industrial accidents had damaged the company's public image in the 2000s. Interaction through social media has become a regular part of the annual screenings, and there are now competitions, live Twitter feeds, and massed sing-alongs. People are also invited to 'tweet' their thoughts at #BPbigscreens. To celebrate the 25th anniversary of the venture in 2014, the ROH streamed the first BP Big Screen of 2014 (*La traviata* on 20 May) completely free on the Internet. This was the first occasion on which the ROH had offered 'a complete opera in real time for free through its website'.[31] The Vienna State Opera announced that in 2014–15 it would be streaming three live performances worldwide for the first time in ultra-HD quality to people's homes, tablets, smartphones, and computers, but these are not available free of charge. Admittedly, the price asked for was low, €14 for each stream, and special offers were available.[32]

The ROH has tried to give its summer screenings a festival atmosphere: 'Come early to get a good spot and relax into the festival feel'.[33] Music festivals have been doing well in attracting attendance over the past few years and, in 2014, summer festivals of opera in the UK appeared to join the trend. *The Guardian* newspaper listed six of them in its festival booklet: Buxton Festival, Dorset Opera Festival, Garsington Opera (Buckinghamshire), Glyndebourne Festival (East Sussex), Grange Park Opera (Hampshire), and Opera Holland Park (London).[34] The ROH also has a Live Cinema Season during which operas are broadcast live to cinemas

[29] 'Your Reaction: *Guillaume Tell*' http://www.roh.org.uk/news/your-reaction-william-tell (accessed 14 July 2015).

[30] 'BP Big Screens 2014', email sent to customers registered with the ROH, 15 May 2014. The screens in 2013 were showing Puccini's *La rondine* and *Tosca*, and MacMillan's ballet *Mayerling*.

[31] 'BP Big Screens 2014', <www.roh.org.uk/about/bp-big-screens> (accessed 10 September 2014). See audiences review at <www.roh.org.uk/news/your-reaction-la-traviata-on-bp-big-screens> (accessed 8 June 2015).

[32] <www.staatsoperlive.com/en/live/?page=1> (accessed 8 June 2015).

[33] 'The sun is shining for the BP Big Screens!' Email message sent to registered customers by the ROH, 10 July 2013.

[34] *Festivals 2014: The Essential Companion to Your Musical Summer*, guide issued by *The Guardian*, 31 May 2014.

across the UK. In 2013–14, the opera house presented simulcasts in 500 American theatres for the first time, beginning with *Turandot* on 24 October 2013, and including seven other operas by mid-May 2014.[35] The ROH announced that its Live Cinema Season 2014–15 would include seven operas and four ballets and be screened live in more than 1,000 cinemas in more than 30 countries across the world.[36]

The history of HD opera broadcasts began with the New York Metropolitan Opera's screening of Mozart's *The Magic Flute* on 30 December 2006, and they were conceived as a supplement to their in-house performances. Very quickly, however, the broadcasts proved to be so successful that it has been predicted that they may become the main feature of the Met's activities, with the traditional performances taking second place.[37] In August 2014, it was reported that *The Met: Live in HD* broadcasts of 10 operas during 2013–14 had been seen in over 2,000 theatres in 66 countries (more than 800 of these theatres were in the USA).[38] This venture generated a total income of $60 million, and if, as is believed, theatre owners were required to surrender half of their box office takings to the Met, then the Met made a profit of around $30 dollars. As this Introduction was being written, the 2014–15 broadcasts were been threatened by a disputed between the Met management and 12 of its 16 labour unions, but the first of 10 transmissions was eventually advertised for December 2014 (delayed from October). Barrie Kosky, the inspirational intendant of Komische Oper in Berlin, is more cautious about broadcasts: he believes that they are purely marketing tools. He warns about overreliance on this medium in an interview with Tom Service:

> Cinemas and live streaming aren't the future of opera. They're just marketing tools. The future of opera is not getting people 12,000 miles away to see Anna Netrebko. That's the death of opera.[39]

This is in line with Kosky's operatic credo:

> In opera, people are experiencing – on an incredibly unconscious level – a return to an archaic form of storytelling ritual that we need. That's why it will survive.

---

[35]   <www.screenvision.com/cinema-events/roh> (accessed 10 September 2014). The Royal Opera House Cinema Season 2013–14 was presented in select US movie theatres by Screenvision.

[36]   <www.roh.org.uk/news/royal-opera-house-live-cinema-season-201415> (accessed 8 June 2015) and <www.roh.org.uk/cinemas> (accessed 8 June 2015).

[37]   This was argued persuasively by Jarlath Jennings in his paper 'Can Technology Help Keep Opera Alive and Relevant to 21st Century Audiences?, delivered at the conference *The Theory, Practice, and Business of Opera Today*, Leeds, 12 April 2012.

[38]   Pamela McClintock, 'Met Opera Standoff Threatens $60 Million Theater Business', *The Hollywood Reporter*, 15 August 2014, <www.hollywoodreporter.com/news/met-opera-standoff-threatens-60-723614> (accessed 8 June 2015).

[39]   Tom Service, 'Barrie Kosky: "When I first saw The Magic Flute, I didn't get it and I didn't like it"', *The Guardian*, 13 July 2015. <http://www.theguardian.com/music/2015/jul/13/barrie-kosky-the-magic-flute-i-was-like-euggh> (accessed 4 August 2015).

It is a special thing and it's a live experience: the human voice coming out of the human body that you can only hear in this space at this time.[40]

To date there has not been a great deal of analysis available to reveal the cultural impact of the use of digital media by opera companies. The Centre for Research in Opera and Music Theatre at the University of Sussex, however, announced in June 2014 that it was soon to be undertaking a new research project with Glyndebourne Opera to examine the effect that 'live cinecasts' have had on the way audiences now engage with opera. The project would also consider how new digital, web-based and mobile media platforms might shape the future forms of opera.[41]

It is tempting to assume that all opera companies are addicted to digital marketing, but that is not the case. Michael Volpe's strategy for achieving his 'opera for all' objective is to make tickets available free of charge for young people, and offer other tickets that can be purchased for £15, a price lower than that for most West End musicals. In contrast to those who believe the big-screen broadcast in the public square is one of the best means of attracting more people to opera, he praises the 'visceral, three-dimensional experience of a live performance',[42] which, he argues, is the best means of countering the perception of opera as an alien world for a privileged social class. Volpe is not a fan of digitization:

In the basket of tools the opera world uses to address the problem [of diversifying the audience] are cheap tickets, cinema broadcasts, big-screen picnics, controversial Twitter campaigns, 'sexy' productions, pop composers *et al.* It is brilliant stuff, risible guff, usually well meant and costly, too.[43]

Opera Holland Park, however, could not survive on profits from ticket sales alone, and needs to rely on corporate sponsorship, aid from the Royal Borough of Kensington and Chelsea (the company's actual owner – Volpe is its General Manager), a substantial number of private donors, and a large Friends organization.

All opera companies need to supplement the funding they acquire through ticket sales, but this does not mean that efforts to sell tickets are neglected. Every company is aware of the necessity of advertising its new productions and trying to attract a large audience. One strategy is to start with the people who have already bought tickets in the past. In June 2013, for instance, ENO emailed its registered customers, sending them press reviews of Glass's *The Perfect American* that praised the opera itself, the 'spectacular' staging, the 'virtuosity' of the designs, the 'inventiveness' of the choreography, the 'superb' cast, and the 'impeccable'

[40]   Ibid.
[41]   Centre for Research in Opera and Music Theatre (CROMT) <www.sussex.ac.uk/cromt/index> (accessed 8 June 2015).
[42]   Volpe, 'Why opera really isn't just for toffs', p. 6.
[43]   Ibid., p. 7.

conducting.[44] It was also possible to click on a video trailer and to view production images. A comment about the opera from whatsonstage.com was given prominence because of its relevance to the debate about public subsidy and opera's narrow social appeal: 'it's likely to fulfil one of ENO's major aims: to bring in a new audience for opera'. Sometimes, attempts to reach out to a broader public are evident in descriptive language that suggests the realm of popular culture rather than that of high art. English National Opera's email message about a production of *Così fan tutte* in May 2014 summed up the opera as follows: 'Mozart's sublime score unfolds to tell a story of love, lust and desire, played out in a world in which the boundaries between what is real and what is make-believe are blurred.'[45]

A final example of the efforts made by opera companies to engage with a broader public is the online broadcast called *Inside Opera: Live*, which was streamed live on YouTube, 10 May 2014.[46] This was the result of a collaboration between ENO, English Touring Opera, Northern Ireland Opera, Opera North, the ROH, Scottish Opera, and Welsh National Opera, and was designed to offer insight into the way opera is created and performed, including backstage action and costume making. People were able to put questions to the companies' artistic directors live via Twitter.

The Scope and Remit of this Book

This book's chapters bring the study of opera up to the twenty-first century, and are distinguished by their concern with the business of opera here and now in a globalized market. That means newly commissioned opera, sponsorship, state funding for opera, and the production and marketing of historic opera in the twenty-first century. Most of the chapters deal with a particular aspect of the business of opera, or with current issues facing those involved in opera in diverse capacities: composers, directors, opera orchestral musicians, and so forth. The chapters incline towards the presentation of individual case studies rather than broad surveys. They are, however, intended to shed light on the difficulties as well as the opportunities that opera practitioners and administrators face in the twenty-first century.

The collection begins with a broad perspective on the business of opera from Nicholas Payne, Director of Opera Europa, who picks up on important shifts in strategy and practice that have taken place in recent years. The important factors that have contributed to the internationalization of opera are, in his opinion,

---

[44]   'The Perfect American', ENO email message, 4 June 2013.

[45]   'See Mozart's stunning *Così fan tutte* this summer at ENO', email message, 9 May 2014.

[46]   The page youtube.com/insideopera is no longer available, but directors' messages can be read on *The Guardian* website <www.theguardian.com/music/2014/may/09/inside-opera-live-why-opera-matters-uk-opera-chiefs> (accessed 8 June 2015).

the redoubling of repertoire, the decline in resident company ensembles and of performances in the original language, the growth of co-productions, a united Europe, the increasing economic strength of Asia, and the transforming effect of digital technology. He goes on to discuss ticket sales, private contributions, and commercial potential as the primary income sources for opera companies. He also touches on labour agreements, a subject that is explored in a specific case study in George Kennaway's later chapter. For Nicholas Payne, a thriving future for opera must, of necessity, be built upon efficient productivity, flexible arrangements, and partnerships across borders. Only in this way will opera companies develop sustainable business models that allow them to balance the needs of creative artists and the demands of contemporary opera audiences.

In the next chapter, Christine Fischer writes on the boom in contemporary productions of Baroque opera, offering insightful observations that help us to understand why there is so often an apparent contradiction between the historic and modern in these productions. To select a recent example, we may consider what happened at Glyndebourne in July 2013. After years of neglecting the leading composer of the French Baroque, Jean-Philippe Rameau, the company decided it would put on his opera *Hippolyte et Aricie*. Immediately there arose the problem identified by Fischer of deciding what is an appropriate balance between the work's historical character and the need to translate its historic intentions in a form that is accessible to today's audience. The allegorical character of the original, written for the Bourbon court, was related to a need to flatter the Sun King, although, at the same time, it contained a moral message for his adulterous great-grandson. Jonathan Kent and Paul Brown, in charge of the Glyndebourne production, move the allegory in a different direction. For example, the debate between the goddess Diana and Cupid about chastity takes place in a giant fridge. Linking chastity to frigidity in this way remains symbolic, but in a way that Glyndebourne's audience can conceptualize readily. In line with Fischer's observation that modern visual impressions often exist alongside a historically informed performance of the actual music, it may be assumed that the experienced conductor of Baroque repertoire William Christie would ensure that there were no reinterpretations of French musical practices (such as turning *notes inégales* into jazz swing).

Sarah Zalfen follows on from this with a study of the recent history of operatic business practices, and analyses what happened following the golden era of state sponsorship of opera in the middle decades of the twentieth century. In that century it seemed that all the major opera houses of Europe had become national or state institutions. The business of opera therefore became a matter for cultural policy and public administration. State dominance has now been eroded, and Zalfen argues that decision-making and power over funding has been relocated from the national to the international level and from the public to the private sector. This she examines with comparative analyses of the operatic environments in Berlin, London and Paris at the end of the twentieth century, showing how these processes have been experienced as crises in each of these cities. These crises include rising costs alongside stagnation or cuts in public subsidy, the decline of opera as a symbol of national prestige, and the questioning by some critics of what they see as opera's artistic elitism in a pluralist and democratic society. Yet, Zalfen, whose varied career has ranged from freelance manager of operatic productions, to fellowship of the Deutsche Bank Opera Today academy and adviser in the formulation of German cultural policy, holds to the argument that the state remains an important agent in the case of opera, even competition is now found from an increasing number of new players and stakeholders, interests, tastes, and values.

The contemporary focus of this book allows the various authors to cover new or largely untrodden ground, such as the linking of the practice of opera to the business decisions that relate to or inform that practice. In Paul Barker's chapter, for example, we have a professional composer writing about how the business of opera affects the composition of music for the stage, its performance and reception, today. He argues that innovative work is largely under-funded and under-resourced, but that does not mean there is an absence of individuals, groups, and organizations that are prepared to take risks. In the next chapter, opera director Christopher Newell explains some of the strategies that may be employed to ensure that the chances of obtaining funding for opera are increased. Funding bodies now place more emphasis than ever on social impact; therefore, Newell argues, consideration needs to be given to what is *generally* beneficial about an opera project, rather than specifically culturally beneficial. In his own work he has been able to link opera to agendas in scientific research, health, new media, pedagogy, and much else.

These two chapters in which aspects of the business of opera have been examined from the perspectives of a composer and a director are succeeded by an account of the ambitious World Opera Project, initiated in 2006 by Niels Lund in Tromsø, Norway. The aim was to create a worldwide multimedia stage for opera that could accommodate performers in multiple locations and create a coherent opera performance for a multi-situated audience. Lund joined up with the sonic artist Jason Geistweidt, who has been aiding in the development of a distributed staging system for the presentation of interactive theatre, dance, and music across high-bandwidth networks. Lund and Gestweidt detail their findings over the course of the project, and assess the problems (political as well as technical and artistic) in creating a global stage. High-speed networks demand a new culture of collaboration, which their chapter attempts to define.

George Kennaway's chapter moves away from grand visions of new operatic practices and returns us to the nitty-gritty of operatic business dealings in an account of the contractual obligations of those playing in opera orchestras. He writes from the perspective of long experience as a professional orchestral musician, and outlines contractual issues that relate to the size and working practices of orchestras, the status of players, and travel arrangements.

In the first of two chapters that focus on Wagner productions, Cordelia Chenault investigates the needs of creative artists and decisions that are made 'behind the scenes' in the context of *Regieoper*. The German term, which translates innocuously as 'director's opera', is much associated with innovative interpretations of operatic texts that startle and shock audiences. Audience reaction can be very mixed, and booing mingled with loud cheering is not uncommonly heard in Austrian and German opera houses. Chenault reveals, however, that directors do not have anything like complete control over productions, and that many practical and business realities play a direct role in shaping a production. Among these are resourcing issues, unexpected budget cuts, performers' health problems, inter-organizational politics, and logistical constraints.

The role of education in building an audience for opera is examined in Jennifer Daniel's ethnographic study of the preparations for Opera North's performances of the music dramas that make up Wagner's *Der Ring des Nibelungen*. She shows how the company envisaged the need for an 'audience development' strategy that differed from the concept the term holds for marketing departments, and she explains how various artistic and educational activities were arranged in order to provide a context that would enable the performances to be enjoyed by those to whom Wagner's epic work was unfamiliar.

No book on the contemporary business of opera could ignore Finland, a country where opera, and new opera no less, has been thriving for many years. In the final chapter, Liisamaija Hautsalo relates the present enormous success of opera in Finland to the historical conditions in which it developed, in particular the support it enjoyed from important Finnish cultural institutions. She also relates its cultural status to the ideology of Fennoman nationalism, which strongly supported the establishment of a national opera company. This company was funded through the national lottery during the 1920s to 1950s. In 1956, it became state funded. The most striking development, however, occurred in the 1990s, when new opera performances began to be given around the country and in astonishing numbers. Each year brought to the stage nearly a dozen new operas by Finnish composers (in 2011 the number was 22). These performances are organized by a diversity of social groups (often acting without state funding), including private sponsors, volunteer helpers, festival companies and foundations.

The contributors to this book engage with the business of opera from an international as well as a local perspective. The authors are themselves an international mixture of professionals and academics who between them represent seven countries (Austria, Finland, Germany, Norway, Switzerland, the UK, and the USA). A book of this size could never hope to cover adequately what is happening in each and every country that has an operatic tradition, and it will seem a disappointing lacuna to some readers that contemporary opera in Italy is missing. In mitigation, the editors would remind the reader that Italy has been well served in the volume edited by Bianconi and Pestelli mentioned earlier in this Introduction. Whatever gaps may be identified in the present collection, it is the editors' conviction that the range of topics covered are sufficient to help provide readers with an informed understanding of the business of opera as it exists here and now, as well as the potential it holds for future development.

Chapter 1
Trends and Innovations in Opera

Nicholas Payne

The (very) English playwright and composer Noël Coward, author of the charming if retrogressive operetta *Bitter Sweet*, held an ambivalent, even bitter-sweet, attitude towards the genre. In response to the criticism that 'the trouble with opera is that it is not what it used to be', he delivered this verdict: 'People are wrong when they say that opera is not what it used to be. It is what it used to be. That is what is wrong with it.'[1]

On the surface, many aspects of opera appear not to have changed. It is performed in grand and historic theatres. The spectacle is often one of extravagant display. It carries a weight of tradition and heritage. Top ticket prices are perceived to be inaccessible to ordinary people. The repertory is dominated by the same old operas.

Under the surface, though, there have been many shifts. Some are structural; others are aesthetic, or presentational. Let us examine the principal ones.

Repertory

When I was introduced to opera nearly sixty years ago, the standard repertory covered less than two hundred years, from Gluck's *Orfeo* of 1762 to the (then) new operas of Britten and Henze. Today, it encompasses more than four hundred years, from Monteverdi's *Orfeo* of 1607 to Birtwistle's, still classically derived, *Minotaur*. The breadth of this much richer heritage is demonstrated by a recent edition of Opera Europa's Future Production Plans database, in which a cross-section of 84 companies lists 730 productions of 377 operas by 211 composers.[2] The downside of this gain is that it can leave less space for new creations, which may be marginalized by the sheer bulk of opera's magnificent legacy. The tenor Jonas Kaufmann, in a radio interview in 2014, confessed to a conviction that 'we are the preservers of an art form whose peak was in the past'.[3] That same Opera Europa database included 73 new operas in its total, representing a not unhealthy share of 10 per cent of the productions and 20 per cent of the opera titles. Yet, that proportion falls well short of the 50:50 balance between old and new to which Nicholas Hytner has aspired as Director of the UK's National Theatre.[4]

---

[1] Noël Coward, *Design for Living*, Act 3, Scene 1 (1933).

[2] Opera Europa Future New Productions 2014–19 (November 2014).

[3] Jonas Kaufmann, interviewed by Tom Service for BBC Radio 3's *Music Matters*, 31 May 2014.

[4] Nicholas Hytner, address to Opera Europa conference in London, 5 March 2011.

Repertoire and *Stagione*

The repertoire pattern of performances, whereby a substantial body of operas may be presented in rotation by a strong resident ensemble, remains the prevailing method employed by the great opera houses of Germany and central Europe. It is by far the most productive system when operated at capacity, as in cities like Dresden, Hamburg, Munich, Prague, and Vienna. But across Europe, repertoire is in retreat. The Italian *stagione* system, already the norm in most of France and Spain, is gaining ground; or variations of it, sometimes categorized as 'semi-*stagione*', are being adopted elsewhere as traditional ensemble companies are being dismantled.[5] The erosion of this precious training ground for opera practitioners is compensated, to some extent, by the potential for improved standards deriving from carefully rehearsed productions with locked-in casts. The emphasis is moving away from developing a company for the long term and towards the more ephemeral achievement of a festival or an 'event'.

Vernacular and Original Language

During much of the nineteenth and first part of the twentieth century, composers expected their operas to be presented in the audience's own language, as with a play. The growing practice of performance in the original language was given an enormous boost by the introduction of surtitles, first in 1983 at the Canadian Opera Company in Toronto, but rapidly spreading worldwide. These titles are the electronic equivalent of the printed libretti made available in the lighted auditoria of the eighteenth and early nineteenth centuries. They are credited with instilling a more concentrated attention in our now darkened auditoria and as an effective educative tool. At the same time, they have contributed to the loss of direct communication between singer and audience in a shared language, which used to underpin the theatrical experience of opera and which may still be cherished at the few remaining companies which regularly use the vernacular, such as English National Opera at the London Coliseum, Berlin's Komische Oper, Munich's Staatstheater am Gärtnerplatz, and the Volksoper in Vienna.

Co-Productions

When most opera companies possessed their own production facilities, sharing sets and costumes was rarely desirable or necessary. Jointly owned or borrowed productions began as a device to maintain or increase the number of new productions

---

[5] *Stagione* (literally 'season') refers to the practice of casting each production separately and performing it for a limited series of performances, whereas a repertory system relies on a permanent ensemble and productions that rotate over extended periods of time.

in a season, but they have become standard industry practice as an increasingly sophisticated means to share both costs and ideas. It is no coincidence that their growth has coincided with a downsizing of many theatres' production workshops and the outsourcing of production-making to independent providers. The loss of these crafts within the opera house weakens self-sufficiency, and the process can cause difficulties between physically or aesthetically incompatible theatres. On the other hand, co-productions have proved an effective way to disseminate the work of important creative artists to a wider and more geographically diverse audience. The composer, and Director of the Aix-en-Provence Festival, Bernard Foccroulle advocates the practice thus: 'It is important that the best new pieces or productions are experienced more widely. The best must be shared. It is not a question of money, but of art. It is not a problem of identity.'[6]

A United Europe

'The Fall of the Berlin Wall' in November 1989 was a symbol of the removal of a much more extensive 'Iron Curtain' which divided Europe into the eastern communist and the more affluent western blocs. The 'triumph of capitalism' has created its own economic problems, not only for the former eastern bloc nations, but it has integrated Poland, the Czech and Slovak Republics, Hungary, the Baltic states, and a growing number of Balkan countries within the Common Market of the European Union (EU). In practice, this open market for labour extends beyond the EU to include Russia and its remaining satellite states. The balance of trade is uneven, and some of the economies remain frail and over-dependent on foreign investment, but the process is irreversible. Germany's success in absorbing the massive economic burden of reunification speaks of its reserves of strength, which is also testified by the survival of the world's most extensive and productive network of opera houses. But the spectacular growth of opera in countries with far less operatic tradition, as distant as Norway and Spain, and the ever more harmonious collaboration evident among the increasing number of Opera Europa members, all show that, for opera at least, the Common Market thrives as a force for development.

Globalization

More than 1,000 singers were auditioned worldwide, from whom 40 were selected for the final rounds of the 2009 edition of the NEUE STIMMEN competition at Gütersloh in northern Germany. None of the seven finalists came from 'old Europe'. The first three prizes were all awarded to Koreans. Here was rather chastening evidence that we live today in a global market and that, as in many other areas, the talent, training, and industry coming out of Asia are contributing

---

[6]   Bernard Foccroulle, Opera Europa conference in Venice, 23 May 2014.

to Europe's future, even in traditional strongholds. The German network is part sustained by the influx of foreign labour; but, where once it was the training ground for well-schooled Americans, it is now the destination of choice for aspiring Asians, especially from South Korea. It initially surprised me when the New National Theatre Tokyo applied to join Opera Europa, later followed by companies from Beijing and Seoul, still more recently by grand new opera houses in Muscat, Oman, and Astana, Kazakhstan; but they all exhibit a hunger for the European model and have proved willing partners in learning and trading. Opera may have been born in Europe, but Europe no longer holds a monopoly in supplying or consuming it.

Technology

Asked to define opera, I would once have described it as a musical and dramatic performance which an audience may experience live and unamplified in a theatre. No longer! Contemporary composers have embraced technology, so that music is written using computer programs and sound enhancement has become common practice in opera houses. Whereas radio broadcasts and the gramophone were adjuncts which enabled live music to be replicated in the home, today cinema screenings are increasingly popular as a means to convey performances by leading artists to distant audiences. The New York Metropolitan Opera already reaches more people in a season with its energetically promoted cinema relays than it does in its large 3,900-capacity auditorium on Lincoln Plaza. With practice, the filming has become more sophisticated and intrusive in conveying a vivid impression of the theatrical experience. Some believe that, in a few years, it will have supplanted the on-site version as the primary offer of the Met.[7]

* * *

All these factors have contributed towards the internationalization of opera. It has been an accelerating trend since 1990, though its origins go back further than that. With hindsight, one might generalize that the first twenty years after the Second World War saw the democratization of the pre-war model, a process enabled first by application of public subsidy from social democratic inclining states, and second by the invention and wide distribution of the long-playing record. During the mid-1960s to mid-1980s, the leading theatres worldwide adopted an international outlook serviced by an elite cadre of top artists, while the domestic level remained wedded to national characteristics. Since the late 1990s, the majority of companies have, to a greater or lesser extent, been affected by the seven principal factors described above. The impact of technology is the most recent development, but its effect on delivery of the core product is spreading rapidly to include online

---

[7]   See the discussion of the Met's HD opera broadcasts in the Introduction to this book.

streaming of performances via an increasing number of outlets, exemplified by the launch of the Opera Europa Digital Platform in 2015.

The changes to opera over the turn of the millennium are not an isolated phenomenon. Similar trends may be noted in pop music, in film, and in painting and the plastic arts. Each has to jostle for the public's attention in an increasingly crowded global market place. If opera wishes to compete, it is inevitable that it will find it harder to be self-contained and reliant on the old values and structures. So, in order to address these changes, managers have had to rethink and adapt their business models, or to adopt new ones. It is a tribute to their ingenuity, or to the enduring appetite for the art form, to discover how well most institutions have survived. Given the high incidence of bankruptcies and takeovers in the commercial world, there have been remarkably few terminal business failures in the operatic world. Hardly any important opera houses have closed in Europe, except for renovation. Magnificent new theatres have been built during the twenty-first century in Copenhagen, Oslo, Tenerife, and Valencia, while others have been expensively restored. Beyond Europe, China leads the way with grand new arts palaces, but the Middle East follows. The highest-profile casualty in the United States has been New York City Opera, but the loss of that 'people's opera' institution has been compensated by the growth of small artist-led groups, almost forty of which now make up the New York Opera Alliance.

For most of the second half of the twentieth century, the top brands would have been recognized as the New York Metropolitan, La Scala Milan, London's Covent Garden, the Paris Opera, and Vienna State Opera. The opening up of Russia has enabled Moscow's Bolshoi and Saint Petersburg's Mariinsky Theatres to establish their premium brands in the international market; and several of the leading German-speaking theatres enjoy worldwide recognition. This eminence is a valuable commodity, because of the growing number of theatres that are now competing to secure the top artists.

Needless to say, solvency is not simply the outcome of virtuous financial practice. The solidity of state support in the traditionally strong artistic economies of Germany and France, Austria and Switzerland, has underpinned their broad national provision. In the less-traditional operatic countries, such as the United Kingdom and Spain, a plural funding model which strikes a balance of public and private support has proved a surprisingly effective compromise between 'old European' and New World ways, though the post-2008 international debt crisis has threatened to derail this delicate equation. Declining funding from the national budget has threatened the status of Italian opera and eroded the productivity of its leading theatres, but even that crisis is beginning to provoke new models. Italy has imposed a *Valore cultura* law (*Legge 112*), which compels 8 out of 14 of its leading lyric institutions to undergo a stabilization programme of reform between 2014 and 2017, the results of which remain uncertain. Likewise, the economic upheavals of the post-communist countries have created instability in Eastern Europe, but are also enforcing fresh thinking and different solutions in capital cities such as Warsaw and Prague. If implemented successfully, they will inform changes to smaller and regional theatres.

Income

Opera has never broken even or made a profit. The question is who picks up the deficit; and the answer tells you where the balance of power lies. In an age when public subventions are static or in decline, the emphasis must fall on other sources of revenue. They are listed below in descending order of importance.

1. Ticket sales are the barometer of public interest. While their importance as a factor in total revenue varies considerably, they remain the single most powerful indicator of approval. A half-empty theatre spells audience indifference, which damages not only the revenue stream but also the confidence of funding bodies. A sold-out house is the best advertisement, because success breeds success. In festivals such as Bregenz, Glyndebourne, and Savonlinna, ticket sales are the primary source of income; but, even for those companies less dependent on sales, the box office percentage is a key economic indicator. Opera is learning from other sectors, such as the travel industry, how to optimize earned income through forms of 'dynamic pricing'.[8] The aim of what is known as 'revenue management' is 'to ensure that companies will sell the right product to the right customer at the right time at the right price'.[9]

2. Private contributions in Europe are unlikely to assume the dominant position they hold in the United States. Whereas an American may individually choose where a proportion of his or her taxes will be spent, thanks to a system of tax incentives which rewards philanthropy, the European still delegates most of that power, and therefore that responsibility, to the state. Yet, there are stirrings of a counter-movement, bred by a disillusion with bureaucracy and, in worse cases, with corruption. Although centralized finance ministries will continue to resist offering tax breaks, they are on the increase. In France, private contributions to the arts increased dramatically after a relaxation of the tax laws. But, whereas such contributions were once primarily made by the corporate sector, the trend is towards an increasing reliance on individual donors.

3. State underwriting of opera is a relatively recent phenomenon. Opera began as a plaything of princes, before becoming an entrepreneurial venture. Handel was a businessman as well as a composer. Today, opera houses are once again exploring the commercial potential of their buildings and of their product. Managements seek to supplement revenue from their core business of presenting opera by exploiting the asset of a large public building with a premium value. The Royal Opera House treats its catering as

---

[8] Dynamic pricing is a flexible approach to setting ticket prices that allows the costs to be adjusted quickly in response to market demands, as practised by airlines, for example.

[9] Tim Baker of Baker Richards Consulting, Opera Europa conference in Venice, 23 May 2014.

a 'cost centre', whose successful operation feeds profits into the production of opera and ballet. Their example will be copied by other theatres with prime city-centre locations and hiring potential. Opera companies are also alert to using modern reproductive technology to making their primary products available through secondary rights in other media, such as cinema, television, and commercial recordings. In most cases, their promotional value is greater than their profitability. Only the Met derives a significant income stream from such initiatives, and its success has naturally generated increased demands from the unions representing the talent being exploited. Conversely, the growth of cinema audiences for the Met's live relays has coincided with a decline in their theatre audiences, resulting in a budget crisis which in 2014 led its General Manager Peter Gelb to counter-propose significant salary reductions. Nonetheless, the Met's success in establishing its global brand is being emulated by others who believe they have brands that may attract followers and perhaps create opportunities to contribute in the mixed economy of opera today.

Opera has remained backward in joining the public/private partnership world. In many parts of Europe, the reliance on state support is still paramount and the philosophy of the state's provision of worthwhile services for its citizens – in culture, alongside education, healthcare and public transport – remains intact. Elsewhere, that consensus is being challenged. Fraser Nelson, editor of *The Spectator*, writing in *The Telegraph* and ostensibly reflecting government 'think-tank' opinion, argued that the reduction of the UK culture budget by a third was a positive move which would lead to more self-sufficient and therefore superior artistic enterprises. Refuting the assertion of Nicholas Serota, Director of Tate museums, that 'this *blitzkrieg* was the greatest crisis in arts and heritage since government funding began', Nelson asserted:

> Today culture in Britain is flourishing more than ever. Again, this is no mystery: the creative life of this country has never depended on a Whitehall bureaucracy. Sir Nicholas's howls of protest sound ridiculous when set against the ingenious ways in which our galleries, theatres and museums have attracted both crowds and sponsors. Society has stepped in where the state stepped back.[10]

English 'country house opera', exemplified by Glyndebourne and its growing army of imitators, is not the only example of this formula or mind-set. At the other end of Europe, Belgrade's Madlenianum Opera and Theatre in Serbia is entirely privately financed, and Saint Petersburg's Mikhailovsky Theatre has been revitalized by private money. There will be more such enterprises across Europe.

---

[10] Fraser Nelson, 'Our tantric Chancellor doesn't realise he's winning the debate', *The Telegraph*, 28 June 2013.

In the comparable worlds of spoken theatre and modern art, there is a more even balance between subsidy and commerce. Not only do they coexist, but they feed off each other. The commercial sector benefits from the longer-term investment of the subsidized sector, while the latter has learned to adopt an increasingly commercial attitude to programming and marketing, in order to thrive in the market conditions. The two leading theatres in England, the National Theatre and the Royal Shakespeare Company, have been notably successful in the commercial exploitation of some of their productions, from the profits of which they cross-subsidize their more experimental work. The need for entrepreneurial skills has influenced the appointment of senior and other managerial positions. These lessons will gradually be applied to opera, too.

Expenditure

As the proportions are adjusted in the mixture of revenue sources, so they will be in the division of expenditure.

Traditionally, opera is very labour intensive, because of its requirements for large forces of singers, orchestral musicians, and technical and administrative back-up. The full-time salary bill can absorb as much as three-quarters of the total budget. That sort of establishment level may be justified, if it delivers a substantial body of work, but the danger is that it may grow ever greater over time until the maintenance of the permanent staff becomes an end in itself. It becomes necessary to ask what services are provided for those salaries, and whether the time-honoured services are what are now required to produce the work. Do labour agreements provide the flexibility to rehearse and perform as today's creative artists and today's mobile audience demand? Do they encompass the secondary rights necessary to disseminate work through other media? How may they be reformed in ways that protect social rights and expectations, while at the same time fitting today's patterns of work?

The answers will vary according to the different practices and priorities of the wide range of institutions in the many countries that make up Europe. It continues to make sense for the leading German-speaking theatres to employ a large ensemble of artists and production staff, so long as they continue to deliver a comprehensive programme of hundreds of performances a year. But, if productivity falls, as a consequence either of reduced funding or of declining demand, establishment levels will be questioned. Progressive cutbacks in output by theatres throughout Europe have undermined the case for permanent contracts. In each case, it will be necessary to strike a balance in the productivity equation, if a long-term future is to be secured. Some companies carry within themselves the capacity for evolution and self-renewal; others may require a more radical revolution, even destruction, if opera is to be born again in their community.

The growing numbers of freelance and guest performers are governed by the law of the market place. At the top end, a relatively few 'world-famous' artists command high fees commensurate with their power to draw in audiences. At the bottom end, there are many who are paid no more than subsistence rates and whose labour may be exploited because of their determination to find opportunities to perform. In between these extremes lie the majority of performers, whose livelihood is sustained by the fragile operatic economy, dependent as it is on public and private contributions. If survival is threatened, the level of recompense, and what it covers, is likely to be questioned. In practice, that has already happened with some Italian theatres paying late and others requesting voluntary reductions of contracted fees. David Pountney, Artistic Director and Chief Executive of Welsh National Opera, has challenged the assembled International Artist Managers' Association with comparisons between singers' and actors' remuneration, asking whether the fee levels for top singers, conductors, and directors are in any way justifiable to voting taxpayers.[11]

The perception of extravagance is a two-edged sword. On one side, it underpins Dr Johnson's definition of opera as 'an exotic and irrational entertainment', an indulgence for rich people. On the other, its very lavishness serves as an attraction to the public. From Roman games through opera to modern musicals or blockbuster movies, a big budget is seen as proof of ambition. The illusion of extravagance is an enticement to public appreciation. For sure, canny production managers seek to find cost savings by using synthetic materials or projected video in place of solid scenery, but sophisticated technology also comes at a price. Managers operating a tight budget increasingly look to outsource non-core services. At first, that applied to catering or cleaning or security, and then spread to financial and some administrative or promotional services. Devolving the making of productions to outside workshops and providers makes it possible to bargain with competing tenders. It adds to the options for controlling costs, while distancing the control of the quality of the product. This erosion of 'in-house' identity represents a loss of traditional values, but it may also help a company to focus on the core values which it is best equipped to deliver. Either way, it is a trend which it will be hard to reverse.

Business Models

Once upon a time, the budgeting process of an opera company began with adding up projected expenditure. The crucial computation was the volume of full-time salaried staff and the levels of their pay including extra payments for overtime and social costs. On top of this total, which might represent between half and three-quarters of all costs, was added the overheads of the buildings owned or inhabited by the company and any ancillary administrative overheads required to sustain the organization. The aggregate of the above was the 'fixed costs' or 'above the line costs'. 'Below the line' were the 'variable costs', which comprised

---

[11]   David Pountney, address to IAMA Opera and Media Day, London, 9 April 2014.

expenditure on productions and performances and, where incurred, touring the product. The income side of the budget was essentially an estimate of what might be expected from ticket sales and any other commercial activities, designated 'earned income', balanced by what had been promised or might reasonably be forecast for 'contributed income' from public and/or private sources. The aim was to 'break even'.

While old habits die hard, the trend today is towards approaching the budgeting exercise from the opposite direction. First, calculate how much may safely be expected from your sources of income; then, decide how you may most effectively spend that income. It will be clear from the outset that this approach places greater emphasis on those areas which generate revenue, such as marketing and fundraising. The ideal for a General Director (GD) or Chief Executive (CEO) moderating the process is to convene a senior management team which can represent a balance between spending and income-generating departments. The complexity of the organization will govern the size of the management structure, but it is reckoned that the optimum number of the senior team is seven. On the spending side, there is likely to be a Music Director or representative of the musical forces such as the orchestra; an Artistic Administrator or Head of Planning responsible for devising the schedule and engaging artists; and a Technical or Production Director who manages those who make and handle the physical aspects of opera production. On the income side, the team might comprise a Marketing and Communications Director responsible for sales; an executive in charge of those raising contributed income; and a Finance or Business Director with a brief to control the budget. The GD/CEO's job is to choose and motivate the team, and ensure that it pursues a common goal in realizing the aims of the opera company. Europe is not America, but it would do well to heed the words of Frayda Lindemann, Vice-President of the New York Metropolitan Opera's Board: 'everyone in an opera company works in development'.[12]

The seven-person management team is not a blueprint. Some prefer a smaller group of, say, five. Other theatres, which incorporate ballet or drama as well as opera, may require more. But the key factor in such a business model is that it starts not by repeating past practice with an allowance for inflation, but from the premise that financial and human resources are to be gathered with the purpose of delivering a programme to an audience.

New Models

While many of the great historical opera houses have successfully managed the transition into the twenty-first century, there has at the same time been a movement towards smaller, more flexible models. Some artists prefer not to be

---

[12]   Interviewed by Marc Scorca, CEO of Opera America, at Opera Europa's conference in Venice 24 May 2014.

bound by permanent contracts. Some managers seek to minimize overheads, and to concentrate resources towards employing freelance workers specific to each project.

In the United Kingdom during 2008–09, the six major operatic institutions supplied 849 performances. During the same period, a further 78 smaller organizations were recorded as presenting around one thousand performances of opera and music theatre, admittedly to smaller audiences. The work of Dutch National Opera at its large Muziektheater in Amsterdam has been supplemented by that of two dedicated companies, Nationale Reisopera based in Enschede and Opera Zuid based in Maastricht, which tour their productions within Holland, and by several smaller-scale troupes. Even Germany, with its rich infrastructure of 84 theatre-based opera companies, is experiencing a growth in alternative and experimental opera projects.

Most of the smaller independent opera groups are artist-led. They reflect the need of composers and conductors, singers and production teams, to express themselves outside the constraints of the big institutions. Many are financially precarious, but light-footed enough to survive economic downturns and, if necessary, to hibernate until warmer conditions return. Crucially, they are moulded to the needs of the creative forces, and can respond to new developments in the art more readily than the larger companies with their obligations to maintain an established staff and the imperative to pursue challenging targets for ticket sales. Viktor Schoner, Artistic Administrator of one of Europe's biggest beasts, the Bayerische Staatsoper in Munich, has issued a refreshingly self-questioning challenge: 'What is opera for? What's our goal? Rather than defend institutions, let us focus on key words: creation, originality, invention.'[13]

It would be wrong to conclude that the flexible smaller-scale models are set to supplant the traditional opera houses. The public continues to seek out the spectacular experience which grand opera can provide. Governments and powerful philanthropists are employing imaginative architects to design imposing buildings for the twenty-first century. Rather, both trends, the small and the great, are part of an increasingly rich operatic ecology. It is significant that the new Oslo Opera House, opened in 2008, was built with a large measure of popular support, has rapidly become Norway's No. 1 tourist attraction, and sees part of its mission as reaching out towards the whole population of its geographically dispersed country which harbours up to 25 smaller, and in some cases tiny, opera groups.

Partnerships

Every artistic institution values its independence. One of Opera Europa's defining beliefs is that each member opera company is unique and autonomous. Yet, the association's purpose is to strengthen opera companies throughout Europe by

---

[13] Viktor Schoner, Opera Europa conference in Venice, 23 May 2014.

means of mutual support and collective action. The watchword is collaboration. After more than a decade as its director, I would judge the dominant impulse to be towards creating working partnerships. Divided, Europe will fall; together, it may thrive. My admiration and sympathy are great for those theatres like the Badisches Staatstheater Karlsruhe or Tiroler Landestheater in Innsbruck or Nationaltheater Mannheim, which maintain strong ensembles and production facilities, capable of staging Berlioz's epic *Les Troyens* or Wagner's *Ring* tetralogy, while eschewing co-productions and private sponsorship. It is a valid model with its own integrity. But the trend is away from such self-sufficiency.

Partnerships may take several forms. The initial purpose behind sharing productions was, in many instances, the desire to save money. It resulted in some uneasy alliances between theatres with very different technical facilities and working patterns. Co-productions have become more sophisticated with experience and the development of mutual trust. The best may help to save costs, but their higher purpose is to share an artistic ideal so that it may reach a wider audience. Although it involves risk, such a partnership can be especially productive when investing in new creative work.

It is not only a question of matching scales of production. Some of the more imaginative partnerships may involve collaboration between a large permanent opera house and a small occasional or independent group, not necessarily from the opera sector. The latter may provide the former with an innovative project, or add expertise from the fields of dance or puppetry or visual arts, while benefiting from the promotional exposure of working with a larger institution. This interdependent model formed the principal theme of Opera Europa's 2010 conference in Rotterdam, under the title of *OPERA sans frontières*, an event which significantly took place in a large city without a permanent opera house but in the context of the 10-day Operadagen Rotterdam with up to 90 disparate events. Several years on, there is pressure to build on that event by creating an environment for further partnership models. That is both evidence of the desire of opera to renew itself by drawing on outside sources of inspiration, and a tribute to the enduring power of opera to inspire new experiments in multimedia theatre, a tradition (in the most positive sense) which embraces Monteverdi and Wagner and Stockhausen.

* * *

More than ever today, the concern is not so much about survival as about adapting to confront the changes and grasp the opportunities that the modern world offers. A summary of the principal topics addressed at Opera Europa conferences over a six-year period offers an indication of the subjects which concern European opera companies; and the locations of those biannual conferences are evidence of the scope and variety of what constitutes this heterogeneous community of more than 150 opera companies and festivals (Table 1.1).

Table 1.1   Opera Europa conferences 2010–2016

London	The Opera Experience
Warsaw	Added Value
Lyons	What Price Sustainability?
Moscow	Through the Iron Curtain
Vienna	Citizenship
Wexford	Discovery
Venice	Italian Journey towards Reform
Brno and Ostrava	Year of Czech Music and Challenges
Madrid	Opera Alive and Online (including launch of The Opera Platform)
Bucharest	Professional Development
Amsterdam	Theatre of the World
Cologne	German Heartland (including European Opera-Directing Prize)

Opera companies throughout Europe are run by inquisitive, energetic, and ingenious people, who are dedicated to finding ways to enliven its presentation and appeal to a widening audience. The obstacles in today's busy, over-crowded, and instant-gratification world are considerable. So are the opportunities provided by that same dynamic world, and the potential rewards. The conflict is contained in a paradox. Opera's advocates find themselves fruitlessly defending a practice which detractors condemn as outmoded, non-cost-efficient and irrelevant to modern society; yet, at the same time, this old-world art is winning new audiences worldwide and demonstrating that it can address contemporary issues.

Any worthwhile art has to seek an internal balance between what its creators aspire to deliver and what its audience is willing to pay to hear and see. Artists, if they are any good, must cross boundaries and risk alienating their public. Consumers have the right to choose what they buy, but also, for their own good, need to be tempted to experiment and discover new things. So, in tracking the trends and innovations as they continue, and at increasing speed, to occur, we have to ask ourselves simple, basic but profound questions:

What do creative artists want?

What do contemporary audiences demand?

How shall we fashion this ancient, but always modern, art to the needs of our new century?

Chapter 2

Baroque Opera, Historical Information, and Business; or, How a Nerd Became a Hipster

Christine Fischer

One of the earliest and probably one of the most influential stage productions of a Baroque opera to occur after that repertoire fell out of favour took place in 1920 in Göttingen. The art historian Oskar Hagen prepared a production of Georg Friedrich Handel's *Rodelinda* and, in the years that followed, of two more Handel operas.[1] It led to the so-called 'Göttinger Händel Renaissance', a first 'boom' of Baroque opera productions, which was focused mainly in German-speaking countries. The ways in which historical information was integrated into these diverse productions during the years that followed were manifold.[2] Before that, early music and opera appeared to have had a relationship dominated by alienation, the outsider position of opera in the early music repertoire being underlined by the instrumentally focused beginnings of the early music movement,[3] with its demand for the depth of absolute music, and its musicological methodology concentrating on the written rather than the performed. After the Second World War, a wave of more positivist approaches to operas of the seventeenth and eighteenth centuries found their way onto stages. Yet, it was not until the aftermath of the Monteverdi cycle by Jean-Pierre Ponnelle and Nicolaus Harnoncourt, staged in the late 1970s in Zurich, that

---

[1]   Oskar Hagen, 'Die Bearbeitung der Händelschen Rodelinde und ihre Uraufführung', *Zeitschrift für Musikwissenschaft* 2 (1920): pp. 725–32; Rudolf Steglich, 'Händels Oper Rodelinde und ihre neue Göttinger Bühnenfassung', *Zeitschrift für Musikwissenschaft* 3 (1920/21): pp. 518–34; Manfred Rätzer, *Szenische Aufführungen von Werken Georg Friedrich Händels vom 18. bis 20. Jahrhundert: Eine Dokumentation* (Halle an der Saale, 2000), pp. 56–7, 64, 69, 73, 113, 185; Isabelle Müntzenberger, '"Händel-Renaissance(n)": Aspekte der Händel-Rezeption der 1920er Jahre und der Zeit des Nationalsozialismus', in Ulrich Tadday (ed.), *Händel unter Deutschen*, Musik-Konzepte, N.F. 131 (Munich, 2006), pp. 67–86.

[2]   See Rudolf Steglich, 'Die neue Händel-Opernbewegung', *Händel-Jahrbuch* 1 (1928): 71–158; Harry Haskell, *The Early Music Revival: A History* (London, 1988), p. 138, summarizes 222 performances within five years on 33 stages of Hagen's edition of *Giulio Cesare* as well as 181 Handel-productions in 37 cities, mostly in Germany, during the years 1920–25. Before that, Handel operas were often regarded as 'too difficult' to be performed and 'not worthy'.

[3]   On the delayed development of research on vocal technique see Peter Reidemeister, *Historische Aufführungspraxis: Eine Einführung* (Darmstadt, 1988), pp. 79–80.

anyone could speak of a 'boom' comparable to that of the 1920s.[4] Now, we are told
that we are experiencing another 'Baroque opera boom'. In times of growing early
music sales within a declining audio business, and of the remarkable success of
live Baroque opera stage productions, early music and opera are challenged in new
ways as a pair. They should, together, attract young audiences, fulfil scientific and
historical as well as artistic claims, and, at the same time, remain true to the anti-
institutional characteristics that the European early music movement once had,
and on which it is still dependent for its self-image.[5]

In German-language newspaper review supplements and academic
publications, the debate about staged performances of Baroque opera is clearly
structured between the two poles of *Werktreue* (fidelity to the work) and
Regietheater (director's theatre), both terms being bound only loosely to conceptual
definition.[6] Although this view of today's Baroque opera world has its undeniable
shortcomings in failing to account for its multifaceted characteristics, it remains
the dominant perspective of the feature pages – as can be seen in a number of
reviews of the production of Handel's *Riccardo Primo* at the Händel-Festspiele
Karlsruhe in March 2014,[7] for which Baroque specialist Benjamin Lazar staged
a visually historicizing production on a candle-lit stage, with singers employing
historic gestures.

In his review of the opening night, Lucas Wiegelmann focuses on the – in his
eyes fatal – interdependence of historicizing scenery and commercial success:

> The idea with the candles must have satisfied the organizers a very great
> deal. […] On the opening night the director of Karlsruher Händelfestspiele
> welcomes the guests […]: 'People back then wanted to see Baroque splendour
> by candlelight. […] I think today it is the same.' On the other side of the

---

    4   Imre Fabian, *Imre Fabian im Gespräch mit Jean-Pierre Ponelle* (Zurich, Schwäbisch
Hall, 1983), pp. 74–80; Max W. Busch, *Jean-Pierre Ponelle 1932–1988* (Berlin, 2002),
pp. 182–204, 347–53; Kristina Bendikas, *The Opera Theatre of Jean-Pierre Ponelle*,
Studies in the History and Interpretation of Music 105 (Lewiston, NY, 2004).
    5   On the differences between the early music movement's characteristics in Europe
and the USA during the 1980s see John Butt, *Playing with History: The Historical Approach
to Musical Performance* (Cambridge, 2002), p. ix.
    6   Christopher Balme, 'Werktreue: Aufstieg und Niedergang eines fundamentalistischen
Begriffs', in Ortrud Gutjahr (ed.), *Regietheater: Wie sich über Inszenierungen streiten
lässt*, Theater und Universität im Gespräch 6 (Würzburg, 2008), pp. 43–52; Hilde Haider,
'Regietheater', in Isolde Schmid-Reiter (ed.), *Opera Staging: Erzählweisen*, Schriften der
europäischen Musiktheater Akademie 9 (Regensburg, 2014), pp. 35–62; Anselm Gerhard,
'Was ist Werktreue? Ein Phantombegriff und die Sehnsucht nach "Authentischem"',
in Gerhard Brunner and Sarah Zalfen (eds), *Werktreue: Was ist Werk, was Treue?*, Die
Gesellschaft der Oper: Musikkultur europäischer Metropolen im 19. und 20. Jahrhundert 8
(Berlin, 2011), pp. 17–23.
    7   Georg Friedrich Handel, *Riccardo Primo*, Internationale Händel-Festspiele
Karlsruhe 2014, musical director: Michael Hofstetter, stage director: Benjamin Lazar.

foyer, packaged postcard sets with five scenes from the candlelit production are offered. For six euros. Posters cost five. The current Handel festival conveys a good impression of the present state of the opera world: sixty years ago Paul Hindemith tried to reconstruct the historical sound of Monteverdi's *L'Orfeo* in a legendary production in Vienna. Since then a whole industry has evolved, specializing in the business of early opera, mainly Baroque opera. If necessary with the methods of André Rieu or the travelling whore.[8]

Wiegelmann's reception logic is, in itself, a journey back in time – back to the 1950s, to the period of Hindemith's *Orfeo* 'reconstruction'[9] referred to in the review, and implicitly to arguments about cultural decline familiar from the writings of Theodor W. Adorno: as soon as commercial aspects enter the cultural scene, art necessarily becomes superficial.[10] Describing the production of *Riccardo Primo* as an emblem of the cheap sensibility of a commercially planned opera event means that it becomes automatically as shallow as André Rieu's music is judged to be; the opera house becomes a whorehouse, and opera becomes the hooker, prompting comparison to the commercial success of the 'poorly informed' genre of historical romance.[11] The role of Hindemith in Wiegelmann's Adorno reenactment remains

---

[8]   Lucas Wiegelmann, 'Wanderhuren aus dem finsteren Zeitalter der Oper', *Die Welt*, 4 March 2014: 'Die Idee mit den Kerzen muss die Veranstalter besonders befriedigt haben. […] Am Abend der Premiere begrüßt der Leiter der Karlsruher Händelfestspiele die Besucher mit dem Mikrofon in der Hand. […] ‚Die Leute damals wollten barocke Pracht bei Kerzenschein sehen. […] Ich glaube, das ist heute nicht anders.' Auf der anderen Seite des Foyers werden abgepackte Postkartensets mit fünf Motiven aus der Kerzenscheininszenierung angeboten. Sechs Euro. Die Poster kosten fünf. Die aktuellen Händel-Festspiele vermitteln einen guten Eindruck vom Zustand der Opernwelt: Sechzig Jahre ist es her, dass Paul Hindemith in einer legendären Wiener Aufführung den historischen Klang von Monteverdis "L'Orfeo" zu rekonstruieren versuchte. Seitdem hat sich allmählich eine ganze Industrie entwickelt, die sich auf das Geschäft mit alten Opern spezialisiert hat, vor allem mit Opern aus der Barockzeit. Zur Not mit den Mitteln von André Rieu und der Wanderhure.'

[9]   Nigel Fortune, 'The Rediscovery of Orfeo', in John Whenham (ed.), *Claudio Monteverdi: Orfeo* (Cambridge, 1986): pp. 78–118; Andres Briner, 'Paul Hindemiths "Versuch einer Rekonstruktion der ersten Aufführung des Orfeo"', in Attila Csampai and Dieter Holland (eds), *Claudio Monteverdi, Orfeo / Christoph Willibald Gluck, Orpheus und Eurydike: Texte, Materialien, Kommentare* (Reinbek, 1988), pp. 162–4; Peter Ackermann, 'Musikgeschichte und historische Aufführungspraxis: Paul Hindemiths Versuch einer Rekonstruktion der ersten Aufführung von Monteverdis Orfeo', *Hindemith Jahrbuch* 23 (1994): pp. 61–81; Michael Schmidt, '"Possente spirto" Monteverdi, Hindemith und die Historische Interpretationspraxis', in Hans-Martin Linde and Regula Rapp (eds), *Provokation und Tradition: Erfahrungen mit der Alten Musik* (Stuttgart, 2000), pp. 365–76.

[10]   Butt, *Playing with History*, pp. 4–8.

[11]   See Iny Lorentz [Iny Klocke, Elmar Wohlrath], *Die Wanderhure* (Munich, 2004); to date, not only have several continuation volumes been published, but there also exists a film adaption (ORF, Sat 1 [TV station], 2010) and a version for the theatre stage (Bad Hersfelder Festspiele, 2014).

unclear: the 'legendary' beginning of 'historical reconstruction of opera' might also be seen as the beginning of its decline, as well as continuing to be an ideal commercial approach to the matter.[12]

In another review of the same production by Dirk Schümer the commercial aspects again appear as a central concern, but this time in a positive light:

> Handel himself, the smart capitalist, drowned some savings in the crisis of Cyprus back then, the so-called South Sea Bubble, and probably hoped ruefully, like many risk investors of today, that state action would reimburse his losses. After all, his homage to the new king [in *Riccardo Primo*] extended the royal income of the composer, who did not have to offset the later bankruptcy of his opera company against his own private fortune and, therefore, many years later, died a multi-millionaire.[13]

If commerce was already at the centre of operatic debate back then, there is no need to criticize similar circumstances surrounding today's productions (with their state subventions) – one may read between these lines. Adorno is defeated by 'authentic' historical facts and by links to the economic troubles of the early twenty-first century. For Schümer, historicizing approaches to Baroque opera create a dilemma when dealing with the loss of the political implications that were essential to opera productions of the past:

> One cannot sense a lot of these political implications in the shining Baroque aesthetic, with its knights' costumes, its military marches accompanied by timpani and trumpets […] on the knight-fortress stage in Karlsruhe. One might imagine this context oneself and, therefore, dive deeply into the magic world of the stage, on which byzantine costumes, metallic bucklers and greased beards blink and glitter in the candlelight. Time-machine views into the Baroque like these do not appear kitschy but, instead, after years of *Regietheater*, exotic and pleasingly alienated. […] Comic and decadent, the naivety and effeminacy of this formal ballet of gestures belong to the consequent counter-world of Baroque

---

[12]   Butt characterizes Hindemith and Adorno as 'two different poles of opinion about HIP in its post-war form', sitting 'both within and without the culture of modernism'. See Butt, *Playing with History*, p. 5.

[13]   Dirk Schümer, 'Das muss man gesehen haben', *Frankfurter Allgemeine Zeitung*, 5 March 2014: 'Händel selbst, der gewiefte Kapitalist, hatte einige Spargroschen in der damaligen Zypern-Krise, der sogenannten South-Sea-Bubble, versenkt und mochte wie manch heutiger Risiko-Investor wehmütig darauf hoffen, dass staatliche Eingriffe ihm seine Ausfälle ersetzen. Immerhin – die Huldigung an den neuen König verlängerte die royalen Bezüge für den Komponisten, der den späteren Bankrott seines Opernunternehmens nicht mit dem eigenen Saldo verrechnen musste und deshalb, noch viel später, als vielfacher Millionär starb.'

opera – located somewhere between a window into music history and a fairy-tale movie in the style of King Thrushbeard.[14]

The political neutralizing of Baroque opera staged in a historicizing way therefore seems inevitable. The only way to convey political implications would be via a modern stage set that offers a translation of those historical circumstances for today's audiences – audiences who might have educated their period ears to a remarkable degree, but are still far from grasping the signification of absolutist and enlightened absolutist state representations found in opera of the seventeenth and eighteenth centuries. On the other hand, abstaining from any attempt to translate meanings visually into the present bestows a sensual immediacy on the productions that an intellectual approach to the matter would destroy:

> A seemingly simple, but highly artificial scenery appears. It sharpens the visual perception; it makes you cock your ears. You drift through the performance, decelerated, even-tempered and content, happy like a naively astonished child and pick one link after another out of Händel's delicious aria-chain […] This 'Riccardo Primo' looks skilfully and curiously into opera's past and at the same time is very honestly present. Just a little diverse.[15]

Here, 'diverse' political implications enter via the back door: present reception patterns favour the hedonistic consumption of Baroque opera, far away from text-centred intellectual interpretations. Interestingly, the historicizing scenery plays a central role in this reception mode by allowing audiences to sharpen their senses and focus on acoustic reception, thereby letting the music take centre stage. To adopt this pattern in a modern production seems to ensure success – from a commercial perspective, too. Adorno's thoughts on the escape from the present,

---

14 Ibid.: 'Von solchen politischen Implikationen der glänzenden Barockästhteik mit ihren Ritterkostümen, mit ihren Militärmärschen im Sound von Pauken und Trompeten […] ist auf der Karlsruher Ritterburgenbühne nicht viel zu spüren. Man darf sich den Kontext getrost dazu denken und dafür tief in die Zauberwelt der Bühne abtauchen, auf welcher byzantinisierende Kostüme, Schilde aus Blech und gefettete Knebelbärte im Kerzenschimmer anheimelnd blinken und funkeln. Solche Zeitmaschinenblicke ins Barock wirken keineswegs kitschig, sondern nach Jahrzehnten des Regietheaters eher exotisch und angenehm verfremdend […]. Komik und Schwulst, die Naivität und das Effeiminierte solch förmlichen Gestenballetts gehören zur konsequenten Gegenwelt der Barockoper – irgendwo zwischen einem Fenster in die Musikhistorie und einem Märchenfilm im Stil von "König Drosselbart".'
15 Manuel Brug, 'Richard Löwenherz: nur echt mir der Goldkante', *Die Welt*, 23 February 2014: 'Eine scheinbar simple, aber hochartifizielle Szenerie ist das. Die den Blick schärft, das Ohr spitzt. Man treibt dahin, entschleunigt, gelassen und befriedigt, glücklich wie ein naiv staunendes Kind und pflückt dabei ein Glied nach dem anderen aus Händels köstlicher Arienkette […] Dieser "Riccardo Primo" schaut könnerisch neugierig in die Opernvergangenheit und ist dabei doch sehr ehrlich gegenwärtig. Nur eben ein wenig anders.'

which he saw in the attempt to explore past musical life, are turned into a positive, up-to-date mode of non-intellectual reception, which Baroque opera (or, better, *opera seria*) can serve to an extraordinarily high degree. As a consequence, the early music movement, which set out in the late nineteenth century to offer an alternative 'nerdy' option to the mainstream music scene, suddenly becomes a kind of 'hipster', at the centre of opera life. It is, at least partly, institutionalized in opera houses, successful and in itself mainstream, particularly in its visually historicizing productions. In their case, to put it unkindly, the more or less hidden implications of 'authenticity' (it is tempting to write 'a single authenticity'[16]), became a brand – and a successful one:

> The king is unsheathing a sword, swinging his purple coat. The crown is shining, the wig fits perfectly, the armour is sparkling. The sounds are swelling and ebbing away, swinging to steep heights and profound depths, cheering, rejoicing, glistening and glimmering. [...] Surrounded by warm, regularly flickering light, in an historic costume, with apparently mannerist, and most gracious gestures, he presents himself as both heroic and vulnerable. He is an antiquated figurine and yet remains always an artist of today: Richard Lionheart – 'only authentic with the golden edge'.[17]

Today, commerce, brands, and cultural events fit neatly together with a scenic reanimation of the musical past. It is noteworthy that the brand 'historically informed opera performance' has been implemented via those parameters – the belief in 'one authenticity' and in the 'work' – that the early music movement left behind in the earthquake-like theoretical debates after the early 1980s.[18] There have also been changes regarding the basic characteristics of what constitutes early music. The preference for grand composers (Monteverdi, Handel, and not much in between and after),[19] as well as a non-ideologically contextualized mode

---

[16]   See Peter Kivy, *Authenticities: Philosophical Reflections on Musical Performance* (Ithaca, NY, 1995).

[17]   Brug, 'Richard Löwenherz': 'Der König zieht das Schwert, schwingt den Purpurmantel. Die Krone strahlt, die Perücke sitzt, der Harnisch funkelt. Die Töne schwellen an und ab, schwingen sich in steile Höhen und profunde Tiefen, jauchzen, frohlocken, gleißen und glimmen. [...] In warmes, gleichmäßig flackerndes Licht getaucht, in einem historischen Kostüm, mit maniriert anmutender, sehr graziöser Gestik gibt er sich heroisch und verletzlich zugleich. Er ist eine altertümliche Figurine und doch immer auch ein Künstler von heute: Richard Löwenherz – nur echt mit der Goldkante.' The closing words are a well-known commercial slogan for a German curtain brand.

[18]   Richard Taruskin, *Text and Act: Essays on Music and Performance* (New York, 1995), containing texts first published between 1982 and 1994; Nicholas Kenyon (ed.), *Authenticity and Early Music* [1988] (New York, 2002); Bruce Haynes, *The End of Early Music: A Period Performer's History of Music for the Twenty-First Century* (New York, 2007).

[19]   Ulrich Frey, 'Was wird gespielt? Eine Bestandsaufnahme', in Isolde Schmid-Reiter and Dominique Meyer (eds), *Oper im 17. und 18. Jahrhundert: L'Europe Baroque*,

of production, runs counter to the early impetus to stage new, unknown repertories and identify social contexts as influences on past sound worlds.[20]

It seems that early music, having been deconstructed by its theorists as a modernist concept, tilts to some degree at the 'whateverism' of postmodernist windmills by seeking a determination of the operatic past unhindered by visible or audible discontinuities that might disturb the illusion of travelling back in time.[21] The success of this concept seems to be rooted in the appealing sensualism of historicizing productions that blur (or endanger, from the standpoint of Adorno disciples like Wiegelmann) the boundaries between high and low culture. By offering an intuitively comprehensible, sensual reception experience they have the potential to enlarge the opera audience beyond its traditional boundaries.

The 'Baroque opera boom', understood to include a small portion of historically informed stage productions, needs to be judged as covering much more than productions that play with glittering superficiality in a negative sense. What is more, the repertories we find on the stages and the audiences' modes of reception are equally diverse and, as already mentioned, cannot be judged adequately via the simple polarities of high and low culture or *Werktreue* and *Regietheater*. Against the background of a non-simultaneity of theoretical debate and practice in the (diverse) early music movement as well as of a discontinuity of the attitude towards commercial aspects in operatic culture as a whole – and (historically informed performance HIP) in its different facets – this chapter sketches various ways in which early music and opera have been able to situate themselves successfully in a field of tensions and contradictions between past and present musical culture. In an old debate, familiar arguments have been turned in a direction that was unavailable while the premises of past centuries were being followed.

Relation of the Arts

Although in most Baroque opera performances nowadays some kind of 'historically informed' approach to music has become standard, things are different where scenery, the visual component of a production, is concerned. The preeminent visual impression of the performance is much more of a factor when the implacable binary of *Werktreue* and *Regietheater* is to be negotiated – implicitly or explicitly dealing with different aspects of the 'authenticities' of a performance.

Schriften der Europäischen Musiktheater-Akademie (Regensburg, 2010): pp. 19–42; Butt, *Playing with History*, p. 7 on the self-aggrandising tendencies in the early music movement of the 1980s.

[20] See Kai Hinrich Müller, *Wiederentdeckung und Protest: Alte Musik im kulturellen Gedächtnis*, Musik – Kultur – Geschichte 1 (Würzburg, 2013).

[21] Thus Wiegelmann, 'Wanderhuren', cites Lazar, the stage director of *Riccardo Primo*, as someone who abstains from 'reconstructions' of historic performances, but sees historical knowledge as his inspiration for contemporary expressions in performances.

In some cases, this leads to a grotesque situation in which productions with highly specialized expert ensembles and modern stage settings are judged to be director's theatre,[22] and thus 'inauthentic' because they serve the self-fulfilment of the stage director rather than the 'intentions' of the piece. Yet, it is evident that productions with historicizing scenery might introduce an impression of authenticity to the audience that fails conceptually when the political and social implications of the historical performances are considered. An audience misses period eyes more than ears, and is thus often unable to bridge the distance between its own perception and the social contextualization of the piece in its historical setting.

Conceptualizing from the audience's point of view leads to productions acting as visual 'translations' of historic intentions. Finding contemporary equivalents of historical affects and effects often leads to 'modern' visual impressions combined with historic music played on period instruments. In some cases, this is not the result of lack of interest in historical performance settings but, rather, an experimental search for ways that might involve audiences in period perception modes. If La Musica is introduced on a show staircase covered with a red carpet, as in Jan Bosse's production of Monteverdi's *L'Orfeo* in Basel,[23] the original intention of the piece, namely to centre the new genre of musical theatre in its musical power, becomes visually clearer at the very beginning of the performance than any scenically historicizing approach could make it. Likewise, the fact that the audience follows Orfeo on his way to the Underworld by walking from the foyer of the theatre (the location of Act I) to the auditorium (the venue for the Underworld) introduces Baroque modes of audience involvement by consciously deviating from the historical venue of the first performance of the opera in 1607. Because most of today's early music specialists also give much room to considerations of artistic authenticity, defining their art in making historically inspired contemporary performances and not 'reconstructions' of the past,[24] the

---

[22]   Not surprisingly, I have never experienced a performance with an 'uninformed' instrumental ensemble and historicizing stage, a fact that underlines the conceptual difficulties of this discourse.

[23]   Claudio Monteverdi, L'Orfeo, Theater Basel, 2008; musical director: Andrea Marcon, stage director: Jan Bosse.

[24]   See René Jacobs speaking with Silke Leopold, *Ich will Musik neu erzählen* (Kassel, Leipzig, 2013), p. 61: 'Was der Sache der Alten Musik nicht weiterhilft, sind Markenzeichen wie "authentisch" oder "mit historischen Instrumenten", wie man es früher sehr häufig auf Aufnahmen lesen konnte. Denn es ist ja nicht so, dass eine Interpretation wertvoller wäre, weil sie auf historischen Instrumenten gespielt wird. Die Marke "authentisch" selber ist ein schwieriger Begriff [...] Probleme entstehen dann, wenn Musiker den Begriff "Authentizität" als eine Art Alibi für einen Mangel an Persönlichkeit oder Fantasie benutzen'. See Butt, *Playing with History*, pp. 16–17; Richard Taruskin, 'The Authenticity Movement Can Become a Positivistic Purgatory, Literalistic and Dehumanizing', *Early Music* 12/1 (1984): pp. 3–12 (p. 3): 'Authenticity [...] is knowing what you mean and whence comes that knowledge. And more than that, even, authenticity is knowing what you are, and acting in accordance with that knowledge.'

combination of HIP sound and modern stages has an undeniable strength: acoustic and visual components do not necessarily work against each other, even if they seem superficially to be different.

Ideas about the relation of the arts on the opera stage are, of course, heavily influenced by a late-nineteenth-century perspective, that of the *Gesamtkunstwerk*, a concept always at hand where Baroque opera is concerned.[25] Setting aside the fact that Richard Wagner's own definition of this ideal varies on the subject of a whether one art is predominant and the question to what degree a *Gesamtkunstwerk* can be implemented practically on stage, the application of the term to Baroque art is a twentieth-century matter. If the term is taken as the point of departure for opening up options that aid the examination of historical performance settings in their specific relation to the staged art of opera, it can, nevertheless, be extremely useful for contemporary opera production, although this is, of course, outside its original purview. Knowledge of the specific relation of the arts can lead to performance modes enhancing the understanding and success of often cryptic pieces. The simplicity of some of the music composed for scenic representations during the seventeenth century should not be judged overhastily as a sign of juvenility or inferior quality. In Alessandro Scarlatti's case, it can be experienced in the course of a production as a conscious strategy of the composer to enhance the affective impact of the scenery, an understanding that can help in finding convincing stage solutions for present-day productions.[26] Moreover, if the unimportance of the concrete plot line for the overwhelming affective force of an *opera seria* is acknowledged right from the beginning of the production, the director is not tempted to try to tell stories visually and thereby disturb the interactions of arts on stage. On the other hand, solutions that create wide stage rooms to give space to the affective, 'unintellectual' power of the music offer unseen and unheard possibilities. Here, a convincing solution does not necessarily need to be a historicizing setting, as Stefan Pucher's impressive production of Handel's *Ariodante* in Basel has shown.[27]

Connecting the discussion of the relation of the arts in opera with thoughts on the contemporary reception of Baroque opera presented in the introductory paragraphs of this chapter leads to a central question: can the hedonistic, sensually focused and success-promising perception mode described above (with the Handel example) be served in productions of operas that in their inherent construction have a predominant art other than music (for example, text)? This is the case in

---

[25]   Christine Fischer, 'Vorwort', in Christine Fischer (ed.), *Oper als 'Gesamtkunstwerk': Zum Verhältnis der Künste im barocken Musiktheater*, Basler Jahrbuch für historische Musikpraxis 33 (Winterthur, 2009), pp. vii–xix.

[26]   Christine Fischer, Johannes Keller and Francesco Pedrini, 'Wissenschaft und Aufführung. Zur Inszenierungsarbeit an *Penelope la casta* (Alessandro Scarlatti / Matteo Noris, Napoli 1696)', in Fischer (ed.), *Oper als 'Gesamtkunstwerk'*, pp. 267–87.

[27]   Georg Friedrich Handel, *Ariodante*, Theater Basel, 2012; musical director: Andrea Marcon, stage director: Stefan Pucher.

many seventeenth-century Italian operas with their lengthy recitatives and simple, non-virtuosic *ariosi* and *ariette*. I suspect even recitative cuts would not help here. A more intellectually centred approach with translations not only of the text, but also of the implications of the plotline on stage seems indispensable. It is doubtful, then, that historicizing scenery can successfully serve the same perception modes as in the case of a Handel *opera seria*.[28]

Reenactment

The turn of HIP away from the belief in the possibility of a single historic authenticity has opened up new perspectives since the late 1980s on the role history plays in and for performance. This development has had remarkable influence on theoretical and practical work within HIP opera productions. John Butt discusses a move away from 'history', as defined by philosophic and scientific arguments, to 'heritage', as a representational form falling between art and history.[29] He describes the importance of living history and the heritage movement within the history of early music up to the 1980s.[30] Although Butt never refers to Robin George Collingwood and the latter's theories on reenactment, which have been much discussed during recent years in neighbouring disciplines such as theatre science, history of art, history, and archaeology, Collingwood is regarded by Bruce Haynes as one of the contributors to the early music movement's theorizing.[31]

The 'non-existence of history' is one of Collingwood's points of departure in his demand for a unity of theory and practice of science through an interfusion of thinking and acting. The past is simply non-existent; and every historian feels this in dealings with it.[32] Since this situation seems to bear traits of similarity to developments in the 1980s, when the proclaimed end of history influenced the early

---

[28] I have not so far been able to witness a scenic performance of seventeenth-century opera or oratorio with historical scenery or gesture. Sigrid T'Hooft seems to prefer later repertories, up to Mozart and Haydn, while Gilbert Blin has staged several earlier operas, among them Monteverdi's *L'Orfeo* (Boston Early Music Festival (BEMF), 2012) and *L'incoronazione di Poppea* (BEMF, 2009), Agostino Steffanis *Niobe* (BEMF, 2011), and *Giuditta* by Alessandro Scarlatti (Opéra de Nice, 2008); of course Benjamin Lazar's productions of Lully operas bring additional influences from the French theatre tradition (for example *Cadmus et Hermione*, Paris, Opéra Comique, 2008).

[29] See Butt, *Playing with History*, pp. 15 and 18, for the role of Karol Berger's distinction between art and history as forms of representation, whereas philosophy and science deal with arguments, and of David Lowenthal's description of a development from 'history' to 'heritage' in the growth of HIP theory on this topic.

[30] See Butt's chapter on 'Historical performance, the heritage industry and the politics of revival', *Playing with History*, pp. 165–217.

[31] See Haynes, *The End of Early Music*, p. 28.

[32] William Dray, *History as Re-enactment: R.G. Collingwood's Idea of History* (Oxford, 1995), p. 146.

music movement so deeply, Collingwood's theories may help in the important theoretical discussion about Baroque opera performances today and their relation to historical information. This would also mean catching up with the practical use of the term 'reenactment' when describing historicizing scenery in Baroque opera performances. For example, a review in 2009 of Gilbert Blin's *Acis and Galatea* production at the Boston Festival of Early Music (BFEM) was entitled 'Baroque reenactment at its very best'.[33]

Kate Bowan authored an insightful paper on the connections between Collingwood and the Early Music movement, underlining the extraordinary position of music history in the writings of the historian, himself a talented musician.[34] In his 'Outlines of a Philosophy of History' of 1928, music history is described as the only branch in which a historian is in need of sensory experience in order to increase his knowledge of historical situations:

> No historian of music deserves the name unless he has studied for himself the old music whose growth and development he is trying to describe. He must have listened to Bach and Mozart, Palestrina and Lasso, and possess personal acquaintance with their works. This means that he must have been present at actual performances of these works either physically or in imagination; and in the latter case the imaginative power is acquainted only by actually hearing similar things performed […] We may therefore boldly say that the *sine qua non* of writing the history of past music is to have this music *re-enacted in the present.*[35]

In Collingwood's later thinking music history is hardly mentioned and all references to practical aspects of reenacts are omitted. Reenactment has turned out to be a historian's method for grasping the thinking of the thoughts that were thought in the past.[36] There seems to have been a division in his theories at an early stage caused by the different roles Collingwood attributed to different perception modes: the visual, which should not be actually acted out, and the acoustic, which requires immediate sensory experience in order to be integrated in the tool kit of the historian.

---

[33] Virginia Newes, 'Baroque Re-enactment at its very best: BEMF's Acis and Galatea', *The Boston Musical Intelligencer: A virtual journal and essential blog of the classical music scene in greater Boston*, 29 November 2009 <www.classical-scene.com/2009/11/29/baroque-re-enactment-at-its-very-best-bemfs-"acis-and-galatea"> (accessed 30 May 2014).

[34] Kate Bowan, 'R.G. Collingwood, Historical Reenactment and the Early Music Revival', in Iain McCalman and Paul A. Pickering (eds), *Historical Reenactment: From Realism to the Affective Turn* (New York, 2010), pp. 134–58.

[35] Robin George Collingwood, 'Outlines of a Philosophy of History', in Jan van der Dussen (ed.), *The Idea of History with Lectures 1926–1928* (Oxford, 1994), pp. 438–95 (p. 441).

[36] See Dray, *History as Re-enactment.*

One of the new ways to deal with Collingwood's theory is to introduce scenic reenactments to stages. His ideas are already evident in the theoretical foundation of theatrical reenactments in recent years.[37] Integrating this research into the discussion of historically informed performances of Baroque opera, which, in its combination of music and scenery, is at the centre of Collingwood's paradoxical answer to the question of practical approaches, might open up new ways for the 'odd couple' opera and early music to coexist.

Collingwood's theories have influenced the analysis of theatrical reenactments such as passion plays, of reenactments of historical events such as the 'Battle of Orgreave', and of reenactments of performances.[38] Jens Roselt and Ulf Otto have tried to define the theatrical events related to reenactments in their volume on *Theater als Zeitmaschine* (Theatre as Time Machine) according to the following characteristics, not all of which have to be met necessarily. Alongside a close connection between popular culture and advanced artistic practice, Roselt and Otto describe their affinity for theatre work with non-professional protagonists. By relating to an historical event, theatrical reenactments develop community- and identity-creating characteristics, often enhanced by the (open-air) venue of the performance. However, for Roselt and Otto the most characteristic feature is one that recollects the reenactment event's own means of composition, created by the transition from one kind of media, mostly written in and referring to the past, to another, present and performative. 'Historical materials […] serve as base for bodily practices'[39] that shape the relation of the event to its historic original. Therefore, theatrical reenactments often include conscious and obvious deviations from the historical event.[40] As can be deduced by these definitions, the actual products of reenactments on theatre stages vary profoundly.

---

[37]   Of course this has been done already in various kinds of living history such as live-action role-play, 'histotainment', experimental archaeology, and so forth. Theatrical reenactments of the near past with their focus on embodiment of knowledge have additional philosophical roots in the phenomenologist school (Martin Heidegger, Maurice Merleau-Ponty, Jean-Paul Sartre) and, later in the twentieth century, in the 'turn to practice' (Jacques Derrida, Jean-François Lyotard, Gilles Deleuze). Arnold Dolmetsch had himself added a diffuse historical touch to halls and to the performance costumes of his concerts; see Bowan, 'R. G. Collingwood', p. 144.

[38]   Erika Fischer-Lichte, 'Die Wiederholung als Ereignis: Reenactment als Aneignung von Geschichte', in Jens Roselt and Ulf Otto (eds), *Theater als Zeitmaschine: Zur performativen Praxis des Reenactments. Theater- und kulturwissenschaftliche Perspektiven*, Theater 45 (Bielefeld, 2012), pp. 13–52; Sandra Umathum, 'Seven Easy Pieces, oder von der Kunst, die Geschichte der Performance Art zu schreiben', in Roselt and Otto, *Theater als Zeitmaschine*, pp. 101–24.

[39]   Jens Roselt and Ulf Otto, 'Nicht hier, nicht jetzt: Einleitung', in Roselt and Otto, *Theater als Zeitmaschine*, pp. 7–12 (p. 10).

[40]   Ibid.

Reenactments like Milo Rau's pieces on the trial of the Ceauscescus,[41] or radio-propaganda during the genocide in Rwanda[42] use mimetic representations of the historical events on stage. They let audiences live through historic moments they have previously experienced themselves 'in reality' (mostly via different public media). Enhanced by the production team's research work with different sources and eyewitnesses of the historical event, the work is meant to increase knowledge and emotional experience about the historical situation. History is recreated by the reenactment, including its preparation and reception before, during, and after the performance. The performance itself and the theatre audience of the performance therefore lose the central position they occupied in conservative repertoire theatre.

In order to reach these or similar aims, theatrical reenactments of performances do not necessarily have to be mimetic. This is amply demonstrated by Rimini Protokoll's reenactment of the first performance of Friedrich Dürrenmatt's *Besuch der alten Dame* on 29 January 1956.[43] The performance was contextualized as a means of understanding the history of the Schauspielhaus Zürich, and Helge Haug, Stefan Kaegi, and Daniel Wetzel worked with eight 'experts' (former workers of the house during the time of the production, and spectators of the performance) in order to recreate it. In the production, these time witnesses conveyed their views of the scenic events, the reactions of the audience, and their own reception during and after the performance on the very stage on which the first performance of the piece had taken place. Rather than being a performance of the piece, it was a performance of the sources of the first performance. Or, to put it the other way around, the attempt to understand a historic performance resulted in a reenactment that consciously and substantially deviated from the first performance by presenting its witnesses and not the performance itself (or, more precisely, what we imagine to have been the performance).

The similarities as well as the differences of these approaches to Baroque opera reenactments and the problems resulting therefrom are obvious.[44] A Baroque opera audience of today has not experienced the original historical event – the first performance – nor is the audience part of a chain of an uninterrupted reception

---

[41]   Milo Rau, *Die letzten Tage der Ceausescus*, Teatrul Odeon Bukarest / HAU Berlin, 2009/2010; see Milo Rau (ed.), *Die letzten Tage der Ceauscescus: Materialien, Dokumente, Theorie* (Berlin, 2010).

[42]   Milo Rau, *Hate Radio*, Kunsthaus Bregenz / Memorial Centre Kigali / HAU Berlin, 2011/2012, see Milo Rau (ed.), *Hate Radio: Materialien, Dokumente, Theorie* (Berlin, 2014).

[43]   See Jörg Wiesel, 'Re-enactment: Zur Dramaturgie kulturhistorischen Wissens bei Rimini Protokoll und Friedrich Dürrenmatt', in Flavia Caviezel, Beate Florenz, Melanie Franke and Jörg Wiesel (eds), *Forschungsskizzen: Einblicke in Forschungspraktiken an der Hochschule für Gestaltung und Kunst FHNW* (Zurich, 2013), pp. 107–13.

[44]   Of course some of the characteristics of artistic research overlap with those of reenactments, like the convergence of science and practice and the focus on embodiment of knowledge. Although this is not the time and place to discuss it at length, I would like to outline that artistic research does not necessarily need to relate to an historic event in the way reenactments do in aiming at (re)creating history.

that might contribute to a recreation of the community-enhancing characteristics that past performances possessed. Crucially, this ignorance makes ideological or political implications hard to convey – other than in the case of Rau's reenactments. The involvement of spectators in aspects of historical performance is, as already mentioned, more easily accomplished by scenic translations than by mimetic approaches. In the scenically historicizing approaches of Sigrid T'Hooft, Benjamin Lazar and Gilbert Blin this distance seems insuperable. The historic scenery and Baroque gesture might be regarded as a weakly outlined, glimmering surrounding for virtuoso singers, such as Franco Fagioli in *Riccardo Primo*, but on the affective side it nurtures a special involvement in a magic world of the past.

If, however, an audience is instructed beforehand in how to act, perceive and understand *like* the historic spectators did during the performance (which is, perhaps, the only way to include non-professionals to a substantial degree in opera performance reenactments), this would necessitate the investment of a huge amount of time before each event. Examples of small steps in the direction of the immersion of audiences into performances are: an audience singing along with a choir,[45] a special seating order that relates to the intentions of the piece,[46] and beginning the performance by defining the auditorium scenically as a museum exhibition hall.[47] The strong pedagogical impetus behind the intention to instruct the audience about its own historical role gives these performances the potential of attracting wider audiences to conventional venues and the opera repertoire. If taken further, this idea might lead to the inclusion in the performance of professional actors playing the audience, so that audiences would watch 'historical audiences' who are watching the performance. Of course, this approach creates several serious problems, especially those of space. I witnessed a step in this direction during a concert of Johannes Ockeghem's *Missa caput* by Ensemble Graindelavoix, when the procession context of the mass was evoked by combining an audio file of the noises of a huge crowd with the sounds of footsteps by the singers, who stamped on the ground at the beginning of the concert. This led to the interesting experience, for a viewer and listener, of being told acoustically how to behave ideally (and with historical correctness) in a context such as this.

The move away from the work itself, as seen in Rimini Protokoll's reenactment of Dürrenmatt's theatre play, is another practical method encountered

---

[45]   Georg Friedrich Handel, *Ariodante*, Theater Basel, 2012; musical director: Andrea Marcon; stage director: Stefan Pucher; the audience was invited to join the musical assistant in the foyer 40 minutes before the beginning of the performance in order to rehearse the choir to be performed by the singers and the audience together at the end of Act I.

[46]   Francesco Cavalli, *La Calisto*, Theater Basel, 2010; musical director: Andrea Marcon, stage director: Jan Bosse; the audience was separated by gender into two identically built sections of the auditorium situated facing each other and separated by a small stage and a water curtain in order to highlight the gender politics of the piece.

[47]   Jean-Baptiste Lully, *Armide*, Théâtre des Champs Elysées, 2008; musical director: William Christie, stage director: Robert Carson.

in contemporary Baroque opera productions: for example, Sebastian Nübling's version of *Dido and Aeneas*, which combined Henry Purcell's music with new compositions by Lars Wittershagen as well as with other historical versions of the subject. This resulted in a convergence of spoken and musical theatre strongly yet convincingly deviating from the musical text of Purcell.[48] Christoph Marthaler's *SALE*, a Handel pasticcio produced in the Zurich opera house in 2012, introduced techniques of spoken theatre such as word loops to Handel's music.[49] Its critique of capitalist consumer society (discussed a little later) lost every trait of a conventional 'work' performance. The intention of these productions, however, was far from that of reenacting a specific historical performance.

Rimini Protokoll's approach, if transferred to Baroque music theatre, would deal with material sources only (texts, music, pictures), since no eyewitnesses are alive today (a similar problem would be faced in transferring Rau's method to Baroque opera). Therefore, audience instruction during the performance would need to increase in order to enhance the process of decentralizing the 'conventional opera performance' inside the production process; moreover, this is something that might often run counter to artistic claims made by the musical members of the production team.

Seen from the reenactment perspective, the inevitable ignorance of the audience (which relates to Collingwood's paradox) has developed into a current problem for HIP opera. It takes much strength of character to experiment with one's own role in the process of performance in order to make reenactment approaches to Baroque opera successful – if you do not take the sensual way out that Collinwood indicated as a possibility. This is where economic factors enter again: part, at least, of the traditional opera audience is not thought to be willing to question their own role in the process of the performance. On the one hand, this explains the traditionalism inherent in the playing schedules of many large opera houses; on the other, it may strengthen existing tendencies to take opera out of its conventional venues (it was not, after all, wholly or even mostly performed in theatres during the seventeenth century) and help it gain new, and perhaps younger, audiences.

Repertoire

The general situation for opera repertoires in the early twenty-first century, falling between diversification and specialization, has been described as contradictory. From an international perspective, only one in a thousand extant operas is

---

[48]   Henry Purcell, Christopher Marlowe, *Dido und Aeneas*, Theater Basel, 2006; musical directors: Lutz Rademacher and Lars Wittershagen, stage director: Sebastian Nübling.

[49]   *SALE*, a project by Christoph Marthaler with music by Georg Friedrich Handel, Opernhaus Zürich 2012, musical director: Laurence Cummings, stage director: Christoph Marthaler.

performed. The repertoire, be it that of big stages, festivals, or independent productions, was never that broad historically until the rediscovery of Baroque opera and of that from the end of the nineteenth century. This is also, in a nutshell, the situation Ulrich Frey describes in his investigation of the performance numbers and repertoire of operas that premiered between 1600 and 1799.[50] Although the number of productions has increased substantially since the 1980s, after the 1990s until 2003 the number of staged and concert performances in France, Britain, and Germany remained about the same – only composer anniversaries have contributed to a higher performance number. Even though more operas of the seventeenth and eighteenth centuries are now performed, the structure inside this repertoire remains conventional, focusing on the 'big composers': Handel and Monteverdi take the leading positions in the Baroque repertory. Gluck's operas are also put on stage, more frequently than Monteverdi's, but one has to bear in mind that his reformed works have enjoyed a nearly unbroken performance tradition. Frey found that only about 4 per cent of opera performances and stage performances of other types are given over to other composers – a number that has not altered substantially since the 1980s. Among them, in order of frequency of performances, the following composers figure: Henry Purcell, Jean-Philippe Rameau, Francesco Cavalli, Giovanni Battista Pergolesi, Antonio Vivaldi, Georg Philipp Telemann, Jean-Baptiste Lully, Johann Adolf Hasse, Christopher Pepusch, Alessandro Scarlatti, and Johann Sebastian Bach. When considering single operas, the situation is even more constricted: 29 per cent of Handel productions are of only three of his operas. So, we have to face not only the prejudice that Baroque opera is Handel *opera seria*, but also the prejudice that Handel *opera seria* is *Giulio Cesare*.

That this Baroque opera boom is, *de facto*, a limited and limiting 'big composers' culture might seem astonishing when considering that the early music movement's drive to discover new repertories was one of its founding features. It might seem less astonishing, however, if one considers that early opera was introduced quite late into a stable opera culture possessing nineteenth-century bourgeois characteristics; characteristics which, in its repertoire focus, fundamentally contradicted the absolutist *stagione* organization of courtly opera life.[51] Although festivals,[52] independent productions, and a few of the bigger stages are willing to risk mounting productions of unknown operas or composers, a large

---

[50]   Frey, 'Was wird gespielt?'

[51]   Mathias Spohr, 'Barockoper zwischen Repertoire- und Stagionesystem: Zu den unterschiedlichen Traditionen im deutschen und romanischen Sprachgebiet', in Schmid-Reiter and Meyer, *Oper im 17. und 18. Jahrhundert*, pp. 43–64.

[52]   Although early music festivals regularly featuring opera, such as Boston, Innsbruck, and Schwetzingen, still seem to be more courageous in putting unknown composers and operas on stage, one should be reminded of the broad festival culture that focuses on the work of one composer, e.g. Handel in Göttingen and Halle, later Karlsruhe, and Mozart in Drottningholm.

part of the Baroque opera boom continues to serve its own attractive (because financially strong) clientele – a clientele that is now aging.

From Nerd to Hipster: Baroque Opera's Career Trajectory

Baroque opera performances were underpinned, from their first 're-stagings', by various ideological subtexts.[53] These included, firstly, the desire for the formation of a new German national identity after the First World War in the Göttinger Handel renaissance, underlined by Oskar Hagen's intention to make opera accessible to wider audiences and by his predilection for the Germanic among opera subjects;[54] secondly, a national-socialist heroic ideal, which featured in Handel productions of the 1930s and early 1940s with their focus on leader characters among the Handel heroes;[55] and thirdly, a socialist heroic touch, which was carved out in Halle productions in the 1950s.[56] Today, it is becoming harder to define national traditions, although discussion about *Regietheater* and *Werktreue* might be rooted deeply in the German-speaking region.[57] In times of globalization and crisis, of capitalism and consumerism, and of sustainability and ecology,[58] the ideological subtext of 'Baroque opera performance *per se*' is equally hard to decipher. Nevertheless, in presenting the following thoughts about two recent examples of Baroque opera productions – for the sake of accessibility both Handel productions[59] – the aforementioned complexity of contradictory ideological currents becomes obvious, in that they exist simultaneously in different approaches.

Benjamin Lazar's *Riccardo Primo*, a festival production, may be seen as a pronouncedly materialist version of a Baroque opera performance. Although ephemeral, its glistening superficiality, highlighted by the shining, metallic sound of voices like Franco Fagioli's (which are in demand right now), as well as the picture postcard sets and posters, conveys ideals of past opulence and wealth. Nevertheless, the viewer is conscious of the vanity of this glitter, because his or

---

[53] See also Butt's discussions of the early music movement between totalitarian and democratic characteristics, *Playing with History*, p. 8.

[54] See Abbey E. Thompson, *Revival, Revision, Rebirth: Handel Opera in Germany, 1920–1930* (PhD diss., Chapel Hill, 2006), pp. 39–42, and Müntzenberger, 'Händel-Renaissance(n)'.

[55] See Haskell, *The Early Music Revival*, p. 139, and Müntzenberger, 'Händel-Renaissance(n)'.

[56] See Haskell, *The Early Music Revival*, p. 147, and Dietrich Helms, 'Westöstlicher Händel: Die "Opernrenaissance" in den beiden deutschen Staaten', in Tadday, *Händel unter Deutschen*, pp. 87–106.

[57] The focus of my examples on the German-speaking region results from my own performance experiences centred in this area.

[58] See Butt, *Playing with History*, p. 169.

[59] It is hard to escape the vicious circle: the more Handel is performed, the more is written about him, and vice versa.

her experience of a performance like this is still new in the twenty-first century.[60] The repertoire has gone through its crisis and been restaged in its 'old' glamour by highly specialized experts. As in past times when the *lieto fine* (happy ending) of an *opera seria* was meant to be conceived as the reinstitution of the God-given absolutist order of society after its having undergone destabilizing developments, the persistence of this repertoire nowadays, and the very opera the audience witnesses, may convey, against all the odds, a belief in the miracle of social and economic success and its sustainability. Therefore, Brug's description of *Riccardo Primo* in Karlsruhe as being 'heroic and vulnerable at the same time' is at the centre of the debate about the attraction of these productions. This implicit reception logic works only if belief in some kind of 'authenticity' of the performance is kept alive in the spectator. For it is only if the historic performance and the actually experienced performance are believed to be substantially the 'same' that the crucial touch of sustainability (of the repertoire and of the story of social and economic success it tells) can be conveyed as a way out of the twenty-first century's economic crisis. Thus, the sustainability characteristics of a production like *Riccardo Primo*, which might be sensed by audiences more than grasped intellectually, are much more than an emblem for a hedonist reception that, beyond responding to a shining, materialistic surface, is devoid of meaning.

Another, strikingly different means by which one might deal contemporarily with Handel was seen in Christoph Marthaler's production of a *pasticcio* entitled *SALE*, staged in Zurich in 2012. Performed at one of the more conservative stages of the opera world in the hometown of the director, who left the city after a quarrel with the Schauspielhaus (his employer from 2000 until 2004), the combination of the name Handel and the title *SALE* already carries connotations of a sell-out of the entire Handel repertoire. Instead of a reanimation of a historic opera performance, Marthaler staged the downfall of a capitalist (opera) culture, accompanied by a *pasticcio* of music from different Handel operas and oratorios. The context of a clearance sale in a formerly well-established department store suggests the ultimate downfall of an old world: from high culture to bargain basement culture, from expensive goods to sell out. This downfall leads to a loss of language, and forces the protagonists to escape into sound, into the music of an elapsed epoch, in the singing which consoles by offering a window into another world (Wiegelmann would have liked it).[61] The division between the visual, textual, and intellectual sides of scenery and text, and the acoustic world of Handel's music might seem to bear similarities with Lazar's production in Karlsruhe, outlined by Brug, but the differences are obvious. Marthaler deconstructs the constitutional characteristics of

---

[60]   Of course there have been candlelight productions before, though they were always exceptions: see Haskell, *The Early Music Revival*, p. 139; also Handel's opera *Riccardo Primo* might not be known to the average operagoer.

[61]   See Marthaler's remarks on these intentions in an SRF programme available as a podcast at: <www.srf.ch/player/radio/echo-der-zeit/audio/marthaler-mit-sale-am-opernhaus-zuerich?id=ad5287b7-9e0c-4e3a-9c7f-e0f4704aead2> (accessed 30 May 2014).

a traditional opera performance by abandoning a concrete plot as well as the work concept (which already existed in Handel's time), and by converging techniques of spoken and musical theatre. His social criticism lets the upper-middle and upper-class Zurich audiences (who, like capitalism itself, have been getting a bit long in the tooth) witness their own, seemingly inevitable downfall in the capitalist crisis of the twenty-first century. Handel's music functions as the incorporation of historic splendour, as in Karlsruhe, but the connotations of this sonic escape are profoundly different from Lazar's approach in Karlsruhe. The sustainability of the repertoire is treated as symptom of the downfall of the opera culture to which it belongs, and not as a possible way to overcome it. Therefore, the productions do not differ as substantially in their approaches to historical information as they do in their intellectual perspective on prevailing political agendas. The question of which attitude is the more up-to-date remains a matter of discussion.

Perhaps, the trajectory of the coupling of opera and HIP since the 1980s can be appropriately (if flippantly) described as a transition from 'nerd' to 'hipster', from a highly specialized alternative and a slightly weird opposition to the nineteenth-century bourgeois opera mainstream, to bourgeois children in historic attire, seeking constantly to preserve a position at the peak of all that is hip. Whether or not this transition, in all its facets, proves to be the solution to the couple's relationship problems, only the future will tell.

Chapter 3

From State Opera to Multilevel Opera Business: The Transformation of Opera Governance in Berlin, London and Paris at the End of the Twentieth Century

Sarah Zalfen

Depuis trois cent cinquante ans,
ce lieu sert de mise en valeur au pouvoir –
et le pouvoir est aujourd'hui économique.[1]

Throughout its history, opera as a business and institution has shown its ability to adapt to new systems, hierarchies, and norms, to survive, and to maintain its relevance as an art form and as a social space and platform for representation. In the twentieth century, opera companies all over Europe left the courts and free markets to which they had belonged and became 'national' or 'state' opera houses. The opera business and public cultural policy became closely intertwined. Despite the different cultural policies and levels of financial involvement, almost all opera business was subordinated to public administration and public values and norms. The conceptual – if not the financial – impact of the state on the development of opera in the twentieth century was very strong, both in countries where the state acts as a strong engineer and in those where it acts as a cautious facilitator and does not intervene directly.[2] Opera houses' budgets were distributed and controlled by parliaments and ministries, and were dependent on political election cycles. Targets of public cultural policy like accessibility, accountability, and artistic excellence were set in line with the democratic values that were also legitimizing the nation-state. Finally, opera houses became cherished symbols and venues for representing national heritage and cultural development, celebrated in galas and state visits.

---

[1] Jean-Yves Kades quoted in Fréderique Jourdaa, *À l'opéra aujourd'hui: de Garnier à Bastille* (Paris, 2004), p. 98.

[2] The differentiation of states into engineer, architect, patron, and facilitator stems from Harry Hillman Chartrand and Claire McCaughey, 'The Arm's Length Principle and the Arts: An International Perspective – Past, Present and Future', in Milton C. Cummings and J. Mark Davidson Schuster (eds), *Who's to Pay for the Arts? The International Search for Models of Support* (New York, 1989), pp. 54–5.

This is a familiar model; it has been documented in many of its facets.[3] The central question of this chapter is therefore: what happens to state opera and its governance when the ideal circumstances credited to the 'golden age of the state' in the 1950s to the 1970s change and the state's dominance fades away, as observed by recent research? Major budget cuts, austerity, and bankruptcy causing major institutional changes were among the notorious operatic problems during the 2000s, indicating that the weakened status of the national state had a severe impact also on the state's opera houses. By comparing the operatic landscapes of Berlin, London, and Paris, I will discuss how these processes become visible as crises of the cities' major opera houses.

I argue that the changes can be understood as a transformation of opera from a state-governed institution to a multilevel governed business. The term of governance, according to Bevir's accurate definition, involves 'all processes of governing, whether undertaken by a government, market or network, whether over a family, tribe, corporation or territory and whether through laws, norms, power or language'. In contrast to 'government', it not only concentrates on the state, its institutions and administration but 'is seen as a set of diverse practices that people are constantly creating and recreating through their concrete activity'.[4] Following this broad understanding, I will not only look at the economic and institutional levels but will show that values and principles, practices, tastes, and symbolic functions – all formally governed by public cultural policy – can also be regarded as part of the transformation of opera.

The Golden Age of the State and the State Opera

The modern state is constituted by the legitimized body politic that is specialized in providing demanded normative goods for a distinct territory and people. Its competences and capabilities to govern, to decide, to order, to implement, and to enforce were monopolized in a historic process, mainly from court, church, and aristocracy. The state's zenith was reached in the twentieth century, showing its powers as both the murderous totalitarian state and the thriving welfare state. The standard form of current statehood in the OECD world developed after the era of world wars and is labelled by political theory as the 'Democratic Constitutional Interventionist State' (DCIS). It is functionally characterized by four dimensions:[5]

---

[3] Ruth Bereson, *The Operatic State: Cultural Policy and the Opera House* (London, 2002); Tuomas Auvinen, Unmanageable Opera? The Artistic-Economic Dichotomy and its Manifestations in the Organisational Structures of Five Opera Organisations (PhD diss., London, 2000); Sven Oliver Müller and Jutta Toelle (eds), *Bühnen der Politik: Die Oper in europäischen Gesellschaften im 19. und 20. Jahrhundert* (Munich, 2008).

[4] Mark Bevir, *A Theory of Governance* (Berkeley, 2013), p. 13.

[5] Michael Zürn et al., (eds), *Staatlichkeit im Wandel – Transformations of the State?* TranState Working Papers No. 1 (Bremen, 2004), p. 3.

1. The *territorial state* holds the monopoly of power and violence as well as of tax collection within a specific territory.
2. The *democratic nation-state* is formed by a common national identity and the feeling of being a community, rooted mainly in the nation-building processes of the nineteenth century.
3. The *constitutional state* recognizes that the state is internally bound by its laws.
4. The *social interventionist* state claims actively to increase wealth and opportunities and to distribute them fairly among the public.

The power of the modern state is, however, not limited to these rather operative elements. Beyond its political functions, it can be described through a variety of images and imaginations, as 'a complex of ideas and values, some of which have an institutional reality. These ideas are diverse in both texture and interpretation.'[6] Besides the monopoly on decision-making, statehood encompasses implementation and retention of ultimate responsibility, the monopoly on symbolic power, or, in the words of Pierre Bourdieu, 'the power to construct reality'.[7]

This ideal type of state had its 'golden age' from the 1950s to the 1970s. Since the early 1990s, however, the DCIS has undergone a gradual transformation. Political theory understands the 'transformation of the state' as the relocation of the aforementioned dimensions of statehood from the national to the international level and/or from the public to the private sector. Territorial boundaries and influences dissolve within the European Union, which is increasingly dominating national law and budgeting, while the European single market and free trade agreements in the globalized world change the scope and range of work and businesses (e.g. through procurement directives). Media and mobility sometimes create global spaces of production, communication, and experience that are almost independent from the locality of an event such as an opera performance. In short, 'international and transnational organizations or regimes take over certain tasks and resources from the nation-state, or appropriate new competences'.[8] Through strategies of liberalization that go along with these changes, a shift from public to private governance is accomplished. Also, former services of general interest, from security to healthcare, public transport to education, are taken over by private agencies, associations, networks, cooperative societies, and businesses, fully or partly independent of state agency.

It has become popular to regard these changes as the final expiration of the (nation-)state. A closer look, however, reveals that the state remains the central anchor of statehood, despite the new forms of governance that might emerge: 'once monopolist, the state is now becoming a manager of political authority'.[9] The result observed is a kind of separating or 'fraying' out of the solid construction

---

[6] Andrew Vincent, *Theories of the State* (Oxford, 1987), p. 11.
[7] Pierre Bourdieu, *Languages and Symbolic Power* (Cambridge, 2003), p. 166.
[8] Zürn et al., *Transformations of the State?*, p. 23.
[9] Phillip Genschel and Bernhard Zangl, *Transformations of the State: From Monopolist to Manager of Political Authority.* TranState Working Papers No. 76 (Bremen, 2008), p. 6.

of the state. Formerly interwoven structures of the dimensions of statehood are split up into different actors, institutions, territorial levels, and so forth and build a network of governing agencies that act with, without, or instead of the state: state and statehood are separating out, because what was once monopolized by the state – statehood – is accumulating among institutions beyond the state.[10]

The golden age of the state can also be regarded as golden age of the state opera.[11] In the first half of the twentieth century, the state as public agency took over opera from the courts as well as from the free market, where entrepreneurs and impresarios once governed. The adoption of opera houses was not always a completely voluntary act as the rising costs of labour, inflation, and the Law of Baumol made it impossible for opera houses almost everywhere to exist steadily without public support.[12] In Berlin, the last of three of its opera houses became a public organization when it failed as a limited corporation in 1925; the others were transformed from court operas into state operas with the end of monarchy in 1918. In Paris, the act of nationalizing all theatres (*Réunion des Théâtres Lyriques Nationaux*) in 1939 ended the bourgeois concession system, in which opera houses had been run under licence by so-called *directeurs-entrepreneurs*. They were bound by contract to the government but acted according to their own executive/ administrative responsibility and financial risk. In London, the Royal Opera did not stand under royal patronage but was part of the liberal cultural market until the final years of the Second World War, when it became the first institution supported by the Council for the Encouragement of Music and the Arts (CEMA), predecessor of the Arts Council. The opera house was in fact an initial place of public cultural policy in Britain.

Thus, by the mid-twentieth century, even in countries that had never seen any significant public support for the performing arts, state or state-governed organizations ran the opera houses. It was above all the increasing costs of labour that brought labour-intensive opera to the edge. It became the norm that the state mainly funded these regular costs of the opera organization (known as the 'fixed costs' in the budget, in contrast to the much smaller amount of the variable costs for the actual artistic productions). As the state had been shown to be much more

---

[10]   Cf. Philipp Genschel and Bernhard Zangl, *Die Zerfaserung von Staatlichkeit und die Zentralität des Staates.* TranState Working Papers No. 62 (Bremen, 2007).

[11]   'State' in this context does not refer to the national state alone, but also to the public agency of the state, which can be located on a regional level. In Germany, for instance, the *Länder* are the subnational level, but have state status.

[12]   According to the 'Law of Baumol' the performing arts sector is mostly independent from the rules of labour productivity growth. Because the numbers of musicians needed to perform an entire Verdi opera or the efforts to sing a bravura aria are the same today as at the time of the premiere 150 years ago there are no productivity gains, while the wages rise as they do in all fields of labour; see William Baumol and William Bowen, *Performing Arts, The Economic Dilemma: A Study of Problems Common to Theater, Opera, Music, and Dance* (New York, 1966); Hans Abbing, *Why are Artists Poor? The Exceptional Economy of Arts* (Amsterdam, 2002).

than the public purse, in the very same move public responsibility linked opera to the norms and principles of the state. The interconnection promised to defuse the (management) risks for opera houses and yet tightened them at the same moment and, as with financial support, opera came under a double control. The first kind of control was that of the public administration: the legal status of opera companies, financial support, regulation, and collective labour agreements all bound the opera to the public agencies of a cultural ministry, department, or an analogue institution. The second, and equally important, form of control was that of public values and norms: the DCIS made the opera a public 'good' in the sense that 'the state finances the cultural good opera on the basis of its social value, thus ranking it among other merit goods like healthcare, education, housing, and defence'.[13] This good status implied various claims for accessibility, excellence, symbolic functions, and accountability, which are shared by almost all national concepts of opera policy, however diverse they may be otherwise. A state that declares opera to be a distinguished cultural and educational asset, and therefore anchors it in the school curriculum and considers the participation of all citizens as desirable, becomes the central point of reference for the art form and institution. This, and not the varying amounts of subsidy, is what makes an opera house a state or a national opera house. Here we find the reason why magnificent landmark buildings are built for operas, even in recent times (the case of the Opéra de la Bastille will be discussed later; Beijing, Oslo, and Dubai are recent examples), why political ceremonies are connected to the opera house (for instance, the premiere of Benjamin Britten's *Gloriana* that took place on the occasion of the coronation of Queen Elizabeth II) and why state visits are regularly made to the opera, the most famous probably being that of the Persian Shah in Berlin in June 1962, which caused lethal riots in front of the opera house.[14]

The four dimensions of statehood are each clearly reflected in the structural and policy objectives of state opera houses throughout Europe:

1. Taxes, monopolized by the *territorial state* are the main source of cultural subsidies; terms like 'state opera' or 'national opera' generally refer to the territorial scope from which this money comes.
2. Not only did particular operas play a vital role in nineteenth-century nation-building processes of the *democratic nation-state*,[15] but the operatic

---

[13] Bernhard Bovier-Lapierre, 'Die Opernhäuser im 20. Jahrhundert', in Arnold Jacobshagen and Frieder Reininghaus (eds), *Musik und Kulturbetriebe, Medien, Märkte, Institutionen.* Handbuch der Musik im 20. Jahrhundert (Laaber, 2006), p. 249 (my translation).

[14] See Sarah Zalfen and Sven Oliver Müller, 'An Interesting Eastern Potentate? Staatsaufführungen für den Schah von Persien in Berlin 1873 und 1967', in Sven Oliver Müller et al. (eds), *Die Oper im Wandel der Gesellschaft* (Munich, 2010), pp. 277–300.

[15] Such operatic discourses of nationalism were, for example, formed by Smetana's *Libuše* in the Czech Republic, Weber's *Der Freischütz* in Germany, Auber's *La muette de Portici* in Belgium, Verdi's *Nabucco* in Italy, Erkel's *Bánk Bán* for Hungary or Zajc's *Nikola Šubić Zrinjski* in Croatia.

repertoires as well as old opera houses are today still regarded and funded as part of a common national cultural heritage and identity.

3. The legal principles of cultural policy are rooted in the *constitutional state*. Above all, the constitutionally guaranteed freedom of art is intended to protect opera from public censorship or constraints of the open market.

4. One main target of opera subsidies is to open the formerly elitist event to everybody wishing to listen to an opera and to provide education to enable people to develop this intention. The *social interventionist* state, one should add, is therefore also a *cultural interventionist state*.

The question investigated in this chapter is that of the extent to which the development described here as the transformation of the state has been affecting the business of opera in recent years. The opera landscapes of the three European capital cities of Berlin, London, and Paris have endured severe crises and decisive reforms in recent decades, as have opera houses in many other places. The three cities' opera houses provide elucidating examples that demonstrate the specific impact the transformation had on opera houses, public cultural policy, and public debates on opera.[16]

Economic and Institutional Crisis: The Case of Berlin

The city of Berlin has three major opera houses. Though this number is owing to a longer tradition, their development under the recent state has been influenced mainly by the history of Berlin as a divided city. For 40 years, its cultural landscape was marked by a parallel evolution: East Berlin, as the capital of the German Democratic Republic, incorporated the former Prussian court opera as the prestigious State Opera (Deutsche Staatsoper) that it had already become in the Weimar Republic and the Third Reich, declaring the smaller Komische Oper to be the opera for the working people. In West Berlin, the Deutsche Oper, developed out of the formerly private Bürgeroper and later City Opera (Städtische Oper), became the cultural embassy and showcase of West Germany. The political targets were clear: the confrontation between East and West was always in mind and on stage; the opera houses were generously funded and, at the same time, loosely controlled by the top echelons of the two (at least in this field) strong states.[17] This was the

---

[16]   This chapter is a very condensed and simplified representation of a more elaborate examination of these crises, available only in German; see Sarah Zalfen, *Staats-Opern? Der Wandel von Staatlichkeit und die Opernkrisen in Berlin, London und Paris am Ende des 20. Jahrhundert* (Vienna, 2011).

[17]   Fabian Bien, *Oper im Schaufenster: Die Berliner Opernbühnen in den 1950er Jahren als Orte nationaler kultureller Repräsentation* (Munich, 2011); Sabine Vogt-Schneider, *'Staatsoper Unter den Linden' oder 'Deutsche Staatsoper': Auseinandersetzungen um Kulturpolitik und Spielbetrieb in den Jahren zwischen 1945 und 1955* (Berlin, 1998).

situation until the unification of the two German states began in 1989, which also explains why, for a long time, the opera houses in Berlin stayed almost untouched by the economic change that the European cultural sector in general started to undergo in these years. What was a relatively slow process elsewhere therefore took place in Berlin in just a few years, as a result of the post-1995 consequences of falling tax incomes, the weakened control of this money, distribution conflicts, lack of legitimacy, and so forth.

When Berlin was voted the new capital of the united country, the opera houses had to meet the expectations that accompanied the new status of Berlin as capital city. At the same time, the lavish showcases of the cultural cold war had to find their way into a new economic reality. This meant firstly modernizing their financial accountability, organizational structure, and management system, extending their funding sources, and justifying their work and existence in a new manner. That the situation at the houses had to be reformed and adapted to new conditions was obvious. With 700 to 1,200 employees in each, most of them with ever-increasing wages, fixed costs already as high as 85–90 per cent of the budget, and huge hidden deficits, the three houses had little chance of survival. Repertoires and playing schedules that were not coordinated in any artistic or organizational sense and an increasing number of empty rows of seats led to the questioning of the actual need for three independent opera houses. The situation became desperate when the structural cost increase could no longer be made up by government grants. Whereas once around half of the city's budget was subsidized by the federal state, this funding was reduced step by step and stopped in 1995, since the city and state of Berlin had lost its special status and the funds related to this. Thus, the idea of opera reform emerged: a major adjustment of the financial, organizational, and artistic status of the opera houses that had occupied the city for almost 15 years. It is impossible to summarize all the attempts, conflicts, and failures belonging to this reform process in a few lines. Some themes, however, dominated the process over the years:

1. The legal status of two of the houses was reformed, thereby creating potential for a merger. Different models were suggested and implemented for each of the opera houses by the administrative part of the municipal authority, making them to different extents more independent from political budgeting cycles and enabling them to act in an economically more effective and efficient way.
2. The opera houses were requested to decrease their expenditures and to increase their income from the box office and alternative funding sources like sponsoring, donations, and royalties. This new income was to compensate for the rising costs that were no longer sufficiently covered by the state as some grants stagnated or were even cut.
3. All three houses were asked not only to coordinate their repertoires and playing schedules but to develop distinct artistic profiles. Due to the years in the separated city, the Staatsoper and the Deutsche Oper had particularly

similar artistic concepts. Annoyed by clashing performances of the same opera on the same night at different opera houses, politicians and the press regularly suggested what their ideal operatic triptych would look like.[18]

Although several extensive reform concepts were developed and many details such as budgeting formats were changed, the actual reform failed again and again. It required the efforts of no fewer than seven cultural ministers (*Kultursenatoren*), who each tried to reform the Berlin opera houses, before a new stable status could be achieved. What, then, prevented progress for such a long time? New funding models and financing strategies for the opera houses were supposed to relieve the public purse but for a long while they caused more problems than they solved. For example, the opera houses were asked to raise more money from sponsors and at the box office and to build up reserves for upcoming projects and later seasons. Their legal status as part of the public administration, however, did not allow them to save anything; fiscal accounting and its principle of deficit financing withdrew all the unspent money. When the Staatsoper found a generous sponsor to fund a sophisticated stage set for a production of Meyerbeer's *Robert le Diable*, the public administration requested that the house put half of the donation into the general budget and not into the Meyerbeer production, because the donation did not meet the formal requirements of an earmarked grant. The efforts of the houses' managements to act in an economically aware manner were thwarted multiple times, when new cultural players, such as sponsors and directors on the partly denationalized boards and control committees, interfered with old political networks or institutional and juridical frameworks. Furthermore, the reforms did not go down easily at the houses. The protection of privileges and the wish for absolute administrative and artistic independence (also in decisions about what to play, when, and with whom) meant that the houses were not very compliant partners in the reform process.

In the end, the three houses survived, became legal bodies in their own right, and, as such, remained largely independent. All workshops and parts of the administration were moved into a new umbrella foundation, coordinated by a more or less willingly accepted general director and governed by two boards, each half made up of public deputies. The framework of the operatic sector in Berlin was thereby, to a large extent, separate from the public structures. In the words of left-wing politician Thomas Flierl, 'the opera reform marks the beginning of the modernization of great cultural institutions. The keyword here is help for self-help [...] the principal means of creating cultural businesses ready for the future is their privatization [*Entstaatlichung*].'[19]

What do these events tell us about the relationship between the opera house and the state? The balancing function of the state, to keep the institution running under

---

[18]   However, it did not prevent the responsible agents in the Berlin government from appointing, for instance, Daniel Barenboim and Christian Thieleman as music directors, who both favoured a somewhat similar repertoire and musical style.

[19]   Thomas Flierl, *Perspektiven durch Kultur* (25 June 2003), <www.kultur-in-berlin. com/archiv/reden/thomas_flierl.pdf> (accessed 8 June 2015).

the conditions prescribed by the state itself (that is, to fully cover the rising fixed costs), came to an end. At the same time, the alternative funding sources of the opera houses became not only more important but also more differentiated. Strategies of sponsorship and marketing now repaid the efforts put into increasing the revenue from the box office and corporate clients, though due to the lack of tradition in private arts funding they still bring in comparably little money. The public purse, which continues to provide up to 70 per cent of financial support, is still the most important source of money but no longer the only one – and also not the only player who has stakes in opera's future. The change of financial strategies was restricted by legal and structural frameworks, so these had to be changed too. The process of economic change, therefore, was not limited to funding. Beyond this, a strategic dimension became increasingly important. To obtain new funding, juridical as well as institutional reforms needed to be implemented. Ensuring reliability outside the public budgeting cycles and political election periods and securing institutional independence and simplifications in employment law were among the institutional and structural changes that were initiated by the economic crisis.

Social Change: The Example of London

A decade before Berlin started its reforms, London opera houses were confronted with a withdrawal of state support. The economic diversification was already more prevalent in British cultural policy and a strong economization was implemented here earlier. In the cultural tradition of Britain, the public sector was always a rather modest patron. Nevertheless, under Keynesian leadership, as documented by the royal charter from 1946, this convention altered and the cultural sector and, in particular, London opera were led by policy principles and targets at least comparable to the continent.[20] This applied to the two large opera houses of London, the Royal Opera House (evolving from the former Royal Italian Opera, used as a dance hall in the years of the Second World War, and revived as an opera house by the Covent Garden Opera Company) and the English National Opera (founded as the Sadler's Wells Company in the 1930s and publicly funded after 1968).[21] Although kept at 'arm's length' by the non-governmental Arts Council executing the arts funding, opera was part of an increasingly active and responsible public cultural policy in the 1960s and 1970s, acting in the name of greater accessibility and of democratizing the art form. The Conservative era of the 1980s, however, tried to reinstate the arts on the allegedly free market: 'Mrs. Thatcher's definition

---

[20]   Frederick F. Ridley, 'Tradition, Change and Crisis in Great Britain', in Milton C. Cummings and Richard S. Katz (eds), *The Patron State: Government and the Art in Europe, North America, and Japan* (New York, 1987), pp. 225–53.

[21]   Ellenor Handley and Martin Kinna, *Royal Opera House Covent Garden: A History from 1732* (West Wickham, 1978); Norman Lebrecht, *Covent Garden: The Untold Story* (London, 2000).

of cultural democracy was based on a commercial mass culture where supply and demand found a "natural" equilibrium in the market place.'[22] Only art that was popular enough to raise the money it needed was worthy of being supported. In terms of its popularity, opera was regarded as an art form with no genuine popular British tradition.

This development might explain why the legitimizing aspect of the popular was also prominent in attempts to revive opera as a public good and to justify more public funding and agency after the Conservative era. The primacy of accessibility, as promoted by all Western cultural policies, developed most strongly in London opera policy. Its power became particularly visible in the aim of New Labour to turn the Royal Opera House into the 'people's opera' after 1997. This concept was paralleled by changes to the National Lottery, which was intended to be a 'People's Lottery' and supported the refurbishment of the opera house at that time. It was exactly these events that catalysed the situation of crisis and reform in London and that reflect well the weakened and often conflicting development of state agency in the *social* realm of opera.

In 1995, the Royal Opera House received a lottery grant of £78.5 million to accomplish major renovations and modifications on the building. The house was in a transitional state after director Jeremy Isaacs suddenly left his executive post after nine years, and the renovation nearly made the opera company of Covent Garden homeless for more than two years. The aim to build a temporary stage at London's Southbank failed, as did the appointment of a new Executive Director. After years of constancy, the opera house faced change and uncertainty and had to prepare for crisis and transformation.

The situation fuelled the old conflict between the lovers and enemies of the opera: 'It is time this rich shower of snobbish parasites were forced to pay for their own elitist hobby', claimed some.[23] Others shrugged such protests off as 'socialist clap trap'.[24] The board of directors responsible constantly declared that the democratization of opera was their principle objective but refused to sit next to 'somebody in a singlet, a pair of shorts and a smelly pair of trainers' as their chairman, Sir Colin Southgate, mentioned unwisely at a press conference.[25] At some moments of this crisis it seemed, as *The Times* pointed out, that London Opera 'almost succeeded in doing what the KGB could not in decades: start[ing] a class war in Britain'.[26]

The government's intention was not really to reconcile the conflicting forces, but rather to state an example of what the new strength of public cultural policy

---

[22]   Christopher H.J. Bradley, *Mrs. Thatcher's Cultural Policy: A Comparative Study of the Globalized Cultural Systems* (New York, 1998), p. 12.

[23]   *The Mirror*, 21 January 1995.

[24]   *The Daily Telegraph*, 1 August 1995.

[25]   Quoted in Lebrecht, Covent Garden, p. 445; almost every newspaper quoted this statement the next day (16 January 1998).

[26]   *The Times*, 29 July 1995.

should be like. The people's opera was the state's attempt to act as an agency of social control and regulation. Alone, it did not work. In contrast to the era of state-governed cultural enforcements in the 1960s and 1970s, the state was no longer the main anchor of cultural regulation. As sociologists have shown repeatedly, the period since the 1990s has been marked by the accelerated pluralization and diversification of cultural interests, tastes and lifestyles, which has not bypassed Britain or the realm of opera.[27] Whether at commercial spectacles at Earls Court Exhibition Centre and in the Royal Albert Hall, public screenings, or more experimental performances in off-West End and fringe theatres, opera acquired many faces for many different people and tastes. They sometimes seemed to offer a similar or even more 'accessible' art than the officially fostered 'high' culture that was explicitly subsidized to make it more accessible. The 'popular' strategy of the new government was increasingly weakened by this development.

Eventually, the Royal Opera House did change in some aspects. Seating arrangements – a historical mirror of the order of society – were modified a little; the foyer was relocated into the glass-roofed Floral Hall, adjacent to the building; the modern escalators to the higher floors symbolized social mobility; the famous 'crush-bar' formerly reserved for some patrons became a floor open for all; and a roof-top terrace invited people to come to the house for casual reasons. But, the most important change was that the old 'black box' of opera was gone.[28] After years of public debate and scandals, the opera probably for good, has lost its status as an impenetrable institution with obscure practices and an untouchable tradition, all of which had been maintained for reasons determined by the 'lofty' approach of cultural policy.

The specific conflict and change described developed out of the very circumstances found in London at that time but the development mirrors the second shift in the relation of opera and the state also to be found elsewhere. The legitimacy of a monolithic authority that controls access to a, for many, outmoded complex of the arts and through this process maintains a highbrow ideal of valuable art became questionable almost everywhere. As cultural historian Robert Hewison has noted, 'the great pyramid of high, middlebrow and popular art forms has crumbled, and people feel free to pick and mix amid its ruins, enjoying opera here, stand-up comedy there'.[29] *Aïda* or Ayurveda, *Carmen* or clubbing – all this became more than ever not a question of status, class, and cultural capital, but of individual choice. Going to a great national opera house has become just one way of enjoying the pleasures the art form has to offer in a world of multimedia and mobility. The educational mandate – one main element of post-war cultural

[27] Gerhard Schulze, *Die Erlebnisgesellschaft: Kultursoziologie der Gegenwart* (Frankfurt, 2005); John Storey, 'The Social Life of Opera', *European Journal of Cultural Studies* 6/1 (2003): pp. 5–35.
[28] Black box theatre was characterized by a flat stage and black walls, which, from the 1960s on, became the preferred space for experimental productions.
[29] *The Times*, 11 June 1995.

policy – that legitimized the state's maintainance and funding of opera is put at risk. The primacy of accessibility promoted by all Western cultural policies is undermined by a pluralization and diversification of cultural interests and lifestyles. It demonstrates not only that the transformation of the state is measurable in numbers of private institutions or large subsidies but also that it refers to the scope and strength of governance as the regulation of cultural needs and tastes.

Fragmentation of Representation: Paris' New Opera House

The developments identified in Berlin and London are similarly evident in the Paris opera crisis. Yet, Paris also draws attention to a third shift within the transformation of the 'state opera'. The case of the newly built Opéra de la Bastille in Paris provides a perfect example of what Monika de Frantz has stated in her analysis of European urban reconstructions: 'as states become reconstructed toward multi-level governance, capital-city culture often turns from a collective good into a contested symbol'.[30] It further shows to what extent this symbolic contest is part of a transformation of state and state opera.

The Bastille was commissioned in the early 1980s by the first left-wing government in post-war France and its president, François Mitterrand, as part of a prestigious architectural programme called *Les Grands Travaux*: 'A new opera, modern and popular, [*moderne et populaire*] will be built at the site of the Bastille. It will give back to Paris the international role it deserves in this domain', as Mitterrand announced in the first year of his presidency.[31] Since its beginnings at the court of Louis XIV, opera in France was an incarnation of power. This function was transferred from absolutism to the revolution, the empire and finally the fifth republic. According to the French opera expert Patureau, 'the Paris opera appeared to be the almost perfect model of an institution capable of traversing the times without damage, despite fundamental differences of regimes and ideologies'[32] As a symbol not only of Mitterrand and his government but of a reinvented state, the idea of the new opera house stood clearly in this tradition.[33] The new opera should be nothing less than a representation of the modern French state. As such a representation, however, the new opera house had to meet expectations that turned out to be almost impossible to satisfy. What makes an opera house modern and

[30]   Monika de Frantz, *Capital City Cultures: Reconstructing Contemporary Europe in Vienna and Berlin* (Brussels, 2011).
[31]   Communiqué du Président 9 March 1982, in Gerard Charlet, *L'Opéra de la Bastille: Genèse et Réalisation* (Paris, 1989), p. 34.
[32]   Frédérique Patureau, 'L'Opéra de Paris ou les ambiguïtés de l'enjeu culturel', in Raymonde Moulin (ed.), *Sociologie de l'art: colloque international, Marseille 13.–14. 6. 1985* (Paris, 1986), p. 83 (my translation). See also Jourdaa, *À l'opéra aujourd'hui*, p. 17.
[33]   Mitterrand's personal art preferences played, as far as is known, a minor role.

popular – and genuinely French? In form and content, this question provoked highly controversial discussions throughout the 1980s.

It started with the architecture. An international competition was to guarantee excellence and cutting-edge modernity for the building. More than 750 proposals were handed in but none really thrilled the jury. As prestige and *génie* were fundamental objectives, the judges chose a design that they assumed had been submitted by the famous architect Richard Meier. When the anonymity was lifted, it turned out that the winning proposal was not Meier's but that of a young and mostly unknown Uruguayan-Canadian architect, Carlos Ott. Once the reputation of the competition had been ruined, attention was focused on the artistic aspects of the opera house. The repertoire and, above all, the opening premier were discussed in a familiar tone. Plans to open the new house with Mozart's *Don Giovanni* or *The Magic Flute* received harsh criticism as they were not seen to be meeting the objectives of the new modern and popular opera house. Even the leftist *Libération* saw it as 'an affront against the cultural identity of France. The new opera has to be inaugurated with Berlioz's great epic *Les Troyens*. The whole world admires it and the most notable experts state unanimously that it is as important as Richard Wagner's *Ring of the Nibelung*'.[34]

These examples could be extended with a long list of struggles, which all revolved around questions of identity, national representation, and authority in cultural decisions.[35] But these debates did not take place in a vacuum. Their background rather reveals that the Bastille opera with its political entitlement was a perfect symbol through which to attack the political order, when after the elections in 1986, an unprecedented situation, known as the first *cohabitation*, emerged. The president of the republic and the prime minister with his government, for the first but not last time in French history, did not belong to the same political party or camp. Since both sides had their stakes in the idea and management of the new opera, the construction site of the Bastille became the battlefield of a proxy war over the authority to define the cultural identity and aesthetic expression of the French nation.[36]

Though the *cohabitation* is a unique element of the French political system, it was caused in this case by a development that politics has had to face almost everywhere in recent history: the pluralization of the political landscape, the vanishing influence of former catch-all parties and unclear majorities after elections, all signs of the decreased stability of the constitutive elements of the democratic constitutional nation-state. In those days, the representation of the state through formally sharp symbols became difficult to fill with a coherent message.

---

34 *Libération*, 31 May 1985.
35 Sarah Zalfen, 'Sera un opéra moderne et populaire', in Deutsch-Französisches Institut (ed.), *Frankreich Jahrbuch 2011: Kulturnation Frankreich? Die kulturelle Dimension des gesellschaftlichen Wandels* (Wiesbaden, 2012), pp. 99–116.
36 Philippe Agid and Jean-Claude Tarondeau, *L'Opéra de Paris: gouverner une grande institution culturelle* (Paris, 2006).

The expectation that opera is a representation of a certain power lies in the art form's tradition and, quite clearly, all kinds of political systems have made use of this function. The case of the Opéra Bastille made clear that where this power is transformed and divided to the same extent as are its institutions and discourses, the vertical gesture of defining an opera house as a display of the 'king's reign' has become impossible. The cultural references that opera conveyed became too multifaceted and, therefore, no one could monopolize it.

The state no longer owns the monopoly on the 'power to construct reality'. Cultural 'stages' are not reserved for sovereign state representation any more and can be used as symbols by a variety of protagonists, creating multifaceted images of 'their' reality. Political, private, corporate, artistic, and many more agents in some dozen countries have argued about the architectural shape of new opera houses in recent years: about their location, their names, the colour of the seats, the repertoire, the chief conductor, and, last but certainly not least, the right to sit in the front seats of the royal box. They all participate in the symbolic governance of opera, which changed in the same way as did the financial and social regulation of opera.

Conclusion

The transformations of opera houses briefly described in this chapter relate in various ways to the transformation of the state. The separating or fraying out of statehood and governance through a multitude of agencies becomes visible not only in the variety of new legal forms, funding sources and decision-makers in former state or national operas but also in the pluralization of cultural preferences and tastes and the fragmentation of representations. The governance of opera has lost its central origin and point of reference in the state in all its dimensions. The shifts from subsidies to more private funds, from public administration to a more independent management, from the public interest to the manifold interests of the public, from the national symbol to a variety of realities, all prove that the state is still an important agent in the case of opera but is now in competition with an increasing number of different new players, stakeholders, interests, tastes, values, social practices, and policies. What 'frays out' here – to return to this term – is not the structure of the institutional state itself, but what the state, with its norms, concepts, and practices of cultural policy referred to and authorized.

The examples made clear that, although the transformation processes of state, politics, and society reflected in the crises of opera were a shared phenomenon, its conflicts were deeply rooted in the very specific traditions and problems of the different countries and their political systems and cultures: the specific topics, dynamics, and discourses of the opera crises reflected transformation processes of state, politics, and society that went far beyond the field of opera. In Berlin, the opera crisis was linked to the disastrous financial deficit of the city, the problems on the way to a finally united city, and to the heritage of history burdening the metropolis. In London, the Royal Opera House stood for the survival of a class society, the fear of interference between politics and art, and the disappointments of market failure. The Opéra Bastille developed into a symbol for the seesaw of the *cohabitation*, for the atavistically monarchical character of a proud republic, and the continued predominance of Paris over the rest of France.

Still, everywhere the crises can be interpreted as ways to deal with the transformation process: 'crisis' was – despite all the different and very serious problems – a colloquial term not an objective state; it became a code, a form of perception and participation, sometimes even a political weapon. Diagnosing a crisis defined (new) chances for and limits of agency and legitimacy in a new political order. To return to Bevir's theory, in the case of opera 'governance [was] explained by the narratives that the relevant actors first inherit[ed] as historical traditions and then revise[d] in response to dilemmas'.[37]

---

[37] Bevir, *A Theory of Governance*, p. 13.

Chapter 4

The Business of Composing Opera:
A Composer's Perspective

Paul Alan Barker

Introduction: Why Opera?

As a composer, my perspective on the business of opera focuses on the process of creating and performing opera. To date I have written 17 operas, but I shall avoid definitions of opera which often seem to be academic arguments in a pejorative sense. I shall however allude to some practices that largely define some of the business of opera from theatre and musical theatre.

Without wishing to compare myself to them, I note that Handel, Mozart, and Britten composed for both the stage and the concert hall. It is not the differences between their music for stage and the concert hall which attract me, but the similarities. My contention is that evidence of an understanding of the theatrical nature of music, once assimilated by a composer, remains implicit in all the compositions.

As an interdisciplinary genre, opera allows for a synthesis of disciplines, which has been an artistic preference and important driving force for me. Pitika Ntuli articulates the lack of synthesis apparent to someone from another culture:

> In my country, and in Swaziland, my country of adoption, the fusion of art forms, to be a poet, painter, sculptor, musician, actor, all in one, can be just a matter of course. Ceremonies, rituals, fuse all art forms, to allow for [...] cross fertilization [...] Arriving in Britain I found myself living, or half-living, in different compartments simultaneously. Each compartment seemed hermetically sealed. Each so stiflingly private.[1]

The epistemological emphasis is evinced by the moral philosopher Mary Midgley, who rails against such atomization in the academy and beyond:

> What is new in this century, however, is the contribution of academic specialization to the splitting process. Mind and body, scepticism and stoicism, god and beast, are now topics belonging to different disciplines [...]Within each discipline, there is a further tendency to keep narrowing the territory; to be

---

[1] Pitika Ntuli, *Storms of the Heart: An Anthology of Black Arts and Culture*, ed. K. Owusu (London, 1988), p. 214.

suspicious of outlying areas and concentrate only on things which can be made
to look perfectly clear and complete.[2]

These are the perspectives from which I perceive opera as the most challenging
form for a composer to investigate. My book *Composing for Voice*[3] grew out
of this experience. Although my primary drive has been composition, I have at
various times worked as a librettist, a singer, a conductor, a director, a repetiteur,
a multi-instrumentalist, a designer, and a producer. Aspects of opera have
gradually encroached on all my other compositions: musicals, music theatre,
and theatre works, but also into much of my instrumental and orchestral music,
which is typically conceived as concert-theatre. Often extra-musical elements are
notated and there is always an expectation for instrumentalists to perform with an
awareness of theatre comparable to that of actors and singers.

The differences between opera, music theatre, and musical theatre have long
been debated. For me the question is pragmatic: the definition is made by the
commissioning body or the venue for marketing reasons. David Pountney supports
this unimportance of differentiation:

> Avant Garde composers in the 60s and 70s who felt the compulsion of story
> telling with music but were embarrassed by the implications of the term opera
> called it 'Music-theatre'; their polar opposites on Broadway and Shaftesbury
> Avenue call the commercialized version 'Musical Theatre'. Spot the difference!
> But Opera simply means 'work' and a quick trawl through its history reveals
> the immense range of entertainments which have fallen into the ragbag of this
> meaningless name […][4]

To paraphrase the writer and lyricist Stephen Clark, with whom I have often
collaborated, opera is the biggest sandpit you can play in. The analogy is important, as
it relates to a substance that is both the plaything of a child and the building material of
adults, an alchemical substance of both semi-liquid and solid qualities transformable
by both imagination and chemistry. Opera is also an amalgam of contradictions, both
base and sophisticated, practical and intangible, a transdisciplinary form, intrinsically
creating more than just the sum of its parts. Edward Cone noted the interchangeable
relationship between song and opera: 'In both song and opera the music transforms
the personalities projected by the original poetic text in two apparently contradictory
ways: it simultaneously particularises them and universalises them.'[5]

Theatre may be seen as a re-embodiment of voice with text, and McGilchrist
cites the crucial importance of gesture in music-making, and quotes John Napier

[2]   Mary Midgley, *Heart and Mind* (London, 2003), p. 10.
[3]   Paul Barker, *Composing for Voice* (London, 2004).
[4]   'The Future Of Opera', speech given on Saturday, 13 February 2000, at the Royal
Over-Seas League, London, UK.
[5]   Edward Cone, *The Composer's Voice* (Berkeley, 1974), p. 21.

on the role of physical gesture as a fundamental part of human communication: 'If language was given to men to conceal their thoughts, then gesture's purpose was to disclose them.'[6] The visual essence of music has been documented by Klaus-Ernst Behne and Clemens Wöllner's research, where even professional musicians have been shown to be led by their eyes rather than their ears.[7]

In respect to opera, Cone evinces a trinity of vocal, instrumental, and complete musical personas. David Pountney makes a similar point when he says: 'An opera is an intricate synthesis of music, text, action and image'.[8] The business of opera creation arises for me through a fascination for three related primary elements: voice, text, and theatre, where theatre and music are indistinguishable. These elements do not exist as abstract, disembodied concepts, but are synergistically connected from conception to performance. Perhaps they represent an important part of human identity: McGilchrist notes that music has been considered the forerunner of language:

> [T]heorists of language, including Rousseau in the eighteenth century, von Humbolt in the nineteenth century and Jespersen in the twentieth, have thought it likely that language developed from music, so that the theories of Mithen and others in the twenty-first century do not come out of the blue.[9]

Laban understands that music might best be seen – as theatre – through embodiment: 'one of the reasons we like to see as well as hear, music performed is exactly that we can better inhabit the former's body, a perception that appears to me intuitively correct'.[10]

Opera may then act as a bridge to both our ontogenic and phylogenic roots.

In the first part of this chapter, I explore the business of creating and performing operas. In the second, I use a case study to illustrate a specific aspect of audience reception in opera.

Creation and Performance

Collaborations with Writers

Collaboration is the most fundamental constituent of the business of opera in respect both to its creation and its performance. A burgeoning process, collaboration

---

[6]   Ibid., p. 71, quoting John Napier, *Hands* (New York, 1980), p. 166.

[7]   Klaus-Ernst Behne and Clemens Wöllner, 'Seeing or Hearing the Pianists? A Synopsis of an Early Audiovisual Perception Experiment and a Replication', *Musicae Scientiae* 15/3 (2011): pp. 324–42.

[8]   Letter to *The Spectator*, 13 February 1999.

[9]   Iain McGilchrist, *The Master and his Emissary* (New Haven, CT, 2010), p. 104.

[10]   Quoted in ibid., p. 122.

might begin with only me and one other person but proceeds to involve many other people through its genesis and performance.

My first collaborative experience grew from an irresistible urge to turn a novel by Doris Lessing into an opera. I wrote and asked her for permission to use her 1980 novel *The Marriages Between Zones 3, 4 and 5* in 1983. I began visiting her regularly with attempts to truncate the 299 pages of her novel into about twenty pages of libretto. Collaboration, I was to learn, is a process which can involve an infinite number of variations; my memory of working with Lessing is of an awed and gauche young man desperately trying to interpret the frequent negative responses she offered my efforts as a sign of how to proceed, which I somehow did, eventually, and to her satisfaction. What I am unable to recall in detail is the degree of gestural communication that passed between us. Despite her monosyllabic responses in respect to my libretto, I felt encouraged to complete the task. I can only ascribe this positivity to the silent gestural language we employed. It remains conjecture, but this early experience underpins my understanding of text, spoken or written, as incomplete until embodied. The composer's business is to embody a text with music, not merely to underpin it. This is a variation on the centuries of argument over the supremacy of word or music begun by Monteverdi when he wrote of the *seconda pratica*.[11]

The screenwriter today might be said to be a modern version of the eighteenth- or nineteenth-century librettist in terms of supply and demand. In the twentieth century, the musical came to require two sorts of writers, the book-writer who dealt with plot and dialogue and the lyricist who provided the text of songs, a division of labour that broadly distinguishes the inheritance of recitative and aria. The film and musical worlds frequently hire and fire successions of writers, but contemporary opera is a far smaller world; the opportunities for employment are few and the formal training elusive if it exists at all. Text occupies a great variety of non-linear relationships to time when it is set to music, and I have outlined this and some other differences in *Composing for Voice*.[12] It is not easy to encounter writers who understand the gamut of macro- and micro-possibilities they might offer a composer and I am privileged to work with some who have. Their scarcity may be the reason why so many composers from Michael Tippett to Judith Weir (along with me) so often have attempted this task themselves.

Collaboration with Directors

My next collaboration was with a director who had heard of my opera and had an opportunity to perform it. He told me the performances were a few months away and asked for my assurance that I was far enough ahead with the work to finish the score in time. I had become completely absorbed with the libretto and not

---

[11]   Monteverdi's thoughts on a 'second practice' were first articulated in an afterword to his *Fifth Book of Madrigals* (1605).

[12]   See, for example, pp. 43–55 and 171–3.

one note was written, and yet I told the director the score was half finished. It is perhaps important to understand the necessity for fabrication of truth as a possible basis for the business of opera, as in any other business. The director Chris Newell remains one of my longest-standing collaborators; after the opera was performed I told him of my deception and he confirmed he would not have gone ahead had he known the truth. Opera is a high-risk business prone to related and pressured forms of behaviour.

The association of voice in the context of opera might understandably lead the reader to consider the singing voice, yet my first operatic experience began as an obsession with an author's disembodied voice in a book, which my imagination was compelled to embody on the lyric stage. Lessing's own voice became a vital source both of permission and encouragement to assemble or extract a suitable text that might be sung on stage. In the opera, her voice was embodied in the character of Malek, the chronicler, who also plays a part in the narrative. This leads me to the director's voice, without which it might not have gone further than the page. The business of opera springs from the business of human communication and collaboration, on and off the stage.

Collaboration with Companies

The Marriages Between Zones 3, 4 and 5 became a chamber opera for four singers, a dancer, a children's chorus largely accompanied by a sarod,[13] and a seven-piece instrumental ensemble. These unusual forces reflected the nature of the story and its *mise en scène* as a myth enacted by a travelling troupe within an extra-terrestrial agenda. Its critical success led to the creation of a company founded by the director and me, the Modern Music Theatre Troupe, which continued to develop national and international projects for a dozen years, until 1997. There were many such companies at the time and together we formed an umbrella organization, through the generous support of the Association of British Orchestras, still known as the Opera and Music Theatre Forum. Typically part-funded on a project basis by the Arts Council, companies like ours provided a very different business and experience of opera from the big houses in the UK. Small to medium in scale, the companies typically staged opera more intimately in terms of cast and audience, and were more diversely popular. The growth of similar companies led to a report by Graham Devlin entitled *Beggars' Opera*.[14] The report clearly demonstrated the iniquities between funding in main opera houses and small- or medium-scale companies. It quoted Kerkhoven's analysis of large-scale opera, which exemplified its resistance to change:

> Doing opera requires a lot of money; the organisation is too big, too expensive to be put at the disposal of experimental artists. They don't usually take chances

---

[13]   Indian stringed instrument of the lute family, an unfretted variant of the sitar.
[14]   Graham Devlin, *Beggars' Opera* (London, 1992).

in opera. They hire artists who have proven their talent with clear success elsewhere. Opera puts all its eggs in a basket of stable values.[15]

The business of opera funding would require an additional chapter, or perhaps a book. The business of the big opera houses was then and still is primarily concerned with a revolving repertoire from Mozart to Puccini, with occasional forays into some musicals and contemporary works. There are exceptions and, as I planned this chapter, Covent Garden announced a bold programme emphasizing new work. Unfortunately, some time later, in this chapter's final draft, their main-house programme could no longer be said to reflect this aim. Such large organizations generally reflect commercial, bureaucratic, and political processes averse to artistic or aesthetic change, which prove Kerkhoven's thesis.

With house singers, and a full-time chorus and orchestra, deviation from the usual voices and instruments and the extra rehearsal time for an unknown work often scares the administrators. Opera on an international level is also built around a star system typified by unpaid rehearsal schedules built around the non-availability of star singers who are able to command enormous fees for a single performance anywhere in the world. The business of opera from this perspective is the star system itself; the core theatre rehearsal process is not valued in the same way.

In theatre and musicals the company rehearsal process represents the heart of the work and is paid. Attendance by the cast is mandatory. Moreover, in opera, the conductor's role is different to the role of the musical director in the musical or theatre work; in the latter the director is in overall control, but in the former the director's role may take second place to the conductor. The lack of collaboration in opera between the conductor and the director, when it occurs, often reflects the potential chasm discovered between music and theatre. This is exemplified by their contrasted attitude to rehearsal, aesthetics and artistic values.

The combination of a reliance on ancient repertoire and the star system has long-since moved the composer out of the opera house in a way that contradicts the experiences of the core opera composers from Mozart to Puccini. Arguably today the experience for a composer in theatre or musical theatre may be easier, where there may be a more flexible and less bureaucratic approach. Thus, the question of where a composer of today might learn the craft, the business of opera, remains elusive. One solution proved successful to Britten and Henze, and this was to create their own companies and their own festivals, and to conduct their own works.

The Modern Music Theatre Troupe enabled me to experiment with opera in unique ways: an abiding perspective was to dispense with the division between the pit and the stage, so the sarod became visible on stage in *The Marriages*, as did the Uilleann pipes in *Phantastes*, where their presence was palpable, not just audible. For the *Pillow Song*, the music was composed around a unique and beautiful set of large temple bells originally played by me, also conducting. In *La Malinche*, the orchestra was in effect a chorus of six sopranos and four baritones; the music

---

[15]   Ibid., p. 12.

was woven around the fixed pitches of a unique set of six large sea-shells that were played on stage by musicians, including four percussionists who surrounded the audience. In *Dirty Tricks* a seated electric bass-guitar was the only instrument behind six male voices and one female voice.

As well as these instrumental adventures, my other compositional business was to play with languages and their perception through the assemblages of texts I made: *The Pillow Song* set Japanese from the Heian dynasty; *La Malinche* made old-world Latin clash with new-world Nahuátl, as English clashed with Cortés's Castillian Spanish; in *The Sirens and the Sea*, the song of the sirens in Homerian Greek resonated alongside with the phonemes and onomatopoeia composed by James Joyce in his *Ulysses*. The discoveries in these works led me to abandon text in *Before the Beginning* and *El Gallo*.

These developments reveal opera's unique ability to articulate something about the nature of language, and they are echoed constantly in the history of the genre. Composers from Gluck to Mozart wrote operas in the language of the country they worked in, requiring translation when changing countries. Verdi and Puccini created a musical language that reflected an Italian sensibility. Debussy and Janáček developed music that reflects characteristics of French and Czechoslovakian respectively; Stravinsky (*Oedipus Rex*) and John Buller (*The Bacchae*) wrote operas entirely in Latin, and Philip Glass used ancient Egyptian (*Akhnaten*); Morton Feldman built an opera out of a single word (*Neither*); Ligeti invented sounds as an integral part of the theatricality of *Aventures* and *Nouvelles Aventures*, as did Berio in many works.

These performances of ostensibly impenetrable texts do not set out to create obscurity, but to challenge how we experience meaning. They resonate and articulate beyond the authority we endow to the written or disembodied word. Mendelssohn is often quoted as saying that music is 'not too *imprecise* to be framed in words, but too *precise*', which contradicts the idea that language is precise and music general in their effect.[16]

Lucile Desblache provides examples of similar trends in popular music:

> In rap for example, transparency of the words for a wide public is certainly not desirable, as slang aims at a particular target audience and a sociolect is created to express identity. Even in less rebellious vocal genres, the exotic or arcane qualities of lyrics are often part of the song appeal. Enya, currently one of the most successful female vocalists as regards commercial sales, includes in her album Amarantine (2005) a song in Japanese, as well as three in Loxian, a fictional language for which no translation is provided.[17]

---

[16]   Letter to Marc André Souchay, 15 October 1842. In Peter le Huray and James Day, *Music and Aesthetics in the Eighteenth and Early Nineteenth Centuries*, abridged edn (Cambridge, 1988), p. 311.

[17]   Lucile Desblache, 'Music to My Ears, but Words to My Eyes? Text, Opera and Their Audiences', *Linguistica Antverpiensia* 6 (2007): pp. 155–75 (p. 156).

Despite the assertion of McGilchrist that 'even now 90 per cent of communication between humans is by non-verbal means, through body-language and perhaps especially through intonation',[18] Patsy Rodenburg argues that the language we speak today has largely been usurped in our consciousness by the language we read in our literate society: 'I think it fair to say that in our schools the written word has triumphed over the spoken word. Literacy has had a far greater impact than oracy'.[19]

This increasing emphasis on disembodiment is seen by Ken Robinson as an educational if not a social weakening:

> One of the outcomes of academic education is a fear of the body, or at least a detachment from it. Academics tend to be disembodied. Academic education is focused on developments from the neck upwards. One result is that people think of their bodies as a form of transport for their heads.[20]

Opera remains one of the few platforms where we may still witness the coalition, synthesis, and collaboration between sound and meaning, text and music. For me and many others, this has only been possible outside the big opera houses. Instead, the performances of my operas came about through a growing network of festivals, venues, and producers. We found earliest support through The Place theatre (before it became a dedicated dance theatre), later the Camden Festival and the annual London Opera Festival. The artistic directors of these shared our excitement at new work and performances there spread when representatives of BBC Radio 3, the British Council and many other festivals attended and invited us beyond London and internationally. Significantly, opera houses remained elusive, perhaps judging correctly that we were working towards a different model. Crucially, we developed a parallel educational and community programme, which soon took specifically designed performances into shopping centres, the outdoors, and street theatre, and onto a sailing barge, through collaboration with other disciplines such as clowning and fashion.

Collaborations with Instrumentalists

Understanding how to compose for unusual instruments is one objective of collaboration with instrumentalists, with both composer and player on common ground. A more testing collaboration is how to entice onstage performances from classically trained musicians, who often find themselves challenged beyond the limits of their academic or conservatoire education and experience. This became clear to me when I was engaged to work with Bill Gaskill at the Royal Academy of

---

[18]   McGilchrist, *The Master and his Emissary*, p. 106.
[19]   Patsy Rodenburg, *The Need for Words* (London, 1993), p. 23.
[20]   Ken Robinson, *Out of Our Minds: Learning to Be Creative* (Chichester, 2001), p. 107.

Dramatic Art on an imaginative interpretation of a Noh theatre classic, *The Fulling Block* (*Kinuta*) by Zeami. I selected four student actors who would become the orchestra and chorus at the back of the Noh stage constructed in the space. We worked on vocalization and the playing of various percussion instruments which I designed: the instruments were largely of wood and unsophisticated but clean and simple, designed to be executed with specific physical gestures. I worked with the actors intensively on performance technique, with the aim of their conveying that each had spent their life dedicated to training in this sort of performance, as is the case in the tradition of Noh theatre. The score evolved in rehearsals on our own and with the cast, and became a list of instructions that were memorized. The effect led to members of the audience asking me from where I had hired the professional percussionists. I do not believe I could have easily found four percussionists who would have been able to absorb the formal, physical manner of performance that endowed the actors with the authority they embodied because musicians are typically educated in Western technique to produce sound – often the specific sound of a specific music or composer – rather than how to perform with their instrument. The instrumentalist does not typically see the stage they play on as the same stage an actor walks on, but the public may do. Yet the two most famous instrumentalists on the nineteenth century, Paganini and Liszt, developed an international reputation for the manner of their physical presence. Here is a music critic on Paganini:

> This man, with his long black hair and pale face, opens to us through a sound a world that we may have experienced before, but only in dreams. There is something so demonic in his appearance that at one moment we seek the 'hidden cloven hoof', at the next, the 'wings of an angel'.[21]

The aesthetic debate they kindled about the value of restraint or indulgence in virtuosity, or modesty over display in performance, led to a schism in the twentieth century. Pop and rock musicians understood through spectacle that we hear through our eyes, as evinced by Behne and Wöllner, and quickly embraced video technology that promoted this, whereas classical musicians either forgot the debate or perhaps were seduced by the idea of a perfect audio recording as an artefact.

Actor-musicianship on the West End stage has become increasingly popular since John Doyle's collaborations with Mary-Mitchell Campbell in Sondheim productions with all performers on stage. On the other hand, it is not uncommon to find in London's West End, such as in the current production of *War Horse* (New London Theatre, 2014), live musicians (an interesting epithet: the history of the phrase 'live musician' deserves another article) sequestered into a back room, with sound transmitted to the audience in the theatre. The role of the musician in this theatre aesthetic does not promote a sense of visual and gestural value or presence

---

[21] *Leipziger Musikalische Zeitung*, quoted in Jane O'Dea, *Virtue or Virtuosity? Explorations in the Ethics of Musical Performance* (Westport, CT, 2000), p. 42.

for either the audience or the musicians themselves. Finding instrumentalists who understand deeper concepts of performance is certainly a challenge, but I have had the privilege of working with many.

Collaborations with Designers

These may be revelatory for a composer. Costumes and sets can be interchangeable with musical instruments and lighting can greatly affect the performance of the musicians and their perception, both negatively and positively, by an audience. My recent work in Spain with the clarinettist Joan Lluna has begun to explore this area of concert-making, allowing the performers to control the tension dynamic on stage through their movements, which affects the audience's response. The invisibility of the orchestra in the opera pit was a device invented by Wagner, and it was justly celebrated for its role in the theatre he designed at Bayreuth. Despite its obvious advantages, it might be usefully noted that the concept, at the very least, destabilizes aspects of collaboration. The composer writing opera with an orchestra should at least be aware of the deception which underpins the choice of an invisible orchestra, as opposed to the Brechtian choice of honesty in its visibility.

Collaboration with Singers

The most dynamic collaborations in my experience have been with singers and they represent for me the front line, the coalface of opera. Although this might seem a truism, there are those works and reviews which suggest that the orchestra might be at least equally prominent in these terms. Critics rarely embrace knowledge or understanding of both theatre and music, as might befit an opera, which might perhaps explain such an opera review about the orchestral music. But in a collaborative, synthetic art form there is a question to be asked about values, equality, and the predominance of any one discipline. Historically we are used to the composer's opera in Wagner, the diva's opera with Callas, the conductor's opera with Haitink, or the director's opera with Zeffirelli. But I would differentiate between the process of opera and the product. Their relationship is not necessarily linear, except in the case of international opera.

Opera houses still largely operate an inherited *fach* system whereby voices are graded industrially to fit certain core repertoire roles. Despite all the benefits of the system born and developed through the most popular era of opera my experience tells me that singers rarely inhabit a single *fach* and are apt to change voices and repertoire throughout their professional lives. I once auditioned and accepted an exciting baritone to later discover he possessed a magnificent bass and tenor voice in addition, with extended ranges, which he could call on at will. As a young singer he worked with three distinct CVs as he was used to people not believing him.

The range of any voice is always unique, as is its tessitura and individual characteristics such as *filato* (the ability to 'spin' a mere thread of sound), tone (the individual colour that makes a certain singer's voice instantly recognizable in any music) and its balance between flexibility and power (commonly, but not necessarily, a strength in one area seems to preclude a strength in the other). Mozart often composed arias for particular singers, as can be seen in the two *coloratura* arias for the Queen of the Night in *Die Zauberflöte*, and it has always seemed to me to be an excellent example to follow. Writing an opera for a soprano would seem to me an abstract idea, demanding changes to be made when the work is cast; I have always preferred to know for whom I am composing in advance.

The collaboration does not stop there, as during the rehearsal process there are so many details which can make the difference between a good or an excellent performance; the fine-tuning, the tailoring of the music to the singer, is best achieved in an atmosphere where the singer in turn is willing to trust the composer's intention, which is not always the case. Whereas opera singers from past eras collaborated with composers as a matter of course, the contemporary preference for dead composers mitigates against collaboration as part of an opera singer's training.

The rift between theatre and opera has also developed into a schism for performers. There are indeed singers who can act and actors who can sing. The phrases echo different aesthetics and are used pejoratively within the professions on both sides. The history of opera abounds with those (epitomized by Callas) who lose control of their voice but not of their performance. Audiences are as faithful to those as they may be to actors who create iconic performances of songs despite vocal or musical challenges. There are many fewer examples of singer-actors of equal virtuosity in both disciplines. The composer's business is to know what sort of a performer his or her music requires.

During the creation of my textless operas *Before the Beginning* (aka *Songs Between Words*) and *El Gallo*, the collaborative element was even stronger. It was never my intention to create a new language the singers would have to learn in order to sing them. Rather it was the reverse, to set the singer free from the constraints of cultural representation and – later I discovered – inadvertently free from rules of pronunciation and diction. I will go into more detail about how these librettos developed in the second part of this chapter.

Audience Reception

Language

From a theatrical perspective, the absence of text in performance has a tradition at least as old as the *commedia dell'arte*, when Italian street theatre learned to evade the Catholic church's ability to imprison and punish that which they deemed blasphemous. By avoiding language, the players found they were able to be both intelligible to their audience and simultaneously incapable of being found guilty of anything; the currency of the legal profession, then as now, was words, which were circumnavigated by nonsense. It was this practice that Dario Fo took up again in countering the fascism that sought to control Italy in the twentieth century. He called his language Grammelot and even used it to accept the Nobel Prize. Peter Brook's collaboration with Ted Hughes saw another invented language presented globally in *Orghast*, as an attempt to discover a universal theatrical language, unrestricted by culture or geography. More recently, the global company Cirque du Soleil and The Sims computer game franchise have developed an attitude to language in performance which reflects global ambitions of presentation: neither use language as such but the former use invented words spoken and sung by the performers which resonate with many cultures, while the latter employed two actors, one male and one female, able to speak freely and copying certain emotional responses in gobbledygook. Opera, on the other hand, has tended to rely on original language performance, and its globalization has led to surtitles in performance or alternative singing translations, except for the small number of contemporary works, such as those mentioned above, which deliberately choose an archaic language. In narrative-based musical theatre (as distinct from juke-box or dance-based), the text is the foundation and is known as the book, the writer of which has an unglamorous role according to Stephen Clark,[22] akin to grouting between tiles; typically with another sort of writer who provides the lyric. According to David Finkle, Elaine Stritch compares singing a Sondheim Song, such as 'Send in the Clowns', to appearing in a three-act play.[23] In so doing she echoes Cone's observation between opera and song.

Beginnings

Before the Beginning grew from a collection called *Songs Between Words*, all *a cappella* without text. I was living in Mexico at the time and the idea grew from a response to the problem of which language to choose to set, realizing that Spanish would be as difficult to English-speaking audiences as English would to those in Mexico. I decided to compose sounds, phonemes ascribed to syllables approximating the practice of words, along with the music. It gave me the opportunity to make sure the singer's art was made as effective as possible by choosing vowels and consonants appropriate to the range and emotional demand of the music. I chose three singers to work with, and their understandable initial resistance to learning a new set of linguistic rules collapsed when they realized that they could make the sounds in a way appropriate to their individuality and replace my ideas with theirs, when they discovered something that worked. These were never designed as abstract songs, and the *meaning* was embedded in the title, such as *Lullaby* or *Blues*; sometimes titles appeared abstract, such as *Turubu*,

---

[22]   Spoken in general conversation with him when working on our work together on our musical *Sigrun's Fire*, 2011.

[23]   'Elaine Stritch in the Stephen Sondheim Stretch', <www.huffingtonpost.com/david-finkle/elaine-stritch-in-the-ste_b_416508.html> (accessed 20 July 2014).

Example 4.1   *Turubu*

but such made-up words were contextualized in the song in such a way that the meaning from an emotional sense was clear. That song, for instance, only uses nine syllables (Example 4.1).

I used the IPA phonetic alphabet to clarify the sound for the score after we chose the syllables. *Turubu* is a celebratory trio, with the voice used in a percussive, rhythmical manner as well as lyrically. The musical notation clarifies the relative stress of syllables and the emotional context that might constitute what is termed meaning, and the limit of paralinguistic sounds is no more a limitation than in, say, Mozart's *Alleluia.*

Once the singers realized that they might create the meaning and thus collaborate in the composition and were given licence to refrain from concerns over pronunciation and diction, the rehearsals were characterized by a great deal of fun and playfulness. We discovered our shared sandpit was enormous, and we worked together with an actor as a sort of Master of Ceremonies, who also entered the spirit and had to eschew any recognizable spoken text; he invented his own nonsense. The inclusion of actors among singers had already become a standard casting approach for me by this time, having learned that when on stage their natural competitive spirit provoked a better all-round performance by all.

A selection of the songs we worked on became the structure for the narrative of *Before the Beginning*, presented in a small chapel in Mexico with a glorious acoustic, a performance which, nevertheless, included elements of cabaret. Individual songs from the collection were taken up by many singers from other countries as well, and the success of the project led me to conceive of the idea on a larger scale.

Around this time I became aware of the work of Martin Crimp and, specifically, his open-text plays. Some of the aesthetic seemed to apply to my work, as I had become aware in working with the singers that their imagination could lead the meaning of the songs into places I had not conceived, albeit within the boundaries proscribed by the title. In Crimp's plays, such as *Attempts on Her Life*, *Face to the Wall* and *Fewer Emergencies*, the dialogue and characters are deliberately unassigned and left for the director and cast to make decisions in rehearsal. While parts in my songs remained clearly for the singer they were designed for, the elasticity of the meaning could allow vastly different interpretations.

My next textless opera became known as *Nye Tand, Eh?* I directed sections of it with Frances M. Lynch and James Meek and we deliberately made two sets of the same scenes, with different characters in contrasted situations. I became curious as to how far this process might take me, and how it might provoke radically different performances of the same work, and the video recordings of these performed excerpts do demonstrate that. But work on *Nye Tand, Eh?* was interrupted by a request to collaborate with the Teatro de Ciertos Habitantes, who were looking for an opportunity to create a music-based work to tour to several continents without recourse to translations or surtitles, as had been their previous practice.

El Gallo

El Gallo became known as an opera without text for six actors and two string quartets, deliberately provoking some kind of synthesis between opera, theatre, and musical theatre. On a practical level, for the Mexico-based international touring company Teatro de Ciertos Habitantes this provoked interest across a wide range of venues and audiences. It defied some of these expectations in respect of the relationship between language, music, and meaning while simultaneously it aimed to communicate character, narrative, and plot to an audience. But there were several steps that led to its discovery.

The Teatro de Ciertos Habitantes under their director Claudio Valdés-Kuri worked in physical theatre and music, usually collaborating with guests for a year to develop a work which would then enter their worldwide touring schedule. The company is unique to Mexico but shares certain characteristics with other companies that devise their own material, such as Complicite In my case this meant travelling frequently to Mexico for several weeks each time during 2008 and 2009 to work with the director and six company members. Beyond the agreement on there being an absence of text, those early collaborations were open-ended and without any clear objective other than to find out how we might work together. They were all experienced company members, originating from Iran, Guadeloupe, Japan, Lebanon, and Mexico, and included two who read music fluently, but only one of whom had a trained voice. In between my visits, Claudio worked with them on their own personal culture and character, discussing how aspects of this might be used to create their stage character. They also worked on their vocal production with Maria Huesca, my long-time specialist collaborator on voice.

My business as a composer was to create material that they might eventually be able to use as the basis for collaboration on a multidisciplinary stage. There were many challenges along the way, such as my producing music which they could not accommodate, and their having to produce a convincing sound on stage, without microphones, as in opera. There were times when I considered the challenge too much for me, as I confided in Claudio; doubtless there were times when the cast felt similarly about my demands. These momentary failures of collaboration became increasingly important for Claudio, who after several visits confided in me his narrative strategy: a composer is given five singers he has never met to learn his music and enter a competition. The plot follows their initial meeting and several rehearsals. It transpires that the composer has his favourite and his nemesis: one singer is unable to hide her lack of musical confidence, frequently disrupting the rehearsal. The composer, however, has no choice but to use this group. The day of the performance (within the narrative) arrives in the second act, after the interval. They perform the work they have been rehearsing as a concert item. At the climax of this substantial piece, when the composer's passion is at his greatest, at the moment of singing her most important phrase, this beleaguered singer is so tense that her voice breaks in the most ugly and artless way. Such a vocal event is called *el gallo* in Mexico, and is roughly equivalent to the English *frog* in the throat. It also means the cockerel, which is a particularly Mexican symbol and thus the title of a work without words can be given a title of words.

But the event, the mistake, the error is so gross that the singers stop singing and the orchestra stops playing; clearly she is the culprit, and the composer – who has been singing and conducting too – is left alone on stage, mortified. The audiences were frequently taken by this device and believed the performance had really collapsed. With much hesitation the cast gradually find their way back onto the stage. The audience are somehow convinced of the dramatic subterfuge and the finale is celebratory; the composer and his five singers have been reconciled with themselves.

The story that Claudio developed mirrored (but with some exaggeration I hope) the experience we had shared in the challenging early workshops. The language or sounds we used evolved between us during the process, and each character chose their own name following a phonetic pattern established in rehearsal: Shaptes (the Nemesis), Shaktom, Jogbos, Thiktum (the Favourite), Shaktas, and Viptim (the Composer).

El Gallo: weeny wobjab nuwi-nuwi

Fno peniuro 'El Gallo' ni efwo cuckarakoo nu chaba. Schnedjhe weji 'Meschikana' ishto djeve dnavuwe. Zhim oodooum djish-kovitch shum 'Entre Palabras' (Quindecim 134): varigoteshki oodooumvosch shin waba-waba, presenschi Meschiko 2004, zhim 'Festival de Mexico en el Centro Historico'. Shibi-shaba Claudio uwischke Paul banga-bango luga-largoscki. Lugu-largo nu, chabamota! Clibobonbon 2 aniosks 6 doo-doo's (Itzia, Irene, Fabrina, Edwin, Kaveh, Ernesto) eeniwoschka widipu shebang-bang Shaptes, Shaktom, Jogbos, Thiktum, Shaktas, Viptim). Sejhenski sinpopozhne!

   Paul showany Kalipadi Kalipadi la la la la. Claudio nemi napo, 'een ai uwi wina yawi nayame wina yame'. Shinofwe – buzhni zheve zhave vu aiu wia – zhiblink chabe: Ernesto (Viptim), oodooumpapapri: niwe papapra eento puweklobongt: 'Shvejishwgvnijmlagenschigcht!' Kaveh (Shaktas) Eduum Hajhne woro udoof Itzia (Shaptes); Edwin (Thiktum) woopi-waas Ernesto (Viptim), een oodooumvoschup eef oodooumvoschlow, wijhne-wojhne www eef mmm (scablickski, djheva!). Irene (Shaktom) eef Fabrina (Jogbos) beetchy-beetchy iwoz toodamkost: 'nemi napo chiwa!' Nuwishni 6 showany, perobut 6 wwwmmm!

   El Gallo powukany 5 presactus eef 1 blevisch, posty-posty. Koabn 1, 'oiuqgfhcnqxj'; koabn 2 (meent 8 oodooumarcos), weeschkum blivny; koabm 3, weeschkum 'da lucha libre*'; koabm 4, wwwv eent mmmv – 'iepiphaneeasch'; koabm 5, oodooum 'el Gallo'; koabm 6 – blevisch, posty-posty, nemoniwi, debiwe dewiya!

*woschish kabakaktpa Meschikana

Figure 4.1   Programme note to *El Gallo*

   The absence of text led to a challenge regarding the content of the programme, in whichever country it was performed. Beyond the standard cast and company profiles, how were we to introduce this work to audiences? I decided to create a programme note using some of the invented sounds from the opera, and this was printed in the programme (Figure 4.1).[24]

   With such a tightly developed work built around specific performers, the idiosyncrasies of their voices, culture, and personalities, one might imagine that only they might be able to perform it, without having to start again. But during the hundred or more performances they have given since 2009, a replacement for one of them had to be found or a leg of a tour cancelled. The Iranian influence the original performer brought was replaced by a Mexican sensibility (including accent, if accent can be discovered in nonsense sounds), and the original improvised cadenza in one of his songs was made repeatable for the first time, but *El Gallo* was still completely recognizable.

   The two string quartets offer gestural, visual, and dramatic as well as musical material for each performance, requiring some memorization for one of the

---

[24]   The complete libretto is available at performances or online, <www.paulalanbarker. net/id2.html> (accessed 20 July 2014).

quartets. Their integration at certain points of the action was as crucial as the choreography of some of their playing gestures, since all were in plain sight of the audience. In the first part they inhabit opposite sides of the stage, offering opposing sides visually and aurally to the drama as it unfolds. As the performances grew and developed they increasingly took part in the acting of the apparent collapse of the performance in the second part, where they would typically regroup as one, confirming the audience's perception of failure.

Conclusion

The business of making *El Gallo* was a unique adventure, drawn out of failure, trust, and collaboration during intense periods of work. To work with such a company, whose dedication and achievements exceed the professional experience of many, is an experience I count as a privilege. It is by no means a typical operatic experience, but then I have never set out with that as my goal. It is, however, one to which the business of opera arguably contributes, and functions, potentially, in a transforming manner.

El Gallo would not be to everyone's taste. Mingling with audiences after performances I overhear people talking about many aspects, usually in a complimentary way, but sometimes less enthusiastically about character, plot, the sense of humour, the music, but never about the absence of text. That had been our aim: for the absence of text not to be noticed as an absence, but instead a means to allow instead the theatre, music, and voices to communicate directly to the audience through the performer's collaborative authority.

I defined opera earlier as a synthesis of voice, text, and theatre. My fascination with opera is that this synthesis is contradictory. Even by omitting any of the three elements, such as I might have been have said to have done with the text in *El Gallo*, it still remains opera. One of my current projects is to work with a synthetic, computer-generated voice (*Of Zoe and the Woman I Sing*). It is a far from new idea and the first score I know of to do so was by Joseph Olive: described by the composer in 1975 as 'Mar-ri-ia-a, An opera for computer voice, music, soprano, and chamber orchestra'.[25] The business of opera from a composer's point of view is essentially the negotiation of a process of collaborative change that may be allowed to question and interrogate the nature of that business.

Music and Opera Examples by Paul Barker Available Online

Turubu (excerpt from *Songs Between Words*): <https://soundcloud.com/paul-alan-barker/14-turuboo>.
El Gallo: <http://youtu.be/GIXdK-FgSXw>; <http://youtu.be/76TPYQzCCX4>.

---

[25] <http://jpoliveconsulting.com/about> (accessed 8 July 2014).

Nye Tand, Eh?: <www.londonmet.ac.uk/thefacility/projects/2005–06/nye-tand-eh-video.cfm>.
La Malinche: <http://youtu.be/i1A77hvjwnk>.

Commercially Available Compact Discs

The Pillow Song & Before the Beginning, on Entre Palabras, Quindecim (2005).
El Gallo, on Quindecim (2012).
Excerpts from *Dirty Tricks*, on *Turquoise Swans*, Sargasso (2000) and *Mono'Dia* by Simon Haram, Sospiro (2014).

Operas by Paul Barker in Reverse Chronological Order

My Voice and Me, a melodrama for avatar, actor, and piano.
Hello, Mr Darwin! Opera for children with two professional singers.
El Gallo, opera for six actors and two string quartets without words.
Nye Tand, Eh? Opera without words.
Before The Beginning (aka *Antes del Principio*). Later published as *Songs Between Words: 48 a cappella, textless songs.*
The Mechanical Operation of the Spirit, interactive Internet opera prototype.
Stone Angels, after *The Lord of the Flies*, by William Golding.
Dirty Tricks, opera drawing on data relating to British Airways vs. Virgin Atlantic.
The Sorceress's Tale, the story behind the story of Dido and Aeneas, from the Sorceress's point of view.
Circus Opera Sailing Barge, Circus Space and MMTT.
The Sirens and the Sea, dramatic cantata for 30 female voices.
Prologue to 'La Malinche', libretto by the composer drawn from historical documents of the conquest of Mexico.
Albergo Empedocle, libretto by Nicholas Till after E. M. Forster.
La Malinche and *Prologue*, libretto by composer after historical sources.
The Pillow Song, libretto by composer after *The Pillow Book*, the diary of a tenth-century Japanese court lady.
Phantastes, an adult fairy-tale opera. Libretto by composer after the novel by George Macdonald.
The Marriages Between Zones 3, 4 and 5, after the novel by Doris Lessing.

Full details of these works can be found on: <www.paulalanbarker.net>.

Chapter 5

Interdisciplinary Support for Opera Practice in the UK

Christopher Newell

In this chapter a model will be proposed to change the perception of middle-scale[1] mainstream operatic practice from exclusively culturally beneficial to more generally beneficial, and thus to increase its chances of receiving support from research funding sources not customarily approached by opera organizations.

Introduction

Public funding and commercial sponsorship for middle-scale 'mainstream'[2] opera are hard to obtain. Being business-like is now a compulsory ethos for opera companies but, although the performing arts and music have both been accorded the status of 'creative industries',[3] it is difficult for opera practitioners to convince decision-makers that the discipline addresses industrial criteria or shows benefits beyond the cultural or artistic domain. One possibility is to reframe the process of opera-making and performance as a 'research opportunity' and seek funding through partnerships with universities, the UK research councils, and the European funding programmes.[4] Interdisciplinary research opportunities may then be sought

---

[1] The focus on middle-scale opera is in accordance with the case studies. There is no reason to suppose that the model proposed herein should not apply equally to large- or small-scale companies and organizations.

[2] I have tried to limit the scope of this chapter to what I call 'mainstream opera'. This may be defined as opera from the standard operatic repertoire rather than new compositions. The reason for so doing is to avoid any confusion with crossover work in contemporary music theatre, musical theatre, and musicals. Clearly this limits the reach of the main arguments set out in this chapter, but some justification can be gleaned from the assumption that 'mainstream opera' offers some of the biggest challenges in terms of the issues addressed herein, particularly impact as construed by the Research Council UK (RCUK) and the Research Excellence Framework (REF).

[3] DCMS, Department for Culture Media and Sport – Creative Industries <www.culture.gov.uk/what_we_do/Creative_industries> (accessed 17 July 2012).

[4] European Commission, 'Research and Innovation', <http://ec.europa.eu/research/index.cfm> (accessed 15 April 2014); European Research Council (ERC) <http://erc.europa.eu> (accessed 15 April 2014).

across the full range of disciplines: science, health, social science, business, and technology, to name but a few. Of course, this requires some adjustment on the part of both opera companies and academia.

One senses that some readers may be protesting at this point. Why should opera companies bother to work with other disciplines? Are we not a significant enough creative force in our own right without selling out to science agendas? Is it realistic or worthwhile to spend the time nurturing such interdisciplinary relationships? How do we come up with ideas for these kinds of interdisciplinary projects? All these points are valid and, for individual companies, may present deal-breaking caveats, but the suggestions found in this chapter are not intended as a generic fix for all circumstances. Nonetheless, for those of us locked into the depressing 'unaffordability issue' of producing mainstream opera, particularly those of us outside the large publicly funded companies, the ideas presented here may be worth considering.

Impact

One reason to seek out more interdisciplinary opportunities is that the research may be perceived as having more 'impact' and the funds awarded to do the research may be correspondingly bigger. 'Impact' is a contentious term, hard to define and possibly even harder to measure, but at present it is a key requirement for any research funded by major bodies such as the Research Councils UK (RCUK).[5] They define different kinds of impact:

> Academic impact: The demonstrable contribution that excellent research makes to academic advances, across and within disciplines, including significant advances in understanding, methods, theory and application.

> Economic and societal impacts: The demonstrable contribution that excellent research makes to society and the economy. Economic and societal impacts embrace all the extremely diverse ways in which research-related knowledge and skills benefit individuals, organisations and nations by: fostering global economic performance, and specifically the economic competitiveness of the United Kingdom, increasing the effectiveness of public services and policy, enhancing quality of life, health and creative output.[6]

In addition, the Research Excellence Framework for 2013 specifies impact as in Table 5.1.

[5] RCUK, 'Pathways to Impact' <www.rcuk.ac.uk/ke/impacts> (accessed 15 April 2014).
[6] RCUK, 'What do Research Councils Mean by "Impact"?' <www.rcuk.ac.uk/ke/impacts/meanbyimpact> (accessed 15 April 2014).

Table 5.1   Indicative range of impacts

Civil society	Informing and influencing the form and content of associations between people or groups to illuminate and challenge cultural values and social assumptions.
Cultural life	Creating and interpreting cultural capital in all of its forms to enrich and expand the lives, imaginations and sensibilities of individuals and groups.
Economic prosperity	Applying and transferring the insights and knowledge gained from research to create wealth in the manufacturing, service, creative and cultural sectors.
Education	Informing and influencing the form or the content of the education of any age group in any part of the world where they extend significantly beyond the submitting HEI [Higher Educationa Institution].
Policy making	Informing and influencing policy debate and practice through interventions relating to any aspect of human or animal well-being or the environment.
Public discourse	Extending the range and improving the quality of evidence, argument and expression to enhance public understanding of the major issues and challenges faced by individuals and society.
Public services	Contributing to the development and delivery of public services or legislation to support the welfare, education, understanding or empowerment of diverse individuals and groups in society, including the disadvantaged or marginalised.

Source: Research Excellence Framework, 'Main Panel D Criteria', <www.ref.ac.uk/media/ref/content/pub/panelcriteriaandworkingmethods/01_12_2D.pdf> (accessed 15 April 2014).

The evaluation of impact may be thought of as seeking to answer the questions: 'what difference is your work making to the world?' or, 'who is going to substantially benefit and how?' It should also be noted that projects receiving funding are likely to be aiming to have impact in several of the areas indicated in Table 5.1. For the opera professional faced with such improbable synergies, it is tempting to defensively proffer the 'cultural life' card; however, this same card is sure to be being proffered by all the competitors of said opera professional.

The Model

My proposed model is intended to anchor the interdisciplinary project in some real-world criteria. It is quite easy for participants in an extreme interdisciplinary activity to become enamoured with 'making new friends' and 'learning new things', almost as if they were participating in network dating, and the result is likely to be weak or inconclusive deliverables that have negligible potential impact. The proposition, here, is that a viable project must have some or all of the following components in varying degrees:

- potential interdisciplinary and collaborative areas of discovery and research;
- challenging and important problem spaces;
- products and tangible outcomes; and
- elements of public engagement.

It should be stressed that these projects must be constituted as partnerships between opera companies and universities or other higher education organizations to be eligible for many of the available sources of research funding.

This model is not intended to be definitive or exclusive. There may be many other ways of increasing the relevance of opera-making and widening the pool of potential collaborators and funding streams that lead to similarly positive outcomes. Educational partnerships, for example, are frequently presented as significant outcomes of opera-practice programmes, and strictly commercial partnerships with industry and broadcast channels are another alternative. This chapter, however, will focus specifically on interdisciplinary research partnerships as an innovative additional strategy.

The Case Studies

This pragmatic approach to finding new ways to fund opera production is supported by case studies familiar to the author, conducted by the Culture Lab[7] at Newcastle University with Co-Opera Co[8] (a middle-scale professional touring opera company), and by the Universities of York and Hull in partnership with opera and music festivals and industrial partners (including Toshiba Research Europe Ltd, Cereproc, and Toby Churchill) in a project entitled the Creative Speech Technology Network (CreST).[9] These case studies include the use of operatic practice to explore user-generated content for collaborative video production, an exploration of the quality of voice popularly known as 'the tingle factor', and consideration of the use of melodramatic techniques derived from opera to improve the expressiveness of computer-generated speech. The modest success of these studies points the way for collaborations between opera practitioners and interdisciplinary researchers on bigger projects, a step up from the tentative 'proof

---

[7]   Culture Lab, 'Newcastle University: Culture Lab', <http://di.ncl.ac.uk> (accessed 15 April 2014).

[8]   Co-Opera Co <www.co-opera-co.org> (accessed 15 April 2014).

[9]   Information on all the industrial collaborators in CreST may be found on line at CreST Network, 'The Creative Speech Technology Network', <http://crestnetwork.org.uk> (accessed 18 May 2013).

of concept' and sandpits[10] towards larger-scale collaborative research proposals, perhaps with some of the major opera companies.

The Economics of Middle-Scale Opera versus Academic Research

Middle-Scale Opera

The author's career in opera has led to encounters with a number of middle-scale opera companies presenting traditional or mainstream opera. They include Co-Opera Co, Mid Wales Opera, and Diva Opera.[11] Full-scale mainstream opera is very expensive to put on. Cheaper middle-scale derivatives with reduced orchestras and cut-down sets, usually without a chorus, find it more difficult to attract audiences, particularly in the big metropolitan centres where the larger companies prevail. They may be obliged to concentrate on touring, where the audiences can be harder to locate, the choice of repertoire may be constrained to a few popular favourites,[12] and the profits achieved from ticket sales are lower. For these companies, productions rarely meet their costs and even more rarely make a surplus for the promoters such that they are able to plan ahead. As a consequence, entering the art form at this level as a producer, director, singer, or conductor is inherently risky. This leads to a relative paucity of opportunities and means that the industry has been slow to develop in terms of new repertoire, new audiences, and new business models. It is a cycle of despair, as less innovation tends to attract less funding from public and private bodies; nor is it easy for emerging opera singers from the conservatoires and colleges to find appropriate opportunities to learn roles and to gain stage experience. Thus the raw material of the opera experience (the singing actor's art) does not have the opportunity to prosper as it might. Conversations within all but the few privileged companies that receive public subsidies sufficient to alleviate some (but certainly not all) existential worries usually end up returning obsessively to the subject of 'how to survive'. Some readers might argue that this is right and proper, and that an art form appealing to a minority audience should have to fight to be seen and heard, and should sink or swim according to public demand. Putting that aside, as the purpose of this chapter permits, middle-scale opera is sometimes a rather depressing place to be.

---

[10]   According to the Engineering and Physical Sciences Research Council (EPSRC), a sandpit has 'a highly multidisciplinary mix of participants, some active researchers and others potential users of research outcomes, to drive lateral thinking and radical approaches to address research challenges'. EPSRC, 'Sandpits' <www.epsrc.ac.uk/funding/howtoapply/routes/network/ideas/whatisasandpit> (accessed 17 July 2014).

[11]   Mid Wales Opera <www.midwalesopera.co.uk>, Diva Opera, <www.divaopera.com>.

[12]   Still heard, anecdotally, are claims by the middle-scale touring fraternity that the only opera able to reliably attract audiences is Bizet's *Carmen*.

Higher Education (Academia)

This position of perpetual financial uncertainty and poverty contrasts with that of the UK higher education sector (despite what many academics believe). While there are plenty of financial difficulties in this sector too, resources are available to potentially allow opera practitioners to do interesting work somewhat protected from the external pressures of the performance industries. At the very least, some universities are likely to be able to offer a performance space, rehearsal studios, academic expertise, participants, and audiences. Universities with larger music or drama departments may be able to offer much more. In general, collaborations do not happen. There are many reasons why this is the case that lie outside the scope of this chapter, but, setting this issue aside, funding is available within academia that is not available to the professional opera world (of course, the converse applies too). Thus the potential for some sort of reciprocal and mutually beneficial arrangement in which the opera company brings expertise in practice and the university in research should be realizable. In general, academic research grants provide larger sums than middle-scale opera companies can expect to attract from arts funding bodies. Of course, the key distinction is the purpose the funding is directed towards. Research funding cannot be used for anything other than research, so even if a new opera production is highly innovative and multidisciplinary, if it does not address a set of research questions it will not receive funding. This issue of 'practice as research'[13] is particularly thorny, but, in essence, the research must be deeply embedded in the practice and cannot be an adjunct or an afterthought. For example, funding will not be provided if the performance alone is used as a method of evaluating a piece of research. One way of rationalizing this complicated concept is to ask whether the research can be done without the performance, and whether the performance can be done without the research. If the answer to both questions is a clear 'no' then the project may be categorized as practice as research. Unravelling viable potential synergies between research in higher education and opera practice may require a more radical approach and a step outside the domain of the arts into less familiar territory.

Multi-, Inter- and Transdisciplinary Activities

It seems unlikely that a professional background in opera would be an asset for a researcher working in a science discipline at a UK university. However, for some years there has been significant encouragement for researchers to work across arts and science disciplines on less conventional, riskier collaborative projects. In fact, it has become fashionable to freely use terms in research proposals such as 'multidisciplinary' (where the integrity of each individual discipline is maintained in the mix), 'interdisciplinary' (where some intellectual exchange occurs between

---

[13]   Estelle Barrett and Barbara Bolt, *Practice as Research: Approaches to Creative Arts Enquiry* (London: I.B. Tauris, 2007).

the disciplines), and 'transdisciplinary' (where the objective is to radically transform disciplinary perspectives in accordance with new knowledge created in the mix). The three terms, while often used interchangeably, may be regarded as points on a continuum from additive through interactive to holistic. Some of the more 'extreme' interdisciplinary convergences provide the case studies later in this chapter.

It is encouraging to note, for those of us with an enthusiasm for the 'extremes', that research funding bodies, whether hosted in the UK or the European Union, are currently unafraid of *insisting* on interdisciplinary components in bids. For example, here are some extracts from the European Horizon 2020 specification for the Future and Emerging Technologies Call. The specifics of the call are not relevant to the argument. The italics are mine, and added for emphasis:

> [...] addresses the *interdisciplinary* fundamentals of knowing, thinking, doing and being, in close synergy with foundational research [...]

> [...] aims at renewing ties *between the different disciplines* studying knowledge, cognition and related issues from various perspectives.

> [...] These *multidisciplinary* studies are expected to go well beyond addressing the perception-action loop [...][14]

The notion of discrete research silos populated exclusively by specialists is arguably on the wane (at least for now); however, it would be wrong to suggest that these more generalist requirements are ubiquitous or indeed will continue to be fashionable. Rightfully, there will always be a place for single-discipline specialist research in areas where only a focused disciplinary approach or at the most a multidisciplinary approach can address the research challenges in the project. Setting this fact aside, the purpose of this chapter is to seek to integrate this trend to connect disparate disciplines into common research programmes with a substantial opera component. These projects are less likely to be significantly supported by conventional arts funding bodies (in the UK, Arts Council England (ACE) or the Arts and Humanities Research Council (AHRC)) than they are by funding programmes for science, innovation, health, technology, social science, or anything else that may emerge from the project and the specifics of the disciplinary mix.[15] That is not to say that sources of funding for the arts are irrelevant; it is just that these programmes are already open to opera-based proposals, and the intention here is to posit new and unconventional funding opportunities rather than restate those that are already addressed intensively by the community.

---

[14]   H2020 Work programme 2 FET <http://ec.europa.eu/research/participants/data/ref/h2020/wp/2014_2015/main/h2020-wp1415-fet_en.pdf>, pp. 14–15 (accessed 17 July 2014).

[15]   All of these disciplines have substantially larger research budgets at their disposal than the performing arts.

So, in answer to the question posed at the beginning of this section: for some of the academics researching the sciences, yes, a background in the arts or even opera can be beneficial, at least in the current climate.

Collaborative Opportunities in Mainstream Opera

Of all the art forms, opera must surely be a contender for being one of the most multidisciplinary. Indeed, Wagner can surely be viewed as an originator of the sort of multimedia immersive environments heralded since the early 1990s as groundbreaking in computer games design.[16] Whether opera can be regarded as interdisciplinary or even transdisciplinary really depends on whether we see the convergent processes that occur in opera production between the arts (for example, performing, visual, and vocal) and other domains (for instance, engineering, management, and pedagogy) as in any way mutually transformative. The answer in most instances is probably 'no'; however, this realization may serve to stimulate a revaluation of the opportunities under discussion in this chapter. Namely, if, as part of designing these processes, they are thought of as transformative exchanges of disciplinary perspectives, then the case for mutually beneficial inter- or even transdisciplinary research activities is clearly viable. In other words, the rich environment of the opera production process – in particular, the inherently multidisciplinary environment – is a naturally fertile ground for the sort of projects under discussion. Being aware of the potential of this resource is the key for any collaboration. It is all too easy to take for granted some of the fascinating processes that take place in any operatic production. This is best illustrated with two anecdotes.

During rehearsal for Co-Opera's production of *The Mikado*, my colleague from the University of Newcastle, who was new to opera and interested in documentary filmmaking, was keen to make more use of user-generated content. This is content that the participants in the opera production could produce for themselves, using devices such as mobile-phone video cameras. He asked if the singers filmed themselves performing and then analysed it later, looking to make improvements, as a football coach might do. I said I was not sure if this occurred and made further enquiries. We found that this was very rarely the case, despite the ready availability of a useful analytical tool. The reasons appeared to be complicated. Notions of etiquette were wrapped up with notions of undermining self-confidence or of getting a false impression of quality. This prompted further enquiries into the pedagogical methods of the company and the gradual emergence of a potential research project to investigate more structured uses of new technology in training for the performing arts.

---

[16] I would argue that *Doom* (1993, ID Software) was the first game that successfully incorporated music, visuals, effects, narrative, and character within a proscenium-like environment. Indeed, the notion of *Doom the Opera* was an unrealized project of the author's.

Here is a second anecdote. Outsiders are impressed by the complex modes of communication and the transfers of responsibility and authority that occur over the duration of the opera production process. From the first solo musical calls in a studio with a single singer and a coach to the full dress rehearsals on stage, a lot is achieved very effectively over a short period, usually under significant time pressure. Another research colleague was eager to understand this process and videoed stage rehearsals of a production of *The Magic Flute*, teasing out the live interaction between the conductor, singers, director, choreographer, dialogue coach, stage manager, lighting designer, and the technical team. We were all surprised when he described the somewhat chaotic process, which we took for granted, as a model of successful collaboration under pressure that he could see being applied to a multidisciplinary design domain, such as computer games development, that works in a similarly intense way.

In opera, large numbers of people have to understand each other's diverse disciplines, retain the integrity of their own, and work towards a common outcome. Opera practitioners are trained to manage the contrasting – sometimes conflicting – viewpoints of singers, conductors, directors, designers, lighting designers, promoters, and, of course, audiences. Clearly the goal of a good performance is deeply embedded in the culture, and such a clear-cut goal may not be as readily apparent in the sorts of interdisciplinary projects this chapter champions. The next section will set out other examples and methods for extreme interdisciplinary collaboration that together constitute the small field upon which the precepts of this chapter are based.[17]

Examples of Collaborations

Research in opera is traditionally a musicological, literary, or dramaturgical specialism, and so far has tended to operate in relative isolation from radical interdisciplinary agendas despite its multimedia credentials. Whereas dance has been quite successful in encouraging convergences with other art forms and science disciplines (particularly computer technology[18]), opera has seemingly presented fewer points of contact for external disciplines. Two comprehensive historical reviews of the convergence between the performing and other arts with new technologies have been published by Stephen Wilson and by Steve Dixon.[19]

---

[17]   Most of the examples are UK based in order that they align with the UK funding models under discussion.

[18]   I. Brown, 'Technology's New Fields of Dreams in Dance' <www.theartsdesk. com/dance/technologys-new-fields-dreams-dance> (accessed 20 April 2014); Dancedigital <www.dancedigital.org.uk/dancedigitaldev> (accessed 20 April 2014).

[19]   Stephen Wilson, *Information Arts: Intersection of Art, Science, and Technology* (Cambridge, MA, 2002), xxiv, p. 945. Steve Dixon, *Digital Performance: A History of New Media in Theater, Dance, Performance Art, and Installation* (Cambridge, MA, 2007), p. 809.

As far as I am aware, opera practice in the UK rarely embeds itself fully into the academic sphere. For example, there are few instances of practising professional opera companies hosted in a university and sharing research and resources. Collaborations do exist between the UK opera companies and the leading music colleges; for example, the Royal Opera House and the Guildhall School of Music & Drama are collaborating on a postgraduate programme in opera-making, but conservatoires, music colleges, and similar institutions tend to operate to one side of the academic mainstream with a distinct focus on practice and less on research. Of the mainstream universities there are a few exceptions.

DARE: A Collaboration between Opera North and the University of Leeds

A number of projects have emerged from this partnership, including new commissions.[20] There is less focus on the standard repertoire and more on new writing and composition. Perhaps the most extreme interdisciplinary domains they have explored are manifest in a series of sandpits that have included Music and Violence, The End of Antibiotics, and Music and Mental Health.[21]

CROMT: Centre for Research in Opera and Music Theatre

This research centre at Sussex University has an ambitious and progressive programme of activities that again tend to exclude mainstream opera. Their focus is principally on multimedia and new work, although they also have PhD students with eclectic research topics including biological systems. They are not specifically aligned to any opera company although there was originally some alignment with Glyndebourne Opera, and they have announced that a new research partnership with that company will commence in October 2014.[22]

OBERTO: The Opera Research Unit at Oxford Brookes

OBERTO has chosen to occupy the relatively safe interdisciplinary domain circumscribed by the humanities; however, it has a stated aim to provide 'a forum for the investigation of opera in all its interdisciplinary richness'.[23]

---

[20]   Opera North and the University of Leeds, DARE <www.dareyou.org.uk> (accessed 13 April 2014).
[21]   Opera North and the University of Leeds, 'DARE Sandpits' <www.dareyou.org.uk/projects/lectures-conferences-debates-and-discussions/dare-think-tank> (accessed 16 April 2014).
[22]   Centre for Research in Opera and Music Theatre (CROMT), 'Opera and the Media of the Future', <www.sussex.ac.uk/cromt/projects/operamediafuture> (accessed 19 July 2014).
[23]   Alexandra Wilson and Barbara Eichner, 'OBERTO: The Opera Research Unit', <http://arts.brookes.ac.uk/research/oberto> (accessed 14 April 2014).

CIRO: Cardiff Interdisciplinary Research in Opera at Cardiff University

CIRO has a membership that includes representatives drawn from Welsh National Opera, Music Theatre Wales, and DARE.[24]

DORG: Digital Opera Research Group (DORG)

This research group at De Montford University Leicester is focused on digital opera.

> The DORG investigates all aspects of digital opera, using analytical, musicological and creative research methods. 'Digital Opera' is deemed to include works that self-define as such and digital works that are conceived on an operatic scale or with operatic intentions. It is a precept of the DORG the art-form 'opera' is being substantially reinvented in the digital age. Our research concerns the nature and consequences of this reinvention.[25]

King's College London

This college has agreed a three-year residency with 'The Opera Group'.

> The Opera Group has developed a successful model of researching and incubating the creation of new opera projects in partnership with non-arts organisations. The first project in this new model, *The Lion's Face*, was developed with the Institute of Psychiatry (IoP) and staged at the Royal Opera House in July 2010, following a successful UK tour. This gave a national platform to ground-breaking research into Alzheimer's Disease carried out at the IoP.[26]

The Lion's Face was supported by the Wellcome Trust, which supports arts projects that explore biomedical topics. Another example from their portfolio is:

> Breath Cycle: Scottish Opera and Gartnavel General Hospital Cystic Fibrosis Service explore whether learning classical singing techniques, including breath control, can improve the wellbeing of cystic fibrosis patients.[27]

In Europe and the rest of the world there are other examples to be noted:

---

[24]   Cardiff University, 'Opera at Cardiff: CIRO' <www.cardiff.ac.uk/music/research/ciro> (accessed 14 April 2014).
[25]   De Montford University, Leicester, 'Digital Opera Research Group. DORG', <www.ioct.dmu.ac.uk/dorg/index.html> (accessed 14 April 2014).
[26]   King's College London, 'The Opera Group' <www.kcl.ac.uk/artshums/depts/music/research/operagroup.aspx> (accessed 14 April 2014).
[27]   'Breath Cycle: Singing and Cystic Fibrosis', www.breathcycle.com/about.html (accessed 13 July 2015).

- The World Opera, led by the University of Tromsø, receives funding from the Norwegian Research Council, academic and industrial partners, to develop technology to make a 'virtual stage' for operas.[28]
- Opera of the Future is a research group at the MIT Media Lab, USA, led by Tod Machover.[29] The work is highly experimental, innovative and influential.
- St Pölten University of Applied Sciences, Austria created a media opera *Pitoti: Echoes of the Echoes*. 'The research focuses on findings that use acoustics to explain the positioning of 4000-year-old rock paintings around their valley home of Valcamonica in northern Italy.'[30]

UK collaborations specifically supported by broadcast channels include:

- BBC Four (TV), *Voice:*[31] a 60-minute programme on the human voice with Professor David Howard of the University of York, an expert in vocal acoustics and electronics. It featured 'Pavarobotti', a synthesized Pavarotti.
- BBC Four (TV), *Castrato:*[32] a 60-minute programme with Professor David Howard of the University of York and Nicholas Clapton of the Royal Academy of Music focusing on the castrato voice in Baroque opera, with contributions including a synthesized recreation of a castrato voice by KTH Royal Institute of Technology Stockholm.
- *The Science of Opera*: produced by the Royal Opera House Covent Garden as a video and lecture, this was a collaboration with neurologists at University College London (UCL) to explore the physiological effects of opera.[33]

The reason for the relative paucity of examples from mainstream opera can only be guessed at. It may be that opera, of all the mainstream art forms, seems far removed from the more utilitarian or experimental objectives of most research in science and technology. It perhaps just feels too absurd to say to a research committee that a scientist or technologist wishes to collaborate with an opera company producing *La traviata* in pursuit of significant scientific research. It may be that opera offers less in its portfolio of accessible linking themes than other performing

---

[28] 'The World Opera (Presentation 2011)' <https://vimeo.com/64383924> (accessed 13 July 2015).

[29] T. Machover, 'MIT Media Lab: Opera of the Future' <www.media.mit.edu/research/groups/opera-future> (accessed 1 April 2014).

[30] Chelsea Wald, 'Revived Echoes Opera Augments Research Results', *New Scientist*, <www.newscientist.com/blogs/culturelab/2011/10/revived-echoes-augment-research-results.html> (accessed 1 April 2014).

[31] BBC Four, *The Voice* <www.bbc.co.uk/programmes/b008s99k> (accessed 17 July 2012).

[32] BBC Four, *Castrato* <www.bbc.co.uk/programmes/b0074spg> (accessed 17 July 2012).

[33] The Royal Opera House, Covent Garden, 'The Science of Opera', YouTube <www.youtube.com/watch?v=0tvNbwZzuaM> (accessed 20 April 2014).

and creative arts – its perceived specificity as a classical, vocal art form may inhibit potential connections. More likely, few opera practitioners and academics have really considered the possibility of exploiting mainstream operatic practice as an interdisciplinary research environment. I am not intent upon suggesting a list of potential new interdisciplinary research projects involving opera, but it may be worth noting at this stage that an opera company is likely to have some if not all of the following resources ripe for research: a large and complex organizational structure, pedagogical processes, technical infrastructure, multilingual requirements, audiences to understand, vocal therapies and training, advertising/PR/marketing, new media distribution channels, live broadcasts, archiving, and curation, as well as the opera itself, its performance, reception, and, for many companies, subsequent revival for a tour or another season. Themes will emerge once a willingness to make connections and to let opportunities grow is established by those companies and academics prepared to try. This is likely to need a playful and open-door policy from all participants, although more strategic approaches, such as those referred to in the case studies (the subject of the next section), may occur.

The Case Studies

The case studies of this chapter all took place in the UK and were partnerships between universities, professional companies engaged in operatic or vocal performance, and in some cases industrial partners. They were not substantial projects, and the maximum budget to deliver the work was in the region of £15,000, with overall budgets of less than £100,000 (not including support in kind from the partner university, which often amounted to a significant sum). Support for the projects came from the Engineering and Physical Sciences Research Council, the Arts and Humanities Research Council, and the universities themselves, as well as from several industrial partners, and, in one case, Arts Council England. The arts organizations also received their own support from their normal sources to support their core activities, so this was extra funding for them to engage in the research process.

It is important to stress that the performing arts companies did not have to radically change what they already did in order to engage with the research. Although they were expected to commit fully to the research programme, this was achieved mainly by making themselves and their resources available rather than having to create something new specifically to accommodate the research. In effect, the benefits from the research flowed back into their core business and did not interrupt or disrupt the activities they were already obliged to deliver.

The Processes behind the Case Studies

Process is not without its difficulties. Key to this task are individual researchers confident enough in the performing arts to understand the opera component, but expert enough in others' research domains to recognize reciprocal interdisciplinary potential. Likewise, for the opera company, it is important that the creative leads are interested in exploring new research areas and are able to provide the flexibility within the company ethos for the project to run successfully.

Each project began with an interesting and hopefully important set of research questions that could be addressed through an interdisciplinary collaboration.[34] In all cases, these questions arose from the academics concerned. As the projects progressed and the companies became more familiar with the academic mind-set they started to present supplementary questions, which were in many cases more interesting than the original ones posed.[35] The questions sprang from the individual researcher's field of interest inflected by the possibilities embedded in the operatic collaboration.

These questions needed to be fully understood by all the lead participants in the project, and questions of a common language had to be addressed early on in order to avoid subsequent misunderstandings. The language of the performing arts and the language of academia are not easily reconciled. Recognizing that the following is a gross generalization, it is my view that the performing arts adopt a language focused on 'making things work', communicating clearly and unambiguously, and achieving goals in a timely fashion. It tends towards the terse and compressed. The academy, on the other hand, delights in complexity and ambiguity. Very often the language adopted by academics encourages irreconcilable uncertainty. It tends to the dense and verbose. This is without consideration of the meta-values embedded in the language, which are even harder to amalgamate meaningfully. As a consequence, it was very important to get to know each other and each other's mode of expression in order to develop a rudimentary common vocabulary. Indeed, most of the budget for all of the case studies was spent on facilitating meetings to ensure that both parties fully understood each other from the outset and maintained good communications once the project was running.

Respect for each other's domains was critical. It was important that the academic participants learned the rigour of the operatic production process in the same way as the operatic participants learned the rigour of academic thought processes. More potential collisions occurred because academics were five minutes late for the start of a 'stage and orchestra' or walked across the stage when the floor was being painted rather than because of more highbrow intellectual disagreements. Likewise, opera companies are very outcome driven and will change something in haste in order to optimize the production or performance. The item being hastily discarded might be a critical component in the emerging academic argument. A cancelled recitative call because a singer is needed for a costume fitting can ruin

---

[34]   There can be no quick fix as to how these questions emerge. If the questions are not apparent to the researchers or opera company, then they probably do not need to pursue the processes suggested in this chapter.

[35]   In future, one would hope that the devising of research questions could be more of a collaborative process.

the culminating analytical opportunity for a pedagogical insight being pursued by one of the academic team.

Despite these bumps in the road, all of the case studies below were modest successes. Papers were written (not all of them published), new prototype technologies designed, public talks arranged, performances and demos presented, chapters written (this one), artists employed (in some cases, artists were paid to contribute directly to the research), questions raised, and the broadcast media engaged. Each of the case studies met most of the criteria specified in the model and reproduced below:

- potential interdisciplinary and collaborative areas of discovery and research;
- challenging and important problem spaces;
- products and tangible outcomes; and
- elements of public engagement.

These are the abstracts of each case study reproduced in full, followed by an informal summary of the way the model relates to each project.

Understanding Tingle in Opera Performances

With HCI venturing more into designing for the cultural and entertainment domain, researchers are engaging with experimental designs and technical interventions to understand how to best consider new technologies for this domain. This paper focuses on audience experience. It presents approaches as to how the HCI community can better support audiences' encounters with deeply engaging peak experiences that are intense, memorable and personally engaging experiences in live performances. We do this by studying tingle experiences encountered during opera performances. Besides contributing to advancing experience design, this work adds to current understanding of liveness, offers ideas about the role of digital technologies to support live performances, and general insights towards designing for audience experiences.[36]

This project successfully stimulated interdisciplinary activity in areas as intellectually wide-ranging as vocal talent competitions such as 'The X Factor' and the quality of Stephen Hawking's speech-synthesis system. Although no new technology was produced, new technology was tested in the form of a set of 'tingle sensors'. The failure to produce a useful result from the technology is, in scientific terms, still a useful piece of research. The opera company received

---

[36] Tuck Wah Leong and Peter Wright, 'Proceedings of the 25th Australian Computer-Human Interaction Conference on Augmentation, Application, Innovation, Collaboration – OzCHI '13; Understanding "Tingle" in Opera Performances', 2013, <http://vbn.aau.dk/files/173308065/OzCHI_2013_Proceedings_preface_.pdf> (accessed 17 July 2014).

additional media coverage at a level well beyond that stimulated by the opera itself.[37] Probably the outcome with the greatest impact was the foundation of a longer-term collaboration between the opera company and the universities leading the research.

In terms of the model and some of the significant points already made:

- The collaboration met the criteria of extreme interdisciplinarity in that it engaged with human–computer interaction, experience design, and digital technology, areas deemed to be important and challenging.
- The generalizable research findings increased the potential for impact beyond the performing arts.
- It sought to develop a tangible product-oriented outcome.
- It was inter- rather than transdisciplinary.
- It was located within a mainstream opera context.
- It made use of what the opera company was already doing, namely putting on performances to a live audience; it did not require them to do anything extra.

Beyond Participatory Video: Supporting User-Generated Video Content Production through Documentary

This work presents insights into how digital systems might be configured in order to support collaboration around the co-production of user-generated video content by communities of interest. We conducted a case study with a London-based opera company, which comprised a parallel documentary production project: one by members of the opera company and one by professional filmmakers. This process was designed to address questions about the 'values', 'qualities' and 'limitations' of existing video production methods. Utilizing insights derived from both interviews and a workshop with participants engaged in this process, we outline a set of recommendations for the design of tools to support participation and collaboration in filmmaking projects by non-professionals in ways not currently supported by existing 'participatory' production methods.[38]

This project was initially presented to one of the major UK-based opera companies together with a major broadcaster. Negotiations began but it soon became apparent that the opera company's nervousness about unmoderated video materials being

[37]   Caroline Roberts, 'Is Stephen Hawking's Voice Music to the Ears?', *The Guardian*, <www.theguardian.com/education/2012/jan/16/research-operatic-singers-speech-generating-technology> (accessed 16 April 2014).

[38]   David Green, 'Beyond Participatory Video: Supporting User-Generated Video Content Production through Documentary', unpublished article, Newcastle University, 2013.

circulated and the reputational and copyright issues that could ensue were going to make things very difficult for the research team. As this issue lay at the heart of the research, in the end a second, smaller, company was approached, who were able to modify the artists' contracts to accommodate this factor.

This project successfully engaged with most of the members of the opera company and the BBC. It supported the opera company's marketing by providing a high-quality trailer of the opera (*The Mikado*). The research itself was complex, and significant issues were found in the third-party technologies employed (again a useful finding). Some members of the company were paid to participate, as they were required to engage in activities outside of their contractual responsibilities. In terms of impact, the project successfully engaged both a specialist academic audience and the general public in a media technology domain somewhat foreign to conventional opera processes. It provided a small but important additional funding stream for the company.

- The collaboration met the criteria of interdisciplinarity but this was constrained within the context of media production. It was not extreme interdisciplinarity.
- Impact was more limited to audience development and the reach of the operatic medium – more akin to increased public engagement.
- It is harder to justify the importance of the problem space, though it is certainly challenging.
- It sought to develop a tangible product-oriented outcome.
- It was multi- rather than inter- or transdisciplinary.
- It was located within a mainstream opera context.
- It made use of what the opera company was already doing, namely producing an opera, but it did require them to make company members available beyond their contractual obligations. This was resolved by paying them.

Can a Computer-Generated Voice Be Sincere? A Case Study Combining Music and Synthetic Speech[39]

This article explores enhancing sincerity, honesty, or truthfulness in computer-generated synthetic speech by accompanying it with music. Sincerity is important if we are to respond positively to any voice, whether human or artificial. What is sincerity in the artificial disembodied voice? Studies in musical expression and performance may illuminate aspects of the 'musically spoken' or sung voice in

---

[39] This project stretches the boundaries of legitimacy in terms of the stated ambitions of this chapter. It was by no means a mainstream opera, nor was it a collaboration with a mainstream opera company. However, the source material for the melodrama was derived from *Pagliacci*, and the piece was produced with the support of the Tête à Tête Opera festival.

rendering deeper levels of expression that may include sincerity. We consider one response to this notion in an especially composed melodrama (music accompanying a (synthetic) spoken voice) designed to convey sincerity.[40]

This project was part of a much bigger interdisciplinary project: The Creative Speech Technology Network (CreST).[41] The strands of support were very complex as they included five industrial sponsors (some contributing cash, others equipment or expertise), the Wingate Scholarship, EPSRC, and Arts Council England, as well as minor contributors such as the Royal College of Speech and Language Therapists, and Hull Truck Theatre. Only some of this support directly contributed to the operatic content. However, in terms of impact, the project as a whole was highly successful, with very significant local, national, and international media coverage, new product development, performances, commissions, and public engagement.

- The collaboration met the criteria of transdisciplinarity with some radical intellectual convergences by the collaborators.
- Impact was strong academically and in terms of public discourse, cultural life and civil society.
- It sought to develop many tangible product-oriented outcomes.
- It was only tangentially located within a mainstream opera context.
- It required CreST to radically reconfigure the conventional network model and as a consequence was a much more complex project to realize than either of the other two case studies.

Coda

This chapter sets out a case for interdisciplinary support for opera practice. The requirements for this innovative way of supporting mainstream opera are presented, and are supported by examples. Such initiatives remain rare, and for researchers and opera professionals this strategy will require us to work to bridge C.P. Snow's famous 'two cultures' through interdisciplinary practice-based collaborations. This strategy is only one of many that the middle-scale opera industry may choose to pursue in order to break the 'affordability' deadlock. Such an approach tallies with the trend exhibited by the principal funding bodies and the pursuit of 'impact' that has become one of the critical measures of viability for any research activity. Fortunately, opera has always known how to have impact, so that's a good start.

[40] Christopher Newell and Paul Barker, 'Can a Computer-Generated Voice Be Sincere? A Case Study Combining Music and Synthetic Speech', *Logopedics Phoniatrics Vocology (Informa Healthcare)* 38/3–4 (2013): p. 126.

[41] Alistair Edwards and Christopher Newell, 'Creative Speech Technology: Editorial Introduction to this Special Issue', *Logopedics, Phoniatrics, Vocology* 38/3 (2013): pp. 91–5.

Chapter 6

The World Opera: A New Global Format for the Business of Opera

Jason E. Geistweidt and Niels W. Lund

Introduction

Marshall McLuhan's vision of a global village – a society intimately intertwined via ubiquitous, real-time communications networks – has arrived.[1] One need not step back too far to realize that most of us are blissfully interconnected via a variety of networked technologies – email, social media, real-time streaming, the cloud, to mention only a few. Though such interconnectivity is nothing new, it is the increasing speed of contemporary communications, the capacity for real-time dialogue across the gulf of time and space, that makes McLuhan's prediction possible. There is now a growing global awareness among people throughout the world, who, in sharing their daily experiences, have come to realize that humanity is a single community, facing common challenges across a host of issues regarding business, culture, politics, and the environment.

A similar collective awareness has arisen in the performing arts, for as long as there has been networked communication available – from telegraph, to telephone, to satellite, and now fibre optics – artistic experiments have been made utilizing the network as both stage and platform for worldwide interactive live performances. Until recently the technology has not been of high enough quality to host longer, more coherent works such as opera, but this is beginning to change.

Founded upon the assumption that the entire planet is one local community, to which we all belong, the World Opera is an international organization working with artists and researchers around the globe to establish the World Opera House, a multi-stage, mixed-reality performance system, allowing local and remote individuals to interact in real time over high-speed, high-bandwidth networks. Currently comprising six nodes across Northern Europe and the Americas, the World Opera and its partners are building the necessary infrastructure for real-time,

---

[1] Canadian media theorist and philosopher Herbert Marshall McLuhan (1911–80) first introduced the idea of the *global village* in his book *The Gutenberg Galaxy: The Making of Typographic Man* (Toronto, 1962). This idea would later be refined to describe a world in which electronic communication technologies create an increasing global awareness, such that society no longer conceives of itself as a group of separate communities, but rather as a single village.

interactive performances across time and space. This article reflects the authors' findings in creating and presenting distributed opera over the past five years, providing an overview of the issues encountered in creating a new opera house for the networked world.

Beginning with an overview of the use of distributed communications within live performance practice, we continue with a discussion of the technologies currently utilized in World Opera productions, introducing the practical challenges and new possibilities distributed performance presents to both artist and producer. This leads to an examination of World Opera productions, focusing primarily on a case study of our first distributed production, Pergolesi's *La serva padrona*, in December 2011. Throughout our production process, we discovered that we were repeatedly encountering issues that we recognized as unique to the distributed nature of the World Opera model.

For example, it is certainly manageable to develop a programme composed of a single production, occurring at a single site for a single audience (the traditional opera model); however, it is a much greater challenge to develop a programme composed of a single production, having a number of distributed, interrelated parts, with artists and audiences interacting between several sites simultaneously.

Similarly, productions are challenged by both the new limitations and possibilities this format presents. In particular, latency between sites alters a performer's innate timing, and the intimate nature of sharing a stage is somewhat altered when real performers are required to interact with virtual projections.[2] Further, coordinating activities across multiple spaces and time zones presents a multitude of logistical hurdles, while the frequency of miscommunication between teams is amplified if everyone is thinking locally in the sense of their local site, not realizing they are a constituent part of the 'multi-site community' spanning local, regional, and national borders.

Consequently, funding a transnational project such as the World Opera can be difficult in a climate where, historically, private and/or public funding policy has been targeted at supporting local, regional, and national institutions. Though this tradition of supporting 'one's own company' in order to provide the local community with an engaging and dynamic cultural milieu is understandable, securing funding for administering long-term international cooperative productions is, simply put, nearly impossible when an overwhelming majority of the funding must stay 'at home'.

When Herbert von Karajan took leadership of the Vienna State Opera in 1957, he quickly dispensed with the tradition of performing all operas (no matter their provenance) in German. He infused new talent into the house by engaging foreign singers in principal roles and initiated collaborative productions with La Scala, sharing both orchestrations and performers. Karajan recognized the synergies that a global approach to opera production could bring to the Viennese stage, as well as

---

[2]   Latency is the temporal delay inherent within any digital system. A more in-depth discussion follows in the technical overview below.

the benefit of projecting his Viennese productions onto the world stage. Likewise, we believe the World Opera model presents a unique opportunity for re-envisioning opera as a dynamic platform for global exchange, discussion, and contemplation, providing a platform for the expression of a growing global consciousness.

Distributed Performance in Practice

Distributed performance can be traced back to the early nineteenth century, when operators would perform music together over the nascent telephone networks; however, the aesthetic use of distributed network technologies having both sound and image has had a relatively brief, though vibrant, history.[3] One of the earliest telematic works was Galloway and Rabinowitz's *Hole in Space* (1980), which utilized satellite networks to relay the sounds and images of pedestrian activity between Lincoln Center and The Broadway department store in Los Angeles for a continuous 72-hour period. As the artists describe it:

> Suddenly head-to-toe, life-sized, television images of the people on the opposite coast appeared. They could now see, hear, and speak with each other as if encountering each other on the same sidewalk. No signs, sponsor logos, or credits were posted – no explanation at all was offered.[4]

For a society in which television permeated daily experience, composed almost wholly of a one-way, top-down broadcast paradigm of 'we report, you decide', *Hole in Space* was astonishing, as it provided a bi-directional means for communication, creating an arena for a type of organic face-to-face interactivity that had not been widely experienced. By placing the most advanced communication network of the time into the hands of the public, *Hole in Space* marked the beginning of an exploration into a networked community that meets neither here nor there, but rather, in an interim, shared space somewhere along the network.

The increasing availability of broadband communication options in the 1990s allowed practitioners to explore the possibilities of communal network space more readily. A notable example is Paul Sermon's *Telematic Dreaming* (1992),[5] which utilized ISDN telephone communications[6] to stream video between two sites

[3]   Carolyn Marvin, *When Old Technologies Were New: Thinking about Electric Communication in the Late Nineteenth Century* (New York, 1988), p. 212.
[4]   Kit Galloway and Sherrie Rabinowitz, 'Hole-In-Space, 1980', *The Electronic Café*, www.ecafe.com/getty/table.html (accessed 24 February 2014).
[5]   Paul Sermon, 'Telematic Dreaming: Statement' and linked pages, <www.paul sermon.org/dream> (accessed 10 June 2015).
[6]   The integrated digital services network (ISDN), developed in 1988 enabled the simultaneous digital transmission of voice, video, and data over the copper wiring of the traditional telephone system.

in Finland. In this work, participants at each site were presented with a duplicate scenario, a small bed with a single camera situated overhead. Participants were encouraged to lie down, at which point their image was captured, streamed, and projected onto the bed at the remote site. The result was an intimate layering of virtual and real bodies appearing to recline together in both local spaces.

These early co-located events are certainly significant for the introduction of (at the time) cutting-edge technologies to artistic practice; however, what makes these works most notable is their interactive nature, with participants at each site contributing to the single event, occurring simultaneously across multiple nodes. Such real-time interconnectivity is an essential aspect of the World Opera model. This is in direct contrast to the most current application of communication technologies to operatic practice, the live broadcast.

Simulcasts[7] such as the Metropolitan Opera's MET HDLive presentations are truly a welcome augmentation of the traditional business model, bringing opera to populations that otherwise might never experience the genre at such a professional level. However, the ability to broadcast live performances globally has been with us for some time, and though the technical preparations for an international presentation are demanding, the dynamics of performance remain relatively unchanged (see Figure 6.1).

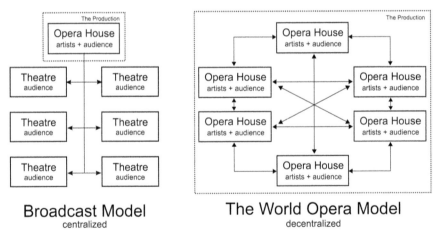

Figure 6.1   The dynamics of performance

From an interaction design perspective, a simulcast can be thought of as a one-to-many transaction that is relatively centralized as regards performance conditions, whereas the World Opera format is a many-to-many exchange of interleaved performance components which is decidedly decentralized (see Figure 6.1). We believe this distributed format not only achieves the goals of the broadcast model – the dissemination of opera to the public – but also presents an

---

[7]   A simultaneous broadcast of a live event or performance to a remote venue.

opportunity for establishing a new operatic practice, requiring innovations in both the technical and creative processes of the opera community.

The World Opera is certainly not the first organization to concentrate entirely upon the production of distributed musical works.[8] The Telematic Circle, an ensemble constituted solely to explore the possibilities of distributed music production, has been in the forefront of networked performance since member Pauline Oliveros' first telematic experiments in the early 1990s. The group defines telematic music as 'music performed live and simultaneously across geographic locations via the Internet'.[9] As technology advanced over the next three decades, the Circle grew to include researchers developing low-latency tools for capturing and streaming high-definition audio and video over high-bandwidth networks. Many of these tools are presently found within the World Opera infrastructure, and we owe a great deal to the collective work of the Circle's members, many of whom are also World Opera partners.

The musical practice of the Telematic Circle is primarily based in improvisation, which is aligned with the aesthetics of Oliveros' Deep Listening Institute, the umbrella under which the ensemble operates. Such an open approach to listening and reacting 'in the moment' works well within a medium that, subject to latency, exhibits temporal flux. Consequently, a majority of telematic musical practice is extemporaneous in nature: works that require tight temporal coordination among performers are difficult to achieve in a distributed setting. For the opera practitioner, this might be a non-starter, as a majority of the standard repertoire could be seen as impossible to present in a telematic setting. However, we see this as an opportunity, a chance to combine contemporary technology with traditional practice, reconfiguring works intended for a single space into distributed productions, and commissioning works that tell new stories via contemporary methodologies.

To do so will certainly require continued advancement in technology, but it also demands the development of a new performance space, or rather a collection of purpose-built and/or adapted venues possessing the requisite infrastructure for producing distributed opera. Collectively, these spaces make up the new World Opera stage.

Technical Overview

In May 2011, Porgy stood in Stockholm while Bess, nearly 9,000 kilometres away in Palo Alto, California, declared her love for him. The accompanist, playing from

---

[8] 'History of Spatially Distributed Performance: aka Milestones in Real-Time Networked Media', <http://srl.mcgill.ca/projects/rtnm/history.html> (accessed 27 May 2014).

[9] Pauline Oliveros, et al., 'Telematic Music: Six Perspectives', *Leonardo Music Journal* 19 (2009): pp. 96–6, https://ccrma.stanford.edu/groups/soundwire/publications/papers/chafeLMJ19-2009.pdf (accessed 31 March 2014).

the stage in California, was heard clearly in Stockholm, and on both sides the voices blended beautifully. Porgy and Bess faced one another from their respective stages, and both audiences experienced two life-sized performers engaged in dramatic dialogue. As Bess plays coy, Porgy responds, and perhaps the true distance between the performers subconsciously amplifies the longing these two characters have for one another.

Such transatlantic demonstrations have served as a proving ground for establishing the infrastructure to facilitate a performance across multiple locations, and with each attempt our technique improves. In addition, these presentations have provided the opportunity for a larger population of artists and audiences to experience the aesthetics of telematic performance. There is no doubt that the technical requirements of the World Opera are demanding, necessitating the coordination of cutting-edge audiovisual hardware and software with high-bandwidth communication networks. Furthermore, the challenge is compounded, as these new technologies must integrate alongside elements of architecture, stagecraft, design, and performance practice that have evolved over the past 400 years of opera's development. However, these difficulties are not insurmountable, and we hope that by providing a brief overview of our technical infrastructure this paper might inform and encourage others to take part in this global effort.

The World Opera Network

The current World Opera Network comprises three sites in Scandinavia – Tromsø, Stockholm, and Struer – and three sites in North America – New York, Montreal, and San Francisco. These sites have been chosen for their proximity to major cultural resources, the availability of high-bandwidth research networks (Internet2, UNINETT),[10] and the presence of corporate or academic partners currently developing World Opera technology solutions.

We have chosen to utilize high-bandwidth networks to transport our digital signals, specifically seeking 10 gigabits of capacity at each of our performance sites. Higher bandwidths afford us the opportunity to move more data in less time, and thus reduce latency within the system. Though there are interesting lower-bandwidth solutions, employing a variety of successful compression schemes, World Opera believes the demands of interactive, networked performance require a level of fidelity and low latency which higher bandwidths can more readily provide. We are also working with service providers (both public and private) to reduce the number of hops between switches within each country, providing robust routing between international gateways.

---

[10]   Internet2 <www.internet2.edu/about-us/> and UNINETT <www.uninett.no> are the respective American and Norwegian high-capacity networks serving higher education and research institutions in the USA and Norway.

Latency

Latency is inherent within any network, and when it comes to a distributed live performance, any delay in the transmission of audio and video assets directly affects the level of interaction that may be achieved, and therefore the type of production that may be attempted. Latency is the greatest hurdle to establishing a mediated performance practice and is the result of minute delays incurred at various points along the signal chain, which may be visualized simply as in Figure 6.2.

Capture Time + Encoding Compression Time + Network Delay + Decoding Decompression Time + Display Time = Total Latency

Figure 6.2   The signal chain

Capture time describes the period required to take in and digitize a signal – that is, the conversion of sound pressure waves and photons into digital audio and video streams, respectively. Additional delay is imparted as the signal is formulated into packets, or *encoded*, for transmission, and large data streams (such as those encountered with video) may necessitate compression, delaying the signal further. *Compression* is the process of algorithmically rendering digital signals into smaller packets, such that more data can be sent per unit time. As assets leave the local node, they are theoretically travelling at the speed of light, though the signal will slow as it traverses the myriad of switches and gateways along the network. Routing data via the most direct physical pathway between sites (minimizing the number of switches and routers traversed) can reduce such *network delay*. At the remote site, the process is reversed with streams *decoded*, *decompressed*, and *displayed* within the space – each step incrementally increasing latency.

Though the latencies presented may appear small – on the order of milliseconds – research has shown (and our practice-based work has confirmed) that audio latencies in excess of 30 milliseconds can noticeably affect coordinated performance of rhythmic music. Furthermore, it appears that musicians are able cope with audio latencies up to 100 milliseconds, though at this point traditional ensemble playing becomes more a follow-the-leader type of affair.[11]

Keep in mind that the latency pathway described above represents only one leg of a two-way trip, for an interactive performance requires action and reaction. Thus, a round-trip time of 60–70 milliseconds (30–35 milliseconds one-way)

---

[11]   Chris Chafe, Juan-Pablo Cáceres and Michael Gurevich, 'Effect of Temporal Separation on the Synchronization in Rhythmic Performance', *Perception* 39 (2010): pp. 982–92, <https://ccrma.stanford.edu/~cc/pub/pdf/temporalSep.pdf> (accessed 25 May 2014). Adriana Olmos, et al., 'Exploring the Role of Latency and Orchestra Placement on the Networked Performance of a Distributed Opera', 12th Annual International Workshop on Presence, Los Angeles, 2009, <http://astro.temple.edu/~tuc16417/papers/Olmos_et_al.pdf> (accessed 24 May 2014).

would be an acceptable amount of latency for the performance of mediated music requiring rhythmic coordination, though the experience would be far from that of the performers being in the same space. For reference, round-trip times from Tromsø to Stockholm (a distance of approximately 1,600 kilometres) averaged 23 milliseconds on the high-bandwidth research network, while the link from Tromsø to Palo Alto (7,780 kilometres) was approximately 210 milliseconds.

Up to this point we have only addressed the effects of audio latency within the context of mediated performance. As previously mentioned, video is much more bandwidth intensive (requiring compression time) and the process of capturing and displaying video assets is, with regards to audio, a much slower process. For this reason we opted to treat audio and video streams as separate entities; this is in contrast to commercial video-conferencing systems offered by PolyCom or Cisco that strive to deliver audio and video in sync. In our system, video arrives slightly later than audio; the result is that performers must rely heavily on auditory cues to synchronize performance and, to some extent, ignore subtle visual cues. This can be difficult for singers who naturally coordinate performances by watching one another's breathing. Consequently, performers regularly mentioned that mediated performance was much more physically and mentally exhausting than performing in a common space. Though an imperfect solution, we believe the extra milliseconds gained by putting audio first results in tighter coordination between spaces.

What follows is an overview of our approach to capture, stream, and display assets for distributed productions. Although we wish to introduce the reader to the common issues encountered in distributed performance, it is beyond the scope of this article to detail the intricacies of digital signal processing, compression schemes, and network optimization, to mention only a few. Our approach to mediated opera performance is a holistic one: we are striving to see what can be accomplished with current technologies within the context of contemporary musical theatre and operatic practice.

Audio

The capturing of audio assets for World Opera performances is achieved primarily by placing the microphone extremely close to the source, allowing for audio assets to be captured without any spatial information or coloration imparted by the local space. We are working on the theory that a true-fidelity performance will present sources resonating in each respective local space. Thus, an orchestra performing in Tromsø will be captured cleanly, with little room sound, and transmitted to the remote site where it will be allowed to resonate naturally, and mix more appropriately, with performers in the remote acoustic. For performers on the go, wireless microphones allow freedom of movement, and audio monitoring is provided for performers on stage with speakers placed to localize the sound to the source (for example, a remote orchestra emanates from the local orchestra pit).

World Opera utilizes CCRMA's JackTrip[12] with Jack Audio Server[13] to both route and stream audio between performance sites. The software is easy to deploy, readily scalable, and the *de facto* standard for audio streaming research. We stream at a sampling rate of 44.1 KHz with a bit depth of 16 bits/second, equivalent to CD-quality sound. As previously mentioned, latency incurred for audio is quite low compared to video, even when uncompressed. Presently, audio encoding/ digitization requires about 6 milliseconds, along with another 6 milliseconds to decode at the remote end – 12 milliseconds one-way and 24 milliseconds round-trip. The physical distance the signal must travel within the network imparts further latency. As an example, network packets can travel from Tromsø to Stockholm, a 1,200-kilometre distance, in about 14 milliseconds, or 28 milliseconds round-trip. Thus, an audio signal originating in Tromsø will be experienced in Stockholm about 26 milliseconds later than it actually occurred. Any response from the Stockholm side would be similarly delayed.

Additionally, there are many communications taking place during an opera, the majority of which are not be heard by performers or audience. This back channel includes conversations between stage management, lighting and sound designers, and other administrative and technical personnel. It has been our experience that this back channel is the most important audio asset during both rehearsals and production. Failure to establish a robust back channel typically results in production delays and miscommunication.

Video

The video requirements for the World Opera are the most challenging aspects of the technical setup. In addition to the latency issues previously discussed, the dynamic environment of the opera stage hinders the capture and display of video assets. Lighting which might be appropriate for the theatre may not be appropriate for video capture, and too much ambient lighting can easily wash out a backlit or projected display. There is a further challenge in capturing and displaying assets that have traditionally moved about the stage with relative freedom. The analogy has often been made that a World Opera production is akin to staging a live film, in which all shots must be previously storyboarded and all assets must hit their mark. It is somewhat of a chess game in which there are no second takes.

For capture of video assets, we have utilized both professional and high-end consumer video cameras. Though these devices offer excellent image quality and acceptable optics, the drawback is their use of the IEEE 1394 interface (Firewire, iLink) to bridge camera and computer, a connection that is relatively slow. With

---

[12]   Juan-Pablo Cáceres and Chris Chafe, 'JackTrip: Under the Hood of an Engine for Network Audio', *Journal of New Music Research* 39/3 (2010): pp. 183–7.

[13]   'Jack Audio Connection Kit', *Jack Documentation*, <http://jackaudio.org/api> (accessed 13 July 2015).

the 1394 interface, a video signal can take up to 80 milliseconds to emerge from the camera; this is before any compression or further pre-transmission processing can take place. One option we are exploring is the use of high-end Ethernet cameras, which process images much more quickly and, due to their Ethernet connectivity, can be located some distance from the encoding computer.

As we increase the number of video streams we wish to use, it will become necessary to compress the video signals to work within available bandwidths. Compression is computationally intensive and increases latency – that is, it takes time to compress a signal. However, total latency can be overcome if the compression scheme employed results in the faster transference of data across the network. Determining the amount of compression necessary to increase transmission speeds while maintaining high-quality video representation is an ongoing investigation between the World Opera and our technical partners.

Video is transferred using McGill University's Ultra-Videoconferencing (UV) software.[14] UV is a low-latency IP transport package capable of transmitting high-definition (HD) video over the network; however, as HD consumes greater bandwidth, we currently stream with the Digital Video (DV) standard that compresses the signal within the camera. UV provides the capability of serving one stream to multiple clients and has the ability to multi-cast, though we have yet to use this function as it is not accessible in the current version. At the remote site the video is decoded, a process that typically is much faster than the original encoding. As with the cameras, consumer display technologies impart significant delay before the image is visualized. More investigation into low-latency capture and display technologies will be necessary in the future if we hope to reduce hardware-induced delay.

Other Assets

A final consideration is the desire for connecting serial devices currently utilized in contemporary opera practice. The ability to sync or operate lighting and sound control boards across the network could be advantageous to coordinating distributed productions. The use of Open Sound Control (OSC),[15] a messaging protocol originally intended for sharing musical data, can serve this purpose well. In future, additional information, such as the location of performers on the stage, might also be captured and relayed among sites utilizing a marker-less motion capture scheme, thus creating an intelligent staging system that reacts in real time to performers' activities, coordinating collaboration across the network.

---

[14] Jeremy Cooperstock, J. Roston and W. Woszczyk, 'Ultra-Videoconferencing Work at McGill', SURA/ViDe 6thAnnual Digital Video Workshop, Indiana University-Purdue University, Indianapolis, Indiana, 22–5 March 2004.

[15] Matt Wright, 'The Open Sound Control 1.0 Specification, 2002', <http://open soundcontrol.org/spec-1_0> (accessed 31 April 2014).

The Aesthetics of a World Opera Production

The World Opera is working to innovate opera production and development through the incorporation of networked technologies, but this is more than a mere technical exercise. We have proposed a new type of stage, a new kind of space; but, in an aesthetic sense, we further wish to adopt a new sense of place. The World Opera, like its predecessors, is producing works for the local community; however, we conceive of the local community in the same way as the Facebook, Twitter, and Google communities see themselves: the local community is a global community.

One major difference between physical communities and the new online communities is their age and history, or, in other words, their traditions for establishing and expressing a sense of community. Many members of a local community may never have face-to-face interactions, but actors on stage are intimately connected through their physical interactions and a sense of shared embodied presence. On the World Opera stage, actors are physically separated from each other and only connected through the technology of cameras, microphones, and networks. Typically, three types of interaction have dominated online communities: *textual communication* via emails, social media, and the like; *oral communication* via Skype and video-conferencing software; and *online gaming*, in which participants simultaneously occupy virtual worlds.

We believe the World Opera stage offers a fourth type of interaction, a hybrid in which actors, audiences, and full-body virtual projections occupy physical space. This interaction is determined not only by the actors, but also by the media (the technology) and the mediators (directors, choreographers etc.). In his article 'Dramaturgy in the Network',[16] Pedro Rebelo outlines three principle forms of networked dramaturgy, or three ways of setting the stage: 1) a projected dramaturgy; 2) a directed dramaturgy; and 3) a distributed dramaturgy.[17]

In the *projected* format, one location is designated as the main node, while other nodes or sites are subordinated, contributing according to the needs of the main node. An example of this format might place an orchestra in the main node with a single soloist or actor contributing to the performance from another site. With the *directed* format, in principle all nodes are equal in their functioning, but in practice are guided by one artistic director who determines the roles of each node. Finally, in the *distributed* format all nodes are equal and autonomous, each possessing the right to contribute what they wish within a predetermined framework defined, or perhaps continually being redefined, by the participating nodes at performance time. Within this classification, as stated by Rebelo, the World Opera suits very well as an example of directed dramaturgy.

In the World Opera case, the leading and defining factor is an artistic director with a particular story to relate to the audience, here the attendees at all nodes

---

[16]   Pedro Rebelo, 'Dramaturgy in the Network', *Contemporary Music Review* 28/4–5 (2009): pp. 387–93.
[17]   Rebelo, 'Dramaturgy in the Network', pp. 389–90.

seen as a whole. As previously mentioned, the majority of telematic works are of an open-ended improvisational character, primarily consisting of instrumental or vocal music and dance. Arguably, the sounds and gestures produced during an improvisational performance are paramount to realizing the work. In contrast, it is the personal and emotional relationships between characters that play the central role in successfully conveying the dramatic narrative of opera. Such complex relationships can be difficult to establish or maintain within the context of performance where artists' relationships are mediated by technology. As Jeremy Cooperstock observed, the singers are placed in a situation where they need to pay full attention all the time to their remote partner in order to keep the emotional connection intact, with no possibilities for taking a short second of a break.[18] Though technology may appear to be a hurdle to conveying narrative, there are opportunities for these technologies to contribute significantly to a distributed production.

In her article 'Distributed Choreography: A Video-Conferencing Environment',[19] Lisa M. Naugle shows how it is possible to use video software to augment a mediated performance in an artistic way by 'treating' the live video stream at performance time (that is, blurring faces, ghosting bodies, and so forth). Here Naugle is not working to present a 'realistic' presentation by imitating a traditional one-site performance at each node, but rather using the technology to inform and affect the personal relationship between the participants in the different nodes as a deliberate part of the dramaturgy. We found within the rehearsal process that artists who were at first wary of mediated performance soon warmed to the idea after being allowed to play around with the technology. Through experiencing the limitations as well as the possibilities offered by this new medium, individuals began to develop their own practice for creating relationships and conveying narrative.

La serva padrona, a Test Case

Our first fully staged distributed production took place in December of 2011.[20] Pergolesi's *La serva padrona* was selected as our test case because it is small in scale, requiring a minimum number of performers, and does not employ excessive theatrical resources, such as multiple scene changes, special effects, or elaborate costuming. Contrary to our global approach, this initial production took place at a single venue – the city of Tromsø's Kulturhuset – across two theatrical spaces: a black box theatre and a general-purpose performance space. Such a focused,

[18]   Jeremy Cooperstock, 'Multimodal Telepresence Systems', *IEEE Signal Processing Magazine* 77 (January 2011): pp. 77–86

[19]   Lisa M. Naugle, 'Distributed Choreography: A Video-Conferencing Environment', *PAJ: A Journal of Performance and Art* 24/2 (2002): pp. 56–62.

[20]   Katrin Beckman, *The Tromsø World Opera Project*, a documentary, 2011, <http://vimeo.com/35689367> (accessed 20 May 2014).

controlled laboratory setting allowed us to quickly troubleshoot problems and have complete control over both spaces as the production developed. The process of incorporating the requisite audiovisual and network technologies into these spaces was technically rather straightforward. In contrast, working in this new format proved the greater artistic challenge.

The Production

One of the more challenging aspects of performing across the network is the way in which the production is conceived in the minds of the creative directors, the performers, and the audience. In our presentation of *Padrona* we adopted a two-node approach placing the vocalists (Serpina and Uberto) in separate theatres. This separation was underscored by a re-envisioned dramaturgy and set design that placed the older Uberto in a New York penthouse with his young mistress Serpina, cast as a kind of trophy wife, living in a Neapolitan villa.

The modified orchestra consisted of a keyboardist and percussionist sharing Serpina's stage, with a violin and cello in Uberto's space. The actor playing Vespone, the mute servant, appeared in both spaces (via a passageway between the theatres), creating a connective presence between local and remote stages. Each space had a sound designer and audiovisual technician while one stage director and one technical director performed double duty, shuttling between the two venues.

Conceptually, the production sits somewhere between Rebelo's classifications of *projected* and *directed* dramaturgy, incorporating the World Opera concept of the two venues existing within a single global community. All participants (artists and audience) are sharing the same story and are fully integrated into the plot. In performance, the activities of both venues complement one another and are interdependent; however, the look, feel, and experience at each node is unique due to the characters present and the dramatic setting presented. We are not attempting to duplicate the same production in both venues, but rather present two sides of the same operatic conversation.

As the performance at one node is dramatically linked to the performance at all other nodes, there is a need for an overall artistic direction to ensure smooth interaction among sites. In our production of *Padrona* we had the luxury of shuttling between venues, but in a fully global production directors and designers will be required to work in a mediated fashion, not unlike that of the artistic personnel. As no one person can envision the production as a single performance (one cannot be in two places at the same time), it is necessary to have assistant directors and designers to realize the production locally. Thus, a single stage or venue is an autonomous entity that is responsible for 1) capturing local assets and streaming these to the remote nodes with the highest possible fidelity, and 2) mixing the incoming streams within their space to guarantee an effective and balanced experience for all *local* participants. Working in such a way requires a high level of trust and collaborative effort between all creative and technical forces across all participating nodes.

The Performers

In our production of *Padrona* we mediated the performers via three video portals, each comprising a pair of video capture/display zones. By stepping into a capture zone, a performer would be projected at life-size proportions into a congruent position on the other stage. By stepping out of the zone, the character would disappear from the remote stage. We made no attempt to conceal the technology; in fact, we encouraged the performers to incorporate the video cameras into their performance. As an example, the angry Uberto scolds Serpina across the network by arguing directly into the lens of a camera, appearing as an enraged giant head at the remote space. Similarly, Serpina may hide from Uberto by avoiding being on camera. Thus, the technology is intimately woven into the performance narrative. The World Opera is not merely a demonstration of technological prowess, but rather a presentation of operatic storytelling within the context of the global village. We exist in a mediated world, a society comprised of separate groups that are no longer separated. The network is the metaphor for expression and we believe opera must engage this paradigm.

The Elements of a World Opera Production

In our future production of Danish composer Per Nørgaard's *Gilgamesh*, we are introduced to the eponymous king of Uruk, an individual who is part human, part divine. As king he is an insensitive and cruel leader, and the prayers of the people are finally answered when the gods create a rival to challenge him: Enkido, a man who comes from the forest, living in balance with nature. This ancient struggle is reflected in Nørgaard's rather specific staging requirements in which the city of Uruk with its suffering inhabitants, the enchanted Forest from which Enkido is spawned, and the divine Underworld where the gods sit in judgement exist simultaneously on the same stage. In addition, the accompanying orchestra is divided among these three worlds, appearing on stage as an integral part of the performance. One final character, the sun god Shamash, assumes the practical role of conductor, coordinating the performance as he moves through the sky. In contrast with many opera productions, all participants in *Gilgamesh* – actors, singers, orchestral musicians, and conductor – have a specific dramatic role in the telling of the story and appear on stage for the entirety of the performance. Nørgaard's epic is an example of an operatic work that adapts well to the distributed nature of the World Opera format. One can easily imagine city of Uruk, the Forest, and the Underworld depicted across three distributed venues with characters shifting from one site to the other as the narrative unfolds.

The Audience

As stated previously, the World Opera conducts a directed dramaturgy, sharing a narrative between performance nodes. Thus the audience at the local venue will not experience the same performance as audiences at other remote sites. In the case of our distributed *Padrona*, some spectators watched the story from Uberto's New York perspective, while others followed Serpina's story from the Italian perspective. In the case of *Gilgamesh*, some spectators will experience the work from the city of Uruk, the Forest, or the Underworld – depending on the theatre at which they attend the performance.

We believe this is one of the most exciting aspects of a World Opera format: the ability to provide audiences with differing perspectives of the central narrative. Not only does this invite multiple viewings, with audiences travelling to different sites to see the work from a different angle, but it further provides audiences a chance to share and discuss their local experience with audiences in remote venues during intervals and following the performance via video-conferencing kiosks. Such face-to-face audience exchanges were accomplished in 2004 during a musical performance connecting Stanford University in California with KTH (The Royal Conservatory of Technology) in Stockholm.[21] Thus, the World Opera audience, though composed of distributed groups, is a single local, global audience.

Towards a World Opera Business Model

Throughout the history of opera, a variety of business models have arisen and we would direct the reader to Lorenzo Bianconi and Giorgio Pestelli's *History of Italian Opera* for a comprehensive overview of the various models.[22] Traditionally, however, opera companies have been tied to geographical regions, typically being *the* opera house for a city, region, or state, usually presenting the same 40–80 well-known works of operatic repertoire on steady rotation. But this is not the totality of operatic practice. Most people are familiar with The Metropolitan Opera in New York, but unbeknown to many, there are actually around sixty opera companies in the New York City area.

These smaller, lesser-known companies are primarily driven by more specific artistic concerns – commissioning new works or specializing in the works of a single composer – and are not necessarily concerned with being the standard bearer of opera for a local community, region, or nation. Additionally, we would point out that it is primarily within these smaller companies that new innovation in opera occurs. In principle, these companies could be based anywhere, as their practice is not tied to a specific geographical place or tradition. The World Opera could be said to occupy a similar position, being an organization that considers the world as its local community, wishing to tell stories relevant to the inhabitants

---

[21]   'Point 25: An Event within the Connected Performances Spaces Project', 18 June 2004. First report, September 2004. <www.r1.kth.se/point25/point25.pdf> (accessed 23 May 2014).

[22]   Lorenzo Bianconi and Giorgio Pestelli (eds), *Opera Production and Its Resources. The History of Italian Opera, Part II: Systems*, trans. Lydia G. Cochrane (Chicago, 1998).

of the global village, and appreciative of, but not necessarily tied to, a specific operatic tradition.

When we introduce the concept of the World Opera to someone for the first time, the most frequently asked question is, 'Where are you based?' Our response has always been that the World Opera stage comprises a collection of individual sites in differing countries, on differing continents, and that company members (both artistic and administrative) can be found at those sites. In our current business culture, such arrangements are far from uncommon. However, in the cultural sector of society, performing arts organizations retain a very high degree of geographical affiliation. Nevertheless, most companies are currently engaged in international business practices, performing a standardized repertoire and sharing productions, designers, and artists. So a culture of collaboration in which companies share resources is already in place. What remains to be seen is whether these companies can share a common stage.

When the Metropolitan Opera goes abroad with its HD Live simulcasts, audiences in theatres throughout the world experience a New-York-based organization presenting a New York production. There is a satisfying aspect of the production that, simply put, resonates *The Met*. However, such productions can only be considered global in their presentation. In contrast, when the World Opera produces a work occurring simultaneously in New York, Denmark, and Belfast, audiences experience a performance that is global as well as local in its production. Each local audience experiences a presentation of a global performance from a unique perspective, and each organization contributes its part to the whole. Such productions require a high level of trust between partnering organizations, as no one entity is every fully in control of the production.

We believe the World Opera, by providing a real-time conduit for cultural interaction, as well as a focal point for global performance, will innovate the operatic art form and reinvigorate its business model. To envision the opera of the future, we may do well to reflect upon the past: perhaps what is needed is a new Florentine *camerata*, a modern group of thinkers, hackers, philosophers, artists, technicians, and scientists who wish to establish a new, global World Opera tradition?

Chapter 7

Opera Orchestral Contracts Considered as a Research Resource

George Kennaway

[Mahler] gave the [timpanist, who had left the performance early to catch a train home] the choice of abandoning either the opera or his home in Brunn, but doubtless finally granted him an allowance to help him to move, for it was then that he learned that some of the musicians earned no more than sixty gulden a month, a sum on which it was impossible to live in Vienna, even as a bachelor.[1]

Mahler's timpanist, who could not stay in the pit until the end of *Lohengrin*, was in a situation familiar to many orchestral musicians today, working in any major city. The suburb of Brunn am Gebirge is approximately 15 kilometres from Vienna's Staatsoper, an unremarkable distance now, but more of a problem in the late nineteenth century. The timpanist worked in what was, and is, perceived as an elite art form, but did not enjoy a comparable level of remuneration. This chapter explores the potential of orchestral contracts as a research area, as a preliminary step towards reconstructing details of the daily lives of orchestral musicians. These documents – when available, which is a major problem in itself[2] – contain information about the working practices of orchestras, the type of work undertaken by the orchestra, the size of the orchestra, and many other aspects of orchestral work. Taken together, they can shed light on the social status of the players. The status of music and musicians is something that has been explored increasingly in recent years, but more work has been done on aspects of the music publishing trade, the consumers of music, the creation of concert series, concert life in general, and so forth.

The groundbreaking work of Deborah Rohr has not been substantially followed up in other periods or countries.[3] Rohr identified a contradiction in the

---

[1] Henry-Louis de la Grange, *Mahler*, 4 vols. (London, 1974) vol. 1, p. 443.

[2] At the time of writing, the archives of the Royal Opera House are closed to researchers, and the Victoria & Albert Museum's theatre collections hold contracts for some onstage performers only. Current orchestral contracts, though technically public documents where state funding is involved, are in practice quite elusive, and I am grateful to colleagues in the musical profession for their assistance in this respect.

[3] Deborah Rohr, *The Careers of British Musicians, 1750–1850: A Profession of Artisans* (Cambridge, 2001) – although see Catherine P. Mulder, *Unions and Class Transformation: The Case of the Broadway Musicians* (New York, 2009).

perceived status of the orchestral musician expressed in her subtitle: 'a profession of artisans'. This neat summation could hardly be bettered. This quotation from the 2004 Musicians' Union survey encapsulates the contradiction:

> For the one in three musicians (35%) earning between £10k and £20k, 38% are part-time, 42% have a degree and 58% have more than 10 years' experience. [...] these income levels are for experienced, full-time, qualified professionals. An important issue for musicians is that they are not generally entitled to progression along a pay spine like many other professionals even when they have the more secure jobs in music. [...] Earnings and career progression compare unfavourably with other professions in the UK [...] A teacher's starting salary, in the UK, ranges from £21k (England & Wales) to £27k (inner London). This starting salary is already better than the current income of 56% of musicians surveyed here. After six years of satisfactory performance, a teacher's salary rises to the top of this pay scale, £31k (England & Wales) to £36k (inner London); this salary is greater than the income achieved by 78% of musicians here. As careers progress the gap widens even further.[4]

This report shows that the issue is as valid today as it was in the early nineteenth century. Musicians are 'professional' in the sense that they are masters of knowledge and skills acquired through years of study, and use this training to undertake highly specialized tasks for a fee. In these terms, they are directly equivalent to doctors, architects, or lawyers – in the nineteenth century this professional class would have also included clergymen and commissioned military officers. But they are also 'artisans', skilled manual workers who practise a functional craft, which can at higher levels approach the creative. Professional musicians are also distinguished from, for example, prominent sportsmen/women, in that the latter are clearly not amateurs. Indeed, in the public mind there is possibly less distinction between a professional and an amateur violinist than between a professional and an amateur footballer.

Even UK income tax regulations struggle to accommodate the precise contractual status of orchestral musicians.

> The status of orchestral players can give rise to problems because of the variety of contracts and circumstances under which they are engaged. [...] The unions have been able to secure a package of measures designed to protect their members [...]. Because these features are more commonly found in an employer/employee relationship, it is natural that an examination of the standard contractual terms may lead to the view that performers/artists so engaged are engaged under contracts of employment. [...] [But] the terms of the contract

---

[4] DHA Communications for the Musicians' Union, *The Working Musician* (Musicians' Union, 2012), p. 9, <www.musiciansunion.org.uk/wp-content/uploads/2012/12/The-Working-Musician-report.pdf> (accessed 27 June 2015).

may not be decisive by themselves, and in the case of artistic workers, such as theatrical performers/artists, the way in which they generally carry on their profession also needs to be considered. Other case law supports the view that [...] individual contracts are not contracts of employment, even though the *prima facie* view [...] may suggest otherwise.[5]

That is, although players can be engaged – even on a full-time, permanent, basis – under contractual terms that are in essence closely comparable to any similar contract of employment in any other trade or profession, including negotiated benefits such as sick pay or pension contributions (which would normally distinguish such employees from their self-employed freelance counterparts), nonetheless these contracts can be interpreted differently in the case of musicians or actors.

Rohr showed that, at the end of the eighteenth century, members of the Royal Society for Musicians had incomes roughly equivalent to those of shopkeepers or the most successful highly skilled artisans, such as instrument makers, jewellers, watchmakers, and fashionable hairdressers.[6] Nonetheless, when the Philharmonic Society was founded in 1813 its members played without a fee,[7] in order that they could be perceived as acting from pure professional ideals, adopting 'the comparative aloofness from the struggle for income' that marked established professionals.[8] In practice this actually contributed to the weakness of the profession. The only way to achieve higher status was to perform chamber music or as a soloist. As it was, musicians remained more artisans than professionals:

> [T]he constant preoccupation with mere subsistence was a grave deterrent to collective efforts that might have helped them achieve professional autonomy, and it prevented many musicians from attaining even the trappings of middle-class respectability and social status.[9]

The strike of the musicians of the King's Theatre, Haymarket, in 1828 shows how this conflicted status was associated with a lack of clarity in industrial relations. The manager having attempted to impose a formal written agreement with the orchestra – an unusual arrangement at this time – 16 players seceded from the orchestra in protest at this attempt to regulate their professional activities. The management wanted exclusivity with regard to the players, who were to be at all times at the disposal of the manager, and could not accept other engagements

---

[5]   HM Revenue and Customs, Staff Manuals ESM4140 and 4121, <www.hmrc.gov.uk/manuals/esmmanual/ESM4140.htm> and <www.hmrc.gov.uk/manuals/esmmanual/ESM4121.htm> (accessed 27 June 2015).

[6]   Rohr, *Careers*, p. 155.

[7]   Ibid., p. 168.

[8]   Harold Perkin, *The Origins of Modern English Society 1780–1880* (London, 1969), p. 256.

[9]   Rohr, *Careers*, p. 154.

without express permission. The management would consider 'how far such indulgence may interfere with the business of the theatre, or how far it may tend to injure its interests'.[10] The new contract specified that 50 performances would be given under the usual terms, but that an additional unspecified number would be given for half pay, and three performances *gratis*. The seceding 16 protested:

> To play on any occasion for *half price* carries with it a degree of degradation, not only inimical to our feelings as men, but also [...] unjust to our reputation as professors. What man of respectable feelings and decent circumstances would subscribe to laws that should leave him, for the time being, scarcely anything of personal liberty?[11]

When in the late 1980s the Orchestra of Opera North (then known as the English Northern Philharmonia) agreed to make recordings for half the prevailing freelance rate, this was seen as potentially reducing available fees across the board by undercutting fees paid to other orchestras. But it enabled the orchestra to begin to make many recordings for Naxos in particular, including the complete orchestral works of William Walton, and within a few years other orchestras had offered even more attractive rates to recording companies. This trend eventually culminated in orchestras such as the Hallé Orchestra and the London Symphony Orchestra issuing live concert recordings under their own labels. (The revised Opera North contract did not apply to recordings of opera, which remained particularly expensive given that the overall requirement for the minimum amount of recording time is set at three hours per 20 minutes of recorded product. An opera lasting three hours therefore requires 27 hours of recording time.) The historical contrast with the dissident theatre musicians of 1828 is obvious. As an orchestral player myself, I do not recall the argument ever being advanced in modern times that to give away a certain number of free recordings annually was to submit to tyranny or professional degradation – it was simply a matter of more effective marketing and, ultimately, of survival.

By the last decade of the nineteenth century it was becoming clear that, notwithstanding the possible loss of professional status, musicians might benefit from some degree of organization. There was considerable discussion about what form this might take, not limited to straightforward unionization. This was additionally complicated by questions of class. Musicians still struggled to reconcile what Rohr called the 'dual identity of literate urban artisans and aspiring professionals'.[12]

---

[10] Ibid., p. 170, quoting 'The King's Theatre', *Quarterly Musical Magazine and Review*, 38 (1828): p. 261.

[11] Ibid., quoting 'The King's Theatre', *Quarterly Musical Magazine and Review*, 38 (1828): p. 262; this passage is also given in 'The Orchestra of the King's Theatre and M. Laporte', *Harmonicon*, 7 (1829): p. 35.

[12] Ibid., p. 166.

One professional body, the Incorporated Society of Musicians (ISM), was criticized for being little more than a talking-shop.

> Its chief aim apparently was to purge the ranks of those who were supposed to be beneath the standard set up by the Society, and so far its only practical work has been a system of musical examinations, for which there was no particular call, and which differ in no essential respect from those conducted by previously-existing institutions. For it cannot be said that the annual conferences of the Society have greatly aided the cause of music. The papers read, and the discussions following, have for the most part been of value to the profession only; and, for the rest, it has pretty much been a case of personal enjoyment, advancement of personal interests, and mutual admiration all round.[13]

The writer also complained that the society did nothing practical to increase orchestral provision in Britain to German levels. The class distinction that applied in the nineteenth century is still evident in our times, in that the present-day ISM primarily acts for instrumental teachers, while the Musicians' Union, as far as classical performers are concerned, acts primarily for orchestral musicians.

The creation of the Musicians' Union provoked an interesting discussion of class issues relating to musicians. Ebenezer Prout was resolutely opposed:

> [T]he object of the Union is to enforce that system of organised tyranny which is the curse of modern trades-unionism in this country, but which, happily, has not yet succeeded in effecting its object, and, thank Heaven! does not appear likely to do so.[14]

Another writer, T.L. Southgate, rejected it if it were to be too inclusive, antagonistic, or led by the wrong sort of person:

> A union of orchestral players properly thought out and with the right sort of people at the head of it would be most valuable and useful; but an association founded in a spirit of hostility to employers, threatening force and boycotting to those who do not join its ranks, admitting anyone to membership, and essaying to reduce all artists to the same dead level will find no support in this journal.[15]

Southgate's highly qualified support for unionization was expressed at greater length in the following year:

---

[13]   Anon., 'What the Incorporated Society of Musicians Might Do', *Magazine of Music* 10 (1893): p. 17.

[14]   Ebenezer Prout, 'The Amalgamated Musicians' Union', *Monthly Music Record* 23 (1893): p. 145.

[15]   T.L. Southgate, 'Questionable Orchestral Associations', *Musical News* 5 (1893): p. 395.

In London and at [sic] Manchester associations have been formed ostensibly to band together orchestral players for the purpose of helping one another, and for protection. This is legitimate enough, and had the schemes stopped there, they would have commanded the sympathy and assistance of those who lead music in this country; but the promoters went much beyond these lines. They proposed to wage warfare against concert-givers and conductors who did not comply with some ridiculous rules emanating from a hole-and-corner clique, who are seeking to do what our American friends term 'boss the show'. And in addition to this, these persons impudently put forth the claim to control all orchestral players in this country, including even the amateurs admitted to their ranks. And they further threaten personal violence to those who stand aloof from their organisation.[16]

The inclusion of amateurs in the proposed union was extremely controversial. It offered uniformity of treatment, and ensured that amateurs would not be able to undercut professional players – but at the same time it also undermined an essential requirement for professional status by removing any requirement for professional training or skills.

Unionization was hampered by a perception that the union was not truly representative, as so many players had not joined. A dispute arose at the 1899 Covent Garden Promenade Concerts, when the season closed prematurely and the players had done more work than was covered by their contracts. One commentator argued for a deposit scheme for concert promoters to guarantee fees, but noted that the players' position was weakened:

This seems to be a case in which the Orchestral Association should be of use in protecting orchestral players. But it cannot be done while so many men stand out from joining an association for the protection of their rights.[17]

The weakness of the union's position was vividly demonstrated in a dispute at the Grand Theatre, Leeds, in 1895.

We will take the case of Leeds, which, by the way, is not the only one available. About a year ago a dispute began at the Grand Theatre in respect to terms to be paid to the orchestra by the new management. No arrangement agreeable to both sides being arrived at, the orchestra decided to 'go out'. The orchestra went out – and another orchestra went in. Forthwith the Union, being a trade union, set all the machinery of trade unionism to work to get the new orchestra put out and the old one reinstated. Boycott, picket, warnings to union members not to deputise or play at the theatre 'blacked' under any circumstances, no matter what remuneration might be offered, black lists for those who paid no heed to

---

[16]   T.L. Southgate, 'The First Step in Musical Trades-Unionism', *Musical News* 6 (1894): p. 57.

[17]   Anon., 'Comments and Opinions', *Musical Standard* 12 (1899): p. 243.

these warnings, appeals to the public not to patronise the theatre – in short, every trade union weapon was used, and everything failed; and although the energy of the Union has never been relaxed to this day, the new orchestra is still there. Hundreds of pounds have been wasted over this one struggle alone, conducted on strictly trade union methods, because those methods are the most effectual to the particular class to which they are applied.[18]

Note the implication in the final sentence of this quotation: trade union methods are inappropriate because they are more effective for disputes involving a different (for which read lower) class of worker. This was in spite of the fact that, at this time, the idea of professional orchestral training was relatively new. Only in 1867 did the Royal College of Music begin to offer courses 'for the benefit and encouragement of those who desire to enter the musical profession as orchestral performers'.[19]

A remarkably detailed account of another theatre orchestra dispute sheds more light on contractual practices and class attitudes.[20] On 1 December 1879, a new production of *H.M.S. Pinafore* opened in the New York, conducted by Arthur Sullivan and Alfred Cellier, a regular conductor at Covent Garden, with Richard D'Oyly Carte present. This was the first authorized American production, after around 150 pirated ones in the USA over the previous two years.[21] The orchestra appears to have demanded an increased fee almost at the last minute before the premiere – $25 per performance, not the $17 or $18 previously agreed with the local manager.

> The excuse they give is that because Mr. Sullivan conducts in person, the event is invested with unusual importance, and they are therefore entitled to larger pay.[22]

Sullivan claimed that such a thing was unknown in England and amounted to swindling. Cellier suggested that managers should unite against organized labour, and Sullivan pointed out that London-based managers had beaten provincial theatre-managers when the latter attempted to withhold fees owed to touring companies. Sullivan and D'Oyly Carte agreed that it was the inferior musicians who were the instigators of strike action.

> 'What I most regard in a professional point of view,' observed Mr. Sullivan, 'is the fact that the cultivated musicians, the men who have spent their lives

[18] Anon., 'Trade Unionism Again', *Musical Standard* 5 (1896): p. 244.
[19] Anon., 'Table Talk', *Musical Standard* 6 (1867): p. 156.
[20] Anon., 'An Interview with Cerberus', *Musical World* 57 (1879): pp. 811–12, reprinted from the *New York Herald* 4 December 1879.
[21] Earl. F. Bargainnier, 'W.S. Gilbert and American Musical Theatre', in Timothy E. Scheurer (ed.), *American Popular Music Vol. 1: The Nineteenth Century: Tin Pan Alley* (Bowling Green, OH, 1989), pp. 120–33 (p. 120).
[22] Anon., 'Cerberus', p. 811.

in hard study, who have come from the conservatories and are earning their daily bread by teaching or in other musical pursuits, are forced into competition with other musicians of a lower grade, who spend their time during the day in other pursuits, and consider an hour or two in the orchestra with much the same practical interest that they contemplate the repairing of an old shoe. I mean to say that there is a difference between your trained professionals and your mere machines.' 'I am of the belief,' said Mr. Carte, 'that it is these machines – the mere mechanics and speculators in music – who are making our trouble.'[23]

Sullivan threatened a dramatic solution:

'If the matter remains unsettled, what will you do, Mr. Sullivan?' 'Promptly telegraph to London for my own people to come. In twelve days I can put before yonder curtain one of the best *Pinafore* orchestras in the world. Meanwhile, as Mr. Carte has mentioned, I will, if necessary, conduct the performance on a grand piano assisted by my conductor, Mr. Cellier, on a harmonium – and I am not sure that *Pinafore* will not even then be presented in a manner that the New York public will thoroughly enjoy.'

Attitudes to orchestral musicians in general remained mired in class attitudes. In 1917, the *Musical Herald* classified performers in precisely this way, ending with a possibly unintentional but still revealing pun.

The virtuoso who plays a solo instrument in a concerto at a symphony concert regards himself as a great artist; but the ordinary members of the orchestra claim to be no more than professionals, whilst the great mass of mere bandsmen rank as artisans, and give the Trade Unionism of the orchestra the artisan tone.[24]

The upper-class virtuoso looks down on the middle-class orchestral players, who in turn rank above the working-class bandsmen. And in 1930, performers in general were put firmly in their lower-middle-class place by the *Musical Mirror*: 'It should be remembered that the performer is little more than a *purveyor* of music – the man behind the counter, as it were.'[25]

If the class status of orchestral musicians is enmeshed in contradiction, the contracts that govern the duties of these players can shed some light. Such documents frequently contain additional information of other kinds. Orchestral contracts from before the twentieth century are rare. However, an early example in the archives of the Hallé Orchestra, from 1908, shows the potential richness of data

---

23 Ibid., p. 812.
24 Anon., 'Musicians Under Control', *Musical Herald* 831 (1917): p. 171.
25 Anon., 'Music To-Day', *Musical Mirror* 10 (1930): p. 309.

available to the researcher.[26] The 1908 contract for a rank-and-file viola player[27] consists of one foolscap side of text only. The contract is between the player and Forsyth Brothers Ltd, a major music shop in central Manchester still trading today. Members of the Forsyth family sat on the board of the Hallé Concerts Society, founded in 1899.[28] It relates to concerts in the 1908–1909 season, consisting of 39 concerts from 14 October to 30 March, in Nottingham, Manchester, Bradford, Leeds, Newcastle, Liverpool, Sheffield, Belfast, Huddersfield, and Preston.

The string strength is specified for each concert, which means that the exact composition of the orchestra can be ascertained for any of the concerts covered by the contract. Some concerts use a reduced-size string section, in many cases the bass section is the same size as the cello section, and the two violin sections are equal in size.

The fee is 1 guinea per concert, including a rehearsal on the day, and one more rehearsal at ⅓ guinea extra, suggesting an annual gross income for a tutti player of approximately 60 guineas (£65) for a player needed for all concerts. Playing for the Hallé was therefore not a full-time job in itself, but there were further restrictions nonetheless. No deputies were allowed if the full orchestra was required, but if the orchestra was smaller a deputy could be used – but only if the deputy was himself a member of the Hallé Orchestra *and* the conductor Hans Richter (who conducted the Hallé 1899–1911) had given written permission. The player could not accept engagements with any other orchestra without written permission.[29] If additional concerts were arranged after the contract had been signed, the player was bound to play, subject to being given three weeks' notice of the concert. Wind instruments were required to be at 'normal pitch'. Travel expenses could be reimbursed subject to limits: train fares for concerts in Manchester were only paid for a distance of up to 35 miles, and concerts out of Manchester attracted the payment of a third-class train fare and an additional overnight allowance as necessary. The player had to join the orchestra's pension fund, and was subject to instant dismissal for unpunctuality, insubordination, or misbehaviour.

A later Hallé contract from 1960 reveals many changes in the work of the orchestra, a greater awareness of the different rankings within it, and a generally greater level of detail. The contract is between the player and the Hallé Concerts

---

[26] I am most grateful to the Hallé's archivist Stewart Robinson for kindly supplying copies of these contracts.

[27] The term 'rank and file' is an exclusively English expression; orchestras in other countries normally use the term 'tutti', with the occasional French 'du rang' being the closest approximation the English term. Dr Bjorn Heile has informed me in a private communication that the expression 'Tutti-schwein' is common in Germany, and much coarser versions of the English term are widely used in British orchestras.

[28] <www.halle.co.uk/halle-concerts-society.aspx> (accessed 10 January 2013).

[29] Correspondence in the Hallé archives shows that in the early 1900s the principal viola, Simon Speelman, organized orchestral work in the summer season at Blackpool for players from the Hallé and other orchestras.

Society (this is still the case), and the highly detailed document consists of three foolscap sides, in small print. In 1960, the player will be given three weeks' notice of the work schedule, but this can be changed up to one week before the actual work. Provision is made for additional payments to players sitting in a higher position than contracted (such as when a tutti player sits as sub-principal). The performance of chamber music is not compulsory for tutti players (but note that 'chamber music' is undefined – see Opera North's contract below). As in 1908, the player cannot accept engagements elsewhere without written provision, but now explicit exceptions are made for teaching, composing, or arranging. The player cannot talk to the press without permission, and cannot advertise himself as being connected with the Hallé Orchestra. The weekly salary is £13.10 – (£13.50) per week, or £700 per annum. (Weekly pay is still a widely preferred salary system for many orchestras, with the notable exception of those belonging to the BBC orchestras, who are paid monthly like other BBC employees.) Union membership is compulsory. The player must be given 13 weeks' notice – or one week in case of *force majeure*.

The early contract governing Opera North's orchestra, the English Northern Philharmonia, established in 1978, remained in force for approximately 15 years.[30] During this time it was successively modified, extended, and refined. Eventually this contract was perceived to be increasingly difficult to administer and too inflexible, and it was replaced with an entirely new one. The most important element of the new contract (modelled on agreements put in place at the Royal Opera House, among others) was that it replaced the three-hour session as the standard unit of work with an hourly-based agreement. Under the older system, any session running over three hours, including a performance, would incur overtime payments, even if the player concerned might (in the case of some instruments) only have worked one or two sessions that week; under the new contract, overtime was only triggered when the player's total working hours for the week exceeded 24. It also enabled the scheduling of rehearsals of different lengths, and allowed for monthly working hours to be exceeded albeit on a strictly limited basis. However, it should be noted that the new contract quickly became longer and more complex than the old one.

Both old and new contracts specify that the orchestra consists of 54 players. This prevents vacancies being filled by cheaper freelance players (apart from covering for absence), and ensures a greater degree of permanence in the ensemble. However, this fact, taken in conjunction with the size of the orchestra pits in Opera North's touring venues, will reveal to future students of performance practice history that Opera North's performances of later romantic repertoire such as operas by Puccini or Strauss (and almost certainly any performance outside London by any regional opera company) must have used considerably fewer strings than are specified in the score. Decisions were taken at the outset as to which

---

[30] Copies of contracts in my possession; I also wish to thank Eileen Spencer for supplying additional material.

instruments should be retained on a full-time basis and which would be supplied by freelance players. Thus, the contract orchestra included strings (10.8.6.5.3), double woodwind, 4 horns, 2 trumpets, 3 trombones, tuba, 3 percussionists, and harp, but not a fifth horn, nor third flute doubling piccolo. This is still the case; the only exception is the harp position, which was redefined as a fractional post when a vacancy occurred.[31]

The question of chamber-music payments at Opera North, referred to above in the context of the Hallé Orchestra, has raised some interesting contractual definitions. Since performances of chamber music incur additional payments, these are not merely academic musicological questions. For example, an earlier contractual definition of chamber music as 'music written by the composer to be performed by one instrument per part' means that a work like Strauss's *Metamorphosen* for 23 solo strings counts as chamber music. But, in addition, each player will be playing as a principal (as, for instance, 'principal 4th cello'), and since many of these will be tutti players, 'sit-up payments' are due. This is a not insignificant sum, given that all such payments apply not only to the concert but to all rehearsals. This definition was therefore modified to limit the overall size of the chamber ensemble to 13 players, a definition that includes Mozart's *Gran Partita for 13 instruments* K.361 but excludes the Strauss work (for which 'sit-up' would still be paid, but not the chamber music payment). The earlier definition produced an interesting result when the orchestra (which had just changed its name to the Orchestra of Opera North) played Kaija Saariaho's *Verblendungen* at the Huddersfield Contemporary Music Festival in 1988.[32] By an odd coincidence, the highly divided writing for strings in this work meant that, quite fortuitously, each string player in the orchestra was playing their own individual line (as, of course, were all the other players). Thus, the work was being played with one instrument per part, albeit by a full symphony orchestra. Although this was not, in fact, the composer's intention, nonetheless a chamber music payment was triggered.

Compared with the three weeks' notice of the work schedule offered to the Hallé Orchestra, the Orchestra of Opera North has always enjoyed six weeks' notice of work, and a minimum of eight free days in each four-week period (although, again, the current contract offers some room for flexibility in this). This is considerably more notice of the work schedule than is available to the chorus (governed by entirely separate contractual arrangements and represented, not by the Musicians' Union, but by Equity).

---

[31]   Personal communication with several members of the orchestra.

[32]   Kaija Saariaho, *Verblendungen*. Performed at Huddersfield Town Hall on 27 November 1988, conducted by Diego Masson. The rest of the programme comprised works by Murray Schafer, Messiaen, and Bartók. My thanks to Andrew Fairley, Opera North's Senior Librarian, for retrieving this information. The same contractual provision also prevented the orchestra from performing Gérard Grisey's *Modulations* at this festival – it was eventually given there by the BBC Philharmonic whose contractual obligations differed. My thanks to Richard Steinitz for this information in a private communication.

The Orchestra of Opera North is unique in the UK in that it performs a full programme of symphonic concerts as well as opera. Contractually, this means that concerts are treated in several distinctly different ways from opera. In particular, freelance players for concerts are paid a fee for the concert which includes a three-hour rehearsal on the day, whereas operas fees are paid at a higher rate and on an individual session basis. There are also important differences in the provision of transport: for opera performances away from Leeds, players are paid standard-class rail fares (an improvement on the early Hallé's third-class fare), but for concerts out of Leeds, the company is obliged to provide a coach to take the orchestra to the venue and return to Leeds. This creates another question of definition where concert performances of opera are concerned – clearly, if a concert performance of an opera is defined as a 'concert', then there is a saving of freelance fees, and coach hire costs are incurred, but if it is defined as an 'opera', the freelance cost goes up as does the cost of travel by train. Note that this definition is entirely separate from the terms used in the promotion and marketing of the event.

While these contracts can provide much information that can clarify aspects of the orchestra's work, and indeed influence repertoire choices, they should be treated with care. Although the first Opera North contract contained a clause governing the scheduling of 'industrial concerts' – a clause which was retained in subsequent revisions of the contract – to the best of my knowledge the orchestra has never in its entire history given such a concert. It cannot therefore be assumed that contractual provisions always necessarily reflect the actual work of the orchestra; circumstances may be anticipated that do not arise in practice.

In terms of the conflicted status of orchestral musicians in general, and opera players in particular, these fine questions of detail and definition confirm the player more as an 'artisan' than a 'professional'. Whereas academics, solicitors, doctors, or other professionals enjoy a regular monthly salary and simply claim for whatever additional expenses they incur in the course of their profession, musicians constantly examine their weekly pay for confirmation that a myriad of additional sums have been paid for overtime, 'sit-up', travel, meals, or (for those carrying large instruments not taken on the orchestra van) porterage. These sums can often be quite small, but they can assume disproportionate importance. An excellent example is found in the long-running contractual dispute over additional payments due for an orchestral concert in Skegness which took place in the middle of an opera tour to various venues in the north of England. Contractually, the company is officially based at whatever venue it is performing. Thus, the rail fare paid to the players between touring venues is for a direct journey from venue to venue without any return to Leeds. Thus, on this occasion, the orchestra was assumed to be travelling from Manchester (opera) to Skegness (concert) and on to Hull (opera). Only the concert required the provision of a coach. This coach was booked to take the orchestra from Leeds to Skegness and back, reflecting the reality of the players' travel intentions. As the coach returned to Leeds after midnight, the orchestra committee requested a late return payment. This was initially refused on the grounds that the company was under no obligation to provide the coach from Leeds in the first place – that, in other words, this had been done as a concession, and no consequential payments were due for a late return. Technically, the management should have offered coach travel from Manchester to Hull via Skegness. After some nine months of negotiation, the matter was resolved by making an *ex gratia* payment on the basis that no precedent was created. The sum involved was approximately £5 per player. Issues such as these are preeminently 'artisanal' in nature.

For a very different kind of contract, in an equally different context, the contract governing the work of the orchestra of the Metropolitan Opera of New York is rich in detail.[33] The document is over 40 pages long, mainly because of the exceptional level of detail covering every aspect of the orchestra's work. Highlights, in the context of this chapter, include the provision of health, disability, and public liability insurance (the first two being a particular concern in the USA); a clothing and instrument allowance of $900 per annum; a built-in annual cost of living adjustment; additional payments for public rehearsals to a non-paying audience; the size of the orchestra being fixed at 90 players; and the management's undertaking to bear in mind individual players' seating preferences when travelling by air. There is an extremely complex system of additional payments for 'split days' (when work is scheduled in the morning and the evening, with a free afternoon), additional performances, and a category of payments due in what are termed 'premium conditions'. Additional maintenance payments for foreign touring are specified in this contract, unlike that used by Opera North, where each foreign tour's *per diem* subsistence rates are negotiated tour by tour. The audition process for new players is set out in great detail, and is much closer to an international music competition than any European model. At each round, each panellist must answer precisely one question, and artistic discussion is explicitly prohibited. Players are appointed initially for a two-year probation period – UK orchestras generally take longer to appoint players, but they are then full members of the orchestra, and in the rest of Europe a one-year probation period is normal. Audition results are decided purely on a majority vote. The cumulative effect is to underline the international status of the orchestra and the considerable prestige conferred on its members, rather than to extend the artisanal status of the player.[34] The foregoing discussion has done no more than highlight the sort of information that can be found in orchestral players' contracts. Taken in conjunction with a historical perspective, further research would show that the current paradoxical status of opera orchestra musicians – employed after years of advanced training,

---

[33]   I am grateful to Sam Magill for this information.

[34]   As of December 2014, the most recent contract for the orchestra of the Metropolitan Opera house has not yet been published. However, it would appear that the original changes required by the management did not materialize, and the contract is substantially unchanged. A reduction in compensation of 7 per cent is to be achieved through reductions in some marginal payments, and the orchestra's health insurance will now entail a higher excess payment. My thanks to members of the company for this information.

to participate in performances of the most expensive Western art form, but also perceived as artisans rather than professionals – has its roots in class attitudes which become visible in the nineteenth century.

Chapter 8
Behind the Curtain: Shaping a New *Siegfried*

Cordelia Chenault

Act II of Wagner's *Siegfried*: a slight, muscular man in brown clothing glides across the forest floor, a slanted disk lit in a mottled, bluish-green. Feathers extend from his graceful fingers. Crouching on an animal skin, stage right, Siegfried notices the dancing forest bird. They begin a musical game on the centre platform: the boy steals a reed from the creature's beak, then blows upon it to imitate the birdsong. The bird beckons the youth closer, coquettishly enticing him to stroke his quills. The boy takes up his own horn, but as he copies the bird's melody, the free-spirited leitmotif transforms to assume a heroic air.

The day after the performance, *Journal Frankfurt* published a half-page photo of the bird: a unitard-clad modern dancer leading Siegfried and his bloodied sword up the outer ramp of the gigantic set, his beak-like jaw angled up to show the way (Figure 8.1). 'Nemirova lets the voice of the woodland bird dance!' declared Christian Rupp; the critic was among the many viewers enchanted by dancer Alan Barnes's onstage embodiment of the character, whose music was sung by the

Figure 8.1   Siegfried and the forest bird

offstage soprano. The majority of reviews of Oper Frankfurt's new staging praised this fresh representation of the forest bird, whose image was repeatedly used by critics to illustrate the 'innovative ideas' in this third instalment of director Vera Nemirova's new *Ring* cycle.

Interestingly, however, the concept presentation seven weeks earlier had included no mention of a dancing bird. Alan Barnes was simply introduced to the cast that day as the second of two assistant directors who would collaborate on the staging. Indeed, a wholly different concept was presented to the *Siegfried* cast and crew: soprano Robin Johannsen, wearing a tracksuit, would encounter Siegfried on a woodland jog in her first appearance as the bird. Three weeks later, however, Johannsen's pregnancy was announced to the creative team, and Barnes stepped onto the stage to fill in for the sick singer at the last minute. His spontaneous presence was enchanting enough to prompt a change of plan: from then on, Barnes would dance the role, with Johannsen singing from the orchestra pit.

This turn of events quintessentially demonstrates a simple point: when an opera production is analysed on the basis of surface-level perceptions of one staged performance, our assertions are hindered by a singularity of perspective. The performance of an opera is a musical-theatrical event in which composers, creators, and audiences all play a defining role. By addressing the piece only on the audience's experience of it in performance, not only do we as scholars fail to consider the people and events that have prepared it for stage, but we also exclude a major vantage point from scholarly consideration: the creative context.[1] Neglect of the creative process can lead us to misconstrue simple truths, and perhaps even to draw false conclusions. I argue that in order to produce judicious analyses, we must also examine the events that bring productions from score to stage.

Opera scholarship since the mid-2000s has already begun to venture down a more comprehensive path. Until recently, Anglo-American musicologists focused primarily on the operatic *Werktreue* in studies that addressed compositional intent, original socio-historical context, or details of the score. Authors usually shied away from discussions of individual productions, particularly recent ones. More recently, scholars such as David Levin and Clemens Risi have re-centred the notion of the operatic text onto individual stagings. This newer trend acknowledges that audiences experience productions, not abstract works, and with that development, the audience perspective has been integrated into the discourse.

Yet with rare exception, the current musicological approach still stops short; scholarship in opera studies still tends to overlook the creative perspective and

---

[1]   Here I place emphasis on the fact that firstly, analysis of a performance tends to imply claims about intentionality of interpretive elements, and secondly, that it can miss many seemingly non-artistic factors that shape the piece, regardless of intentionality. Other reasons also exist for why an analysis confined to a scholar's impression of a sole performance is flawed: namely, that each live performance is (at least to some extent) its own performative event, and differs from other performances of the same production. For more, refer to Carolyn Abbate's 'Music: Drastic or Gnostic?' *Critical Inquiry* 30/3 (2004): pp. 505–36.

context of a production. Moreover, the indisputable influences of logistics and business details draw nary a comment. Interestingly, however, useful work addressing the contextual and business factors that influence musical institutions has been initiated and proven useful in fields adjacent to musicology: *In Search of a Magic Flute*, David Ranan's 2003 public-policy study of opera funding in England and Germany, shows how financial matters can affect artistic content. Anthropologist Georgina Born addresses similar logistical issues, also following a more scholarly and theoretically grounded approach. Her 1995 ethnography of the avant-garde musical institution IRCAM, *Rationalizing Culture*, has effectively shown how that body is guided by inter-organizational and personal politics, the mundane practices of daily operations, as well as the larger artistic and philosophical goals espoused by the establishment's creative personae.[2]

Indeed, my work in this chapter is closely modelled after Born as I attempt to provide a 'backstage' analysis of the preparations for Oper Frankfurt's 2011 premiere of *Siegfried*, which shows how this production was shaped by the concerns of its creators, the manner of its preparation, and the business concerns of the opera house's artistic directors. Like the music addressed in Born's study, this opera staging also bears the indelible traces of the people and events that brought it to stage – both creative personnel and those from the artistic administration.[3] The turn of events that transformed Alan Barnes from the assistant director into the dancing woodland bird is one of many examples that show the need for the multiplicity of analytical perspectives to be gained through production-based analysis, but it also reveals the value in addressing the unique contributions of a web of involved individuals. These points will form the basis of my analysis of the 2011 *Siegfried*, producing a colourful illustration of an improved analytical approach that reaches beyond simple discussions of a staging in performance as it examines the individuals and developments that enabled the production of this new reading.

It must be pointed out here that my research methodology differs significantly from approaches utilized by most other musicologists. My analysis has been influenced by my unusual position as a dramaturgical collaborator and member of the creative team for the Nemirova *Ring* cycle: I was offered the rare chance to undertake this kind of research as part of my larger dissertation project, an institutional history of the Oper Frankfurt since 1979, from which the analysis in this article is taken. The ability to work alongside the cast, directors, designers,

---

[2] Georgia Born, *Rationalizing Culture: IRCAM, Boulez, and the Institutionalization of the Musical Avant-Garde* (Berkeley, 1995).

[3] Understanding the contributions of individuals – in many different roles – is essential to this work. For this reason, I use the word 'creators' intentionally to refer to both traditional members of the creative team – directors, designers, and dramaturges – as well as to the performers, and also some artistic administrators involved in some creative matters. In the course of this analysis, it will become clear that it is important to understand the nature of staging as a collectively authored process, steered alternately by *many* creative individuals within the web of the production team at the opera house.

and administrators has provided me with an unusual insight into the issues that would normally remain private. Without this intimate level of access, many of the factors discussed in this chapter would have been unknowable. Likewise, it is essential to recognize that my perspective on the decisions made and their import is by no means a neutral one; the understandings and analysis to be presented in this chapter are inherently biased, informed by the experience of collaboration on the daily tasks and decision-making involved in a production process.

This *Siegfried* is the third instalment in the most recent setting of Wagner's full *Ring des Nibelungen* initially presented at Oper Frankfurt in 2010–2012. The 30 October 2011 premiere revealed a straightforward interpretation with stunning aesthetics: the staging exhibited an array of eye-catching stage pictures and highly physical depictions of the character tensions. The new reading adhered to many of the emphases in the original Wagnerian productions, with few thematic additions; the visual narrative, too, remained true to the libretto.[4]

Wagner's *Siegfried* on a Striking Set

The Nibelung blacksmith, Mime, finally tells his orphaned ward, Siegfried, about his origins. Mime learns the of the young man's destiny from a mysterious Wanderer, the disguised god Wotan, in a knowledge wager. Siegfried re-forges his father's sword, then fells the dragon, Fafner. After tasting the dragon's blood, the boy gains the ability to understand the language of a forest bird. He learns that Mime plans to poison him, then kills his foster father in self-defence. Led by the bird, he goes to seek his bride.

The Wanderer holds conversations with Alberich and Erda in an attempt to alter his dire predicament, to no avail. He is equally fruitless in swaying Siegfried's support, and the sword of the ignorant youth shatters Wotan's spear.

Siegfried comes upon Brünnhilde's enchanted rock, where the former Walküre sleeps, surrounded by a ring of fire. He summons the courage to cross the enchantment, and awakens her with kisses. Greeting the sun, Brünnhilde warms to her rescuer, and the two fall in love.

The most interesting feature of this *Siegfried* – and, indeed, of the full *Ring* cycle – is the set design (Figure 8.2). The massive construction features four concentric rings, each motorized to rotate separately. Designer Jens Killian's playing field allows for a seemingly endless array of configurations: when the rings are rotated to different degrees, the resultant shape resembles the planet Saturn. During the opera, the set morphs into multiple landscapes; the rings seem to imply cliffs, caves, or forest paths. The colossus is still as the curtain rises. A disc consumes the stage, tilted at 35 degrees, ascending back from the orchestra pit.

---

[4] For more on themes brought out in the original Wagnerian stagings at Bayreuth, see George R. Fricke, James Andrew Deaville, and Evan Baker (eds), *Wagner in Rehearsal 1875–1876: The Diaries of Richard Fricke*, No. 7 (New York, 1998).

Figure 8.2   Set design, *Siegfried*

Despite its enormous flexibility, this set was nothing new by the third opera in the cycle. Furthermore, other design elements also showed mindful construction. The costumes, for example, which were drawn from subtly mixed historical periods, typically reflected the major themes of the narrative, occasionally offering reinforcement of minor interpretive ideas.[5] As will become clear in later discussion, stage pictures were breathtaking, and a handful of clever tricks led to poignant moments. Yet only the set elements were striking enough to distinguish this *Siegfried* from other settings conceptually; no other feature of the staging was woven into the fabric of the Nemirova staging thoroughly enough for it to be taken as a new directorial 'concept'. Nevertheless, this enchanting version presented Wagner's text in overt, colourful, and often playful visual language. Deft combinations of movement, characterization, and technical elements foregrounded the driving tensions in the music, text, and subtext. At the heart of the interpretation lay the conflicts and internal struggles of highly human characters.

Character, *Konzept*, and Creation

Portrayal of the relationship between Mime and Siegfried in Act I was particularly compelling, and their contrasting physical animation propelled the drama. Peter Marsh was both sympathetic and grotesque as the neurotic Mime; despite his contorted physical caricatures, he was intensely human. Lance Ryan's Siegfried was awkward and sullen, if also innocent and vulnerable. Unsure of his unwieldy body, the frustrated title character flung his own limbs as liberally as the cooking pots.

---

[5]   The costumes of Fafner and the woodland bird were thought-provoking: the dragon's suit illustrated the ideas 'man versus the machine' and 'society as machine' as he took the form of skinless human in a painted bodysuit, while the bird's simple costume and long expressive feathers provided extraordinarily demonstrative fingers with which to build a relationship with Siegfried, foreshadow danger, and embody the virtue and power of nature against the villain of an evil, monstrous society.

Mime, by contrast, shrank away from the brutish child, clinging to his anvil when threatened. The physical juxtaposition of Siegfried's explosive temperament against Mime's timidity made visible the emotional familial tensions between the surly youth and his physical antithesis of a foster father.

The 'fire dance' towards the end of Act I was also particularly effective. As Siegfried smelted his sword, the stage darkened. The barefoot dance took place atop the innermost ring, the platform temporarily replaced by glowing red plexiglass. The protagonist's trance-like ritual pulled him down towards the core of the rings to make a primal connection with the earth – an idea reinforced by the descending stepwise motion in the brass.

The battle in Act II offered the only additional hint of a directorial *Konzept*. When Siegfried entered the dragon's lair, the rings rotated wildly in a science-fiction-inspired attack. The enormous construction seemed to become the dragon as the hero battled on the skeletal structure of the monstrous apparatus. Fafner emerged from within, clothed in the bodysuit of a skinless man, transformed into a giant horror of exposed muscle and bone draped in gold chains. Siegfried easily defeats this odd villain, but the nightmarish machine is slower to halt. The scene emphasizes society's capacity to manipulate and destroy as the hero battles the disfigured giant and the constructed monstrosity. Ignorant of human society, befriended by birds, Siegfried is nature's defender. His status as social outsider is reinforced as he sorts through the hoard – he throws the riches from the cave, puzzled by and uninterested in the symbols of wealth and power.

The dancing forest bird plays an ominous protector during this and the next scene as it watches over Siegfried when he first 'hears' the murderous thoughts behind Mime's duplicitous words. Cunning use of supertitles did much to clarify the double-texted scene: the soothing, deceptive words that Mime presumably speaks are displayed on the screen above the stage while he sings his true thoughts. The incongruence between the sung and displayed texts creates a moment of Brechtian estrangement. Like Siegfried, viewers with an eye on the supertitles will probably experience a confusing disjunction of sight and sound, just before the two-faced reality of the situation becomes clear. Despite the fact that I personally had created the supertitles, and was therefore well aware of the conflicting texts, my first experience of watching the staged scene as part of a run-through jolted me mentally out of the onstage narrative, away from the singers: I briefly became preoccupied with the uncomfortable experience of the double-texted trick before returning to the story.

The final scene of Act III also offers examples of what might be considered a weakness of the staging: heavy reliance on the spectacular stage technology sometimes usurped attention from the narrative and musical development. Furthermore, when the technical effects fell away, though they were mesmerizing, the effect of the stage pictures shifted starkly; stripped of the accustomed power and movement produced by the technical elements, the naked stagework left the scene energetically weak by comparison. The beginning of Act III, scene 3, for example, featured a gargantuan ring of suspended flames that dominated the stage.

Yet with its disappearance, the effect of the following duet was pale; after the marvel faded into darkness, the momentum of the scene dwindled. The stunning glow of the ring had enhanced the awe of Susan Bullock's harp-accompanied awakening and the charm of Lance Ryan's bashful kisses, but the remainder of the scene lacked the visual sparkle that had up to that point been taken for granted. As a result, even the rich and expressively performed music suddenly seemed incomplete without the support of the by-now-familiar visual sheen. The staged variations in blocking and body language seemed empty, by comparison, and the extremely slow pace of development in non-musical elements left stage pictures stale. Put simply, with the fire ring extinguished, there was too little action to support the remaining 32 minutes of singing before the curtain finally fell.

The aforementioned observations can all be traced back to how the creative team handled matters that arose during production. Each moment was painstakingly crafted by the designers, cast, and crew. In the seven tightly scheduled weeks of the production period, the group confronted questions of an artistic nature while they simultaneously handled mundane, practical matters. Furthermore, artistic ideas were fitted to the available personnel, resources, and technology.

Issues addressed in rehearsal profoundly affected the shape of this *Siegfried*. The treatment of set elements and technology played an especially important role. The gigantic set was of major concern in this rehearsal process, and its construction was time consuming. The process of assembling the motorized rings was slow, and their safe operation involved numerous precautions. Each ring was driven by a separate crewmember; the technical team was entrenched in mastering its operation for the first 10 mainstage rehearsals. The singers, too, had to learn proper navigation on the rings; even the slightest loss of attention could easily lead to a dangerous fall or being caught between platforms. Staging on the outermost ring, in particular, demanded a great deal of time due to its extraordinary height.

The prioritization of the technical effects seems to have been a reason for the lacklustre effect of the final scene. Four of the six rehearsal days allotted for its staging were spent exclusively on the first quarter of the scene; nearly all the work revolved around handling the fire ring. The burning form posed a number of unexpected problems. Lance Ryan's costume began to smoulder during rehearsal one afternoon, prompting reconstruction of the scene's costumes out of fire-retardant fabric. Another near-accident occurred when the cabling went slack; the flaming apparatus plummeted several metres over the head of a terrified Susan Bullock before the suspension mechanism could be controlled. The next day included an extra four-hour session: an impromptu rehearsal, purely technical, solely to practise the safe raising and lowering of the blaze. As the hours devoted to the matter dragged on, the time allotted for those scenes dwindled, with the end result that later portions of the scene were only scantily developed – the copious number of hours devoted to the fire ring might have been useful for the elaboration of the following scene.

In addition to the handling of technical concerns, daily rehearsal meetings were occupied with the implementation of the artistic vision of many different individuals. Within the walls of the off-site rehearsal stage and the two in-house rehearsal rooms, members of the cast and crew strongly influenced the contents of the end product. Each player brought a particular set of skills and knowledge into rehearsal, and thus the ideas and concerns raised were driven by the respective backgrounds and skill sets of the collaborators.

Collaborators and the Creative Team

As mentioned at the opening of this piece, assistant stage director Alan Barnes is a dancer. He came to Frankfurt in 1989 as a new member of William Forsythe's cutting-edge modern dance company, which at the time was loosely affiliated with the opera. When the Forsythe company declared insolvency, Barnes was transitioned into directing: a technicality of German contract law demanded that he be provided another job with one of the city theatres. He also continued to work as a freelance dancer. In *Siegfried*, his replacement of the pregnant Johannsen was intended as an interim solution to enable the continuation of the day's rehearsal, but his movements prompted a flash of inspiration. Adjustments were made to his contract, and Barnes assumed a second role.

A number of other moments were influenced by the backgrounds of team members. Siegfried's fire dance, for example, originated in the Bulgarian Nestinarii ritual. Nemirova's own background plays a clear role in the development of this element: the director emigrated to the former East Germany from Bulgaria as a young girl. The stage director and her mother, who was present for the last four rehearsal weeks, held heated conversations about the fire dance in their native tongue during mid-rehearsal breaks, resulting in significant adjustments afterwards to the blocking and choreography.

Singers Lance Ryan and Peter Marsh brought a wealth of ideas into the very first rehearsal. Ryan came to the production having already sung multiple versions of the Siegfried character and so his well-practised character was in place from the start. This production offered Marsh his first opportunity to sing the role of Mime, but the singer arrived replete with his own clearly defined version of the dwarf's personality. Nemirova's voice was seldom heard during the first week of rehearsal. She articulated a few constraints, but primarily allowed the actors to 'play', to experiment with movement and character. The two singers essentially staged the scene themselves; the start–stop pattern so typical of early staging was non-existent here. The directing team drew inspiration from the pair, and after a few days intermittently interjected minor enhancements: one clear example was the development of a chalk-drawing lesson about fish and bird families on the walls of the cave, which accentuated Marsh and Ryan's character contrasts and intensified the dialogue. Even that visually mesmerizing moment arose with heavy input from the singers: without their substantial contribution, that powerful stage picture would have appeared quite different.

The various influences discussed up to this point have primarily addressed how actions, ideas, and concerns of various artistic collaborators involved in *Siegfried*'s creation heavily influenced the final shape of the piece. Yet matters of a less obviously 'creative' nature also had an impact on the eventual form of the performed work. Indeed, matters more obviously related to business and logistics – and in particular, the structure of rehearsals – also affected the extent to which creative work could take place. For that reason, it would be a mistake to omit discussion of such operational details, although at first glance matters such as the structure of rehearsals may seem relatively mundane. In fact, organization of rehearsal schedules, the availability of in-house resources, the presence and technical setup of rudimentary set pieces, and the selection of collaborators present during particular rehearsal phases bear heavily on the final shape of the production, because all these factors have the potential to either limit or enable the extent of the creative work.

Furthermore, such business concerns are not as arbitrary as they might seem. On the contrary, such organizational details are highly revelatory about the priorities and artistic vision of the company's direction. Operational concerns, which extend into decisions about season programming, casting, budgeting, and marketing, not only affect the types of work eventually produced, but they also reflect the artistic goals of an organization.[6] As such, examination of the structure of the rehearsal period and other production-related activities can provide greater understanding of company priorities. With this in mind, this next section will discuss the organization of the *Siegfried* rehearsal period in relation to two analytical tasks: first, to show how logistical matters during rehearsal shaped the process of creation itself, and second, to reveal how such business-focused matters can reflect priorities of the artistic management.[7]

The Production Period: Priorities and Logistical Realities

The structure of the *Siegfried* production period dictated how long scenes could be rehearsed, under what conditions, and by whom. Rehearsals at Oper Frankfurt fall into distinct phases that can most easily be understood as a multi-stage process cycling through the various rehearsal locations. As the house uses the *repertoire*

---

[6]   Both motivations and consequences of an opera production's logistical organization can be oblique and complicated to trace within the final product. Yet such details play an important role in how the piece took shape. I contend that, despite the difficulties, scrutiny of such operational detail is worth undertaking, and will nonetheless allow salient points about the production – particularly with respect to house priorities – to emerge.

[7]   These priorities may be either overt or latent. I deliberately avoid any arguments here about intentionality on the part of the house's artistic administration, as both unintentional and intentional priorities are certainly involved but, regardless of intent, the effect is identical.

Siegfried Probenübersicht Stand: 16. September 2011

	Vorstellung	Bühne	Röhdelheim	Probebühne 1	Probebühne 2	Orchester	Foyers	Verfügbarkeiten / Sonstiges
MO 12.9		7 TE Etoile	Siegfried Einrichtung	10 Etoile	10 Siegfried / 18 Siegfried	10 Oa Etoile / 19 OS Etoile		Probenbeginn Ryan, Marsh
DI 13.9		7 TE Etoile / 18 ProT Etoile	Siegfried Einrichtung	10 Etoile	10 Siegfried / 18 Siegfried	OF		
MI 14.9		10 Pr Etoile / 13:30 Bel. Etoile / 19 Pr Etoile	Siegfried Einrichtung		10 Siegfried / 18 Siegfried	10 Oa Konzert Weigle / 19 Oa Konzert Weigle	Salon 14 Dispo	
DO 15.9	19:30 PENTHESILEA	10 Pr Etoile	Siegfried Einrichtung	18 Etoile	10 Siegfried / 18 Siegfried	10 Oa Konzert Weigle		
FR 16.9	19:30 TOTE STADT		Siegfried Einrichtung	10 Etoile / 18 Etoile	10 Siegfried / 18 Siegfried	10 Oa Konzert Weigle		
SA 17.9	19:30 PENTHESILEA		Siegfried Einrichtung	18 Etoile	10 Siegfried	AO 10:30 GP Konzert Weigle		
SO 18.9	AO: 11 KONZERT Weigle / 19 COSI							
MO 19.9	AO: 20 KONZERT Weigle	7 WE Etoile / 19 Pr Etoile	18 Siegfried	10 Etoile			10 Konzept +mus. Probe	Probenbeginn Stensvold, Schmeckenbecher, Baldvinsson, Arwady, Bullock, Kasper
DI 20.9		10 Pr Etoile / 13:30 Bel. Etoile / 18 ProT Etoile	10 Siegfried / 18 Siegfried			OF		Stensvold, Schmeckenbecher weg
MI 21.9		8 Bel. Etoile / 19 Pr Etoile	10 Siegfried / 18 Siegfried			10:30 OS Etoile	Salon 14 Dispo	Stensvold, Schmeckenbecher weg, Baldvinsson in Köln
DO 22.9		10 BO 1 Etoile / 13:30 Bel. Etoile / 19 BO 2 Etoile	10 Siegfried / 18 Siegfried					Stensvold, Schmeckenbecher weg, Kasper weg

Änderungen vorbehalten! – Bitte beachten Sie den jeweiligen Tagesplan

Figure 8.3   Rehearsal schedule, *Siegfried*

system, a handful of different productions must be prepared at any given moment, each at a different development stage in the process.[8]

The first page of the *Probenübersicht* (rehearsal schedule overview) for *Siegfried* illustrates the multi-phase nature of this process (Figure 8.3). On any given day, the *Bühne*, or Main Stage, is occupied with either a later-phase technical rehearsal or a performance, while two in-house rehearsal stages on the fifth floor of the main building on Willy-Brandt-Platz, *Probebühne 1* and *Probebühne 2*, are occupied with other productions. The *Rödelheim* rehearsal studio, a generous off-site space in the Frankfurt-Rödelheim neighbourhood (25 minutes from the opera house by subway) is used for the first weeks of staging rehearsals. The *Orchester* rehearsal space on the seventh floor is the site of musical rehearsals. With this collection of rehearsal spaces occupied at full capacity, as many as three mainstage productions may be in preparation at any given time.[9] In addition, a handful of offices and studios are booked for musical and diction (language) coachings for individual singers throughout all stages of production. Finally, the *Foyers* are used as a gathering space for the full cast on a small number of special occasions, including the first full meeting of the cast and creative team known as the *Konzeptionsgespräch*.

The initial concept talk for Siegfried was held on Wednesday 14 September in the *Foyers*, followed by the start of rehearsals for most members of the cast, as visible in the column marked *Verfügbarkeiten/Sonstiges* (Availability/Other) on the far right of the chart (*Probebeginn Stensvold, Schmeckenbecher, ...*). Preparations for the rehearsal period had actually begun with rehearsal set building (*Einrichtung*) on the prior Monday (see column *Rödelheim*, MO 12.9–SA 17.9) and, atypically, singers Lance Ryan and Peter Marsh had also already begun rehearsals of Act I on *Probebühne 2* at the start of that week. At this phase of the process, the orchestra had not yet begun rehearsing, as it was still deeply entrenched in end-stage preparations for Chabrier's *L'Étoile* (dir. David Alden), which would eventually premiere four weeks prior to *Siegfried* on 2 October. The final blocking rehearsals for the Alden staging took place during the same week on *Probebühne 1*, while run-throughs of the *L'Étoile* scenes already staged were simultaneously held on the *Bühne* from Monday to Thursday. That weekend, however, the Étoile

---

[8] Most creative personnel (including directors, dramaturges, costume and stage designers, assistants, and performers) are assigned solely to one production at a time. The exception to this is the musical staff, including the conducting staff, coach/accompanists, and the orchestra, many of whom are involved in multiple productions simultaneously. For a comprehensive explanation of the differences between the *repertoire* and the *stagione* systems, see Ranan, *In Search of a Magic Flute*, pp. 204–5.

[9] Mainstage productions are designated for performance at the opera house, but additional stagings may also be in preparation as well. Pieces not designed for the Main Stage consist of two groups: those performed at Oper Frankfurt's intimate Bockenheimer Depot space, and those designed as educational productions for young audiences, which tour to schools and community centres throughout the region.

rehearsals on the Main Stage were paused to allow for three other performances: *Die tote Stadt*, *Così fan tutte*, and *Penthesilea* (column *Vorstellung* [Performance], FR 15.9–SO 18.9). *Penthesilea* had premiered on 4 September and was midway through its initial run, while the other two operas were *Wiederaufnahmen* (revival performances) from the 2009 and 2008 seasons, respectively.

After the *Konzeptionsgespräch*, the *Siegfried* team spent three weeks staging in *Rödelheim* from 19 September to 6 October, with additional individual coaching sessions taking place in small studios at the opera house. After a three-day rehearsal pause – during which the stage ring mechanism was dismantled, transported back to the opera house, and rebuilt – a new rehearsal segment of approximately a week began there on Monday 10 October, utilizing both Rehearsal Stage 1 and the Main Stage. This second phase was used to work on the coordination of lighting and other technical aspects, as well as for additional run-throughs that gradually integrated the finalized versions of props, costumes, and set pieces, while simultaneous music rehearsals began in earnest upstairs on the orchestra level. This period culminated in three *Orchestersitzproben* (seated musical rehearsals with orchestra) from Thursday 13 October to Monday 17 October. The third and final rehearsal phase ran from Tuesday 18 October through to Wednesday 26 October. During this last phase, the stage director stepped back to allow the conductor to take over the direction of rehearsals, which consisted of act-specific rehearsals on stage with the orchestra (*Bühnenorchesterproben* or BO 1–3), one full run-through with a rehearsal pianist (*Klavierhauptprobe* or KHP), and, finally, a run-through with orchestra (*Orchesterhauptprobe* or OHP). Performances effectively began with the ticketed dress rehearsal (*Generalprobe*) on Thursday 27 October, an uninterrupted run-through three days before the premiere, open to a special audience of invited patrons, friends, family, sponsors, and opera employees.

The structural constraints of this rehearsal plan affected the work that could be accomplished during the process. During the Rödelheim phase, the fully functional set of the four motorized rings was present in the spacious studio, and singers were able to work with simplified versions of props and in rough rehearsal costumes, so that use of important pieces of the intended stage elements could begin to be explored, at least on a rudimentary level. Singing was typically 'marked' (half-sung) or spoken.

Rehearsals were led by the stage director, Vera Nemirova, with input from assistant directors Hans-Walter Richter and Alan Barnes, the set designer Jens Killian or his scenic collaborator Katia Gehrke, dramaturge Malte Krasting or myself, and costume designer Inge Bernerth or her assistant Carl-Christian Andresen, all of whom were intermittently present. Also in attendance were one of several members of the company's coach-accompanist staff (who rotated duties as rehearsal pianist), the prompter Barbara Kornek, and any one of several junior members of the conducting staff, depending on the day. At this early stage, some absences and travel were still permitted to the singers, which naturally limited the scenes that could be prepared in this period. Because of this, rehearsals during the whole of this initial three-week phase were restricted to just a few scenes, the blocking progressing painstakingly slowly. The main assets in Rödelheim were a full version of the complicated set, and the requisite space to focus on movement. Therefore, rehearsals in the space centred on two elements: firstly, the more complicated choreography and staging work that involved quickly rotating rings (this could not be accomplished in *Probebühne* 1 and 2 due to the lack of a full-scale rehearsal set there), and, secondly, on Nemirova's style of *Personenregie*, which focused intensely on the embodiment of characters and their physical actions and interactions.

Perhaps not surprisingly, the most effectively developed examples of choreography and the most dynamic characterizations of this *Ring* cycle were staged in Rödelheim. The intricate rotating battle between Siegfried and Fafner, for example, was rehearsed there for four full days. The physical realization of the contrasts between the characters and the precise execution of their struggle on the wildly spinning ring were among the most visually powerful and energy-filled moments of the production – a fact that can be attributed at least in part to the extensive hours given to their precise choreography in Rödelheim. A similarly stunning example of the detailed choreographic work prepared in that rehearsal studio under Nemirova's concentrated eye occurred again during preparations for *Götterdämmerung* in January 2012. A similarly long stretch of four days was also consumed with the intricate personal choreography of the Three Norns (Meredith Arwady, Claudia Mahnke, and Angel Blue) as they wove a large web of red yarn across the full cast of frozen characters and the three angled rings to create a dynamic stage picture that spanned the full surface of the rings.

The relaxed tone and comparatively long stretch of time designated for this first stage of detailed rehearsal work, in which many of the resources and personnel were still quite limited, was not without drawbacks. The example of the difficulties in Act III, scene 3, which included the visual stagnation at the close of the production, makes this point well. Despite Susan Bullock's polished musical interpretation – her material was already thoroughly prepared and vocally expressive even at the first rehearsals – her initial days of rehearsal were not scheduled with scene work in Rödelheim. Rather, she had a relatively light schedule primarily composed of musical coachings and costume fittings; the staging of her sections of Act III was left for rehearsal until the second and much shorter phase at the opera house. Bullock was also granted leave for a large stretch of the Rödelheim rehearsal period, which also included the first days of the second rehearsal phase, from 26 September to 10 October, and permission for her to be elsewhere seems consistent with the relaxed pace of the first rehearsal phase. Yet granting the soprano absence from the Rödelheim phase, during which intense attention was given to *Personenregie* and complex choreographic blocking, was not without consequences. Especially when combined with the technical problems that developed during the shorter second phase of rehearsal when Act III was finally staged, both the *laissez-faire* approach to the Rödelheim period and the lengthy stretch of time allotted to scene work were to the detriment of the creative development in the presentation of Brünnhilde in this final scene – and of Act III, scene 3, in general.

Particularly with respect to this last example, the setup and workings of the *Siegfried* rehearsal process at Oper Frankfurt begin to provide some indication of the greater concerns and priorities of the company. Just as the experiences and priorities of individual team members directly affected the stage piece, so did matters of importance to the company; both aspects are traceable within the rehearsal period, and within the production as a whole.

Starting with the problematic visual consequences for the presentation of Brünnhilde in Act III, scene 3, it becomes clear that, ultimately, rehearsal time with Susan Bullock was focused minimally on stage movement, blocking, and her scenic interactions with Siegfried. Rather, her relatively scant schedule of rehearsals involved so few hours on blocking and characterization compared to scene work with other cast members that the focus of her contribution to the scene seems to have been left to her singing alone. Of course, scheduling Bullock for so little rehearsal time is also understandable due to her very minor role in this opera: the soprano appears only in the final scene. Yet the fact that she was allowed such a substantial absence precisely during the important staging weeks in Rödelheim emphasizes the position of intense esteem that high-profile singers occupy within the company: prized for their voices, celebrities such as Ms Bullock are afforded some unusual privileges and scheduled somewhat differently from the majority of the singers in either the ensemble or the chorus.[10] As she is an extraordinarily high-profile soprano with a longstanding history as a guest artist at Oper Frankfurt, it seems worth the company's while to create a rehearsal structure amenable to her needs. With this understanding, the reasoning behind the granting of her leave as well as the preponderance of musical rehearsal within her work schedule becomes clear.

Oper Frankfurt, Past and Present

Oper Frankfurt is certainly not the first opera company to place high-profile singers in the foreground. Indeed, the extent to which this is done in Frankfurt is still fairly

---

[10]   According to a 24 June 2010 interview with Malte Krasting (2 of 3), to be published in my forthcoming dissertation, 'ensemble' members at the Oper Frankfurt are singers contracted with the company for a certain number of productions each season. Fairly common in Germany and within the system of repertory houses, such singers can expect a certain amount of work with the house every year in either lead or *comprimario* roles, and depending on their position within the ensemble, some are also afforded the ability to work with other companies. 'Chorus' singers, like the orchestra, are offered a long-standing (essentially lifelong) position with the company, and can also count on a steady amount of work every year. Contract terms and rehearsal expectations for both groups are fixed, and in Germany, these aspects are well regulated: they are handled by the *Betriebsbüro*, an internal department concerned with handling the personal interests of employees, who are also regularly reviewed by representatives of the musician's division of the Vereinte Dienstleistungs-Gewerkschaft (VERDI), the German freelancers' union.

moderate, especially in light of the number of ensemble singers regularly used for lead roles in new productions. However, when the present-day prioritization of the matter is compared to practices at the house in the 1980s, a shift of emphasis becomes visible: there is an increasing focus on star singers who draw in audiences. As discussed in chapter one of my forthcoming dissertation, operas staged during 1979–87, known also as the 'Gielen Era', were approached from a distinctly different standpoint.[11] Guided by an intentionally politicized and avant-garde approach to opera as a musical-theatrical craft, pieces of the Gielen Era were bold both in terms of their unconventional artistic perspectives and with respect to their creative methods, which prioritized the import of ensemble work and the collaborative nature of making (musical) theatre. These early days of *Regietheater* were marked not only by provocative readings, but also by a consistently team-driven approach to conceptualization and creation when staging a new version of a canonized *Werktreue*. Remnants of this collectively authored approach certainly remain visible in *Siegfried* – indeed, the cooperative atmosphere seen among director Nemirova, conductor Weigle, designers Killian, Bernerth, and Winter, dramaturge Krasting, and the numerous singers and collaborators continues to echo that theme, albeit to a lesser degree than three decades before. Yet a growing number of allowances reveal a real, if also subtle, shift of guiding vision.

A number of factors could account for the change. Certainly, attitudes of the artistic direction play an obvious role in questions of operational priority, and an understanding of key personnel within the artistic leadership can shed some light on the evolution of the house's current tactics, goals, and artistic vision. The Intendant at time of writing, Bernd Loebe, assumed his position in 2003, following many years as a journalist in London. As detailed in an interview with Malte Krasting, one of Herr Loebe's strengths is the cast of 'world-class' singers he has been able to assemble for recent productions: based on his own longstanding professional acquaintance with many leading world voices, Loebe's emphasis on their recruitment has placed a spotlight on 'excellent quality' singers (both well-established and those with growing careers) at Oper Frankfurt.[12] This effort has been a conscious one, as further evidenced by the *Liederabend* series created shortly after his arrival, designed precisely for this purpose through the established Frankfurter Museumsgesellschaft.[13] The opportunity to offer a concert in this series

---

[11]   Cordelia E. Chenault, *Behind a Flourishing Avant-Garde: An Institutional History of Opera in Frankfurt am Main* (Stony Brook, NY: Stony Brook University, forthcoming).

[12]   Taken from my interview with Malte Krasting, No. 3, 24 June 2010, as published in the appendix to Chenault, *Behind a Flourishing Avant-Garde*. Krasting immediately raises the notion of quality when asked about any guiding mission for the company. In the follow-up interview No. 4, Krasting uncomfortably admits that he has been considering the fact that he has no further definition for the term, though it is frequently used by the artistic administration when speaking to the public about their work.

[13]   See Paul Bartholomäi, *Das Frankfurter Museumsorchester* (Frankfurt am Main, 2002), pp. 7–11. The *Museumsgesellschaft* (Museums Society) is a cultural board of

typically accompanies a new guest artist contract; it provides singers with the relatively rare and coveted opportunity to present a solo programme of art song, and has become an enticing draw for a number of both blossoming and established international artists, including John Tomlinson, Alice Coote, Cristiane Karg, Anne Schwanewilms, and Anne Sophie von Otter, to name just a few of the celebrity appearances since 2011.[14]

Qualität, Vielfalt, Emotion

With respect to both the singing and the artistic work produced at the house, the reference to 'quality' is verbalized distinctly and frequently in Oper Frankfurt's current building on Frankfurt's Willy-Brandt-Platz. Both my interviews with Krasting and unofficial conversations with various members of the direction returned to that theme on numerous occasions. According to Krasting, *Qualität* was also one of three points of organizational focus identified for Oper Frankfurt by a private consulting agency, *McKinsey & Company, Inc.*, who performed a detailed review of and report about the opera company's business structures in 2006. Based upon extensive interviews and workshops with members of the artistic direction designed to provide the organization's leadership with a clearer sense of their (unspoken) goals, the McKinsey report was undertaken with the ultimate goal of helping the company improve the consistency of their presentation to present and potential audience members. The results of that work identified the words 'Quality, diversity, and emotion' (*Qualität, Vielfalt, Emotion*) to best summarize the company's profile.[15] These three points, perceived by the artistic direction to reflect the needs of most attendees, were also taken from a larger list, which had originally also included 'reliability', 'innovation', 'openness to risk', 'sensuousness', 'intellectualism', and 'provocation', although these other suggestions were eventually struck from the final collection.[16] Interestingly, the report also contains a second group of terms, which included the artistic direction's perception of another audience subset: potential and infrequent audience-members. Traits identified as appealing to this group were 'intellectual challenge', 'provocation', and 'emotional distance' – some of the very words included on the list of discarded suggestions.

In this context, the choice to forsake 'challenge', 'provocation', and the simultaneous lack of any word similar to 'collaboration', or another term

---

Frankfurt citizens which has existed since the 1780s, an organization that guides many of the artistic institutions in the city.

[14]   A basic overview of the Liederabend series, which has been offered every season since 2003–2004, can be seen on the Oper Frankfurt website: <www.oper-frankfurt.de/en/page681.cfm> (accessed 27 June 2015).

[15]   Internal report by McKinsey & Company, 'Oper Frankfurt' (2006), p. 16.

[16]   Ibid., p. 15.

to address the nature of the artistic process, seems to indicate another shift of emphasis. Indeed, current priorities within the Oper Frankfurt leadership seem to have shifted away from emphasizing the artistic nature of the work – meaning both the prioritization of collaborative methods and encouragement of experimental artistic content. Instead, emphasis is placed upon providing work of 'quality', a word that neither Krasting nor the McKinsey group ever defines, but which is by definition linked to perception and expectations, and therefore reception.

This notion of 'quality' therefore indicates a distinct focus on the perceived needs and reactions of the majority of operagoers. Interestingly, the same page of the McKinsey report continues on to identify the messages that the artistic direction would like to publicly communicate. These include two statements that indicate a complex and undecided perspective within the direction on the matter of provocative stage work: 'Intellectual stimulation and emotional impact are not mutually exclusive', states one bullet point, while the next articulates the complexity of the company's present perspective on this controversial issue: 'the house stands for innovation – but not for thoughtless provocation'.[17] Regardless of whether or not the artistic direction is aware of the link between their perception of high-quality music and audience desires, the company's struggle to articulate a clear stance on the subject of theatrical provocation seems rooted in their own intent to please a general audience and therefore also to the pull away from riskier artistic work.[18]

Conclusion

It hardly seems surprising, then, that the 2011 *Siegfried*, like most mainstage works produced at the house in recent years, can neither be taken as risqué, nor aligned with the provocative style of work termed *Regietheater*. The latter offers wholly new conceptual layers to the presentation of a canonized work, and is generally understood to represent the avant-garde side of today's opera industry. As earlier discussion of the production has already implied, despite the dynamic, mechanistic set design, the extreme subtlety of the directorial *Konzept* implied by the costume and stage design of the Nemirova *Ring* cycle left the audience with a relatively

---

[17] Translations are mine.
[18] Interestingly, two of my interviewees, both of whom asked to have this part of their interviews remain anonymous, confessed that they would like to see the present-day company more willing to offer pieces featuring challenging interpretations. The significant internal conflict within the company over the extent to which theatrically provocative work should be produced is a larger topic addressed in my dissertation. At present, the company solution seems to be to leave the Main Stage for less controversial work, but to present smaller-scale productions of a more experimental nature at the company's second space, a former railway station that has been renovated into the theatre space known as Bockenheimer Depot.

typical interpretation of Wagner's music dramas – and therefore is unlikely to be identified as *Regietheater* according to prevalent definitions. As Stephan Mösch has articulated about this type of contemporary productions:

> The transport of themes can only work when they are anchored on many levels, or rather, possible to anchor (in that fashion). *Regietheater* immediately and necessarily falls flat when directors equate the transport of themes with the transport of the text.[19]

While Nemirova's style of work does offer some new conceptual elements, they are implemented subtly enough to be overshadowed by her intense focus on transporting the meaning of the text through expressive embodiment and relatable transmission of human emotion. Furthermore, the visually dynamic set pieces and costumes seem to work on a wholly different level from the emotional intensity delivered by the singers, while the singing and orchestral music attends to still other goals. With that disjuncture, the various creative elements of *Siegfried* each seem to present singular ideas – all interesting, but with little overlap or reinforcement of other elements. While the various themes raised by set, costuming, lighting, musical choices, and the *Personenregie* were all undertaken with a great deal of forethought, and offer moments of interest, the themes raised are neither underscored with enough repetition, nor addressed on the multiple levels necessary to sufficiently rise to the surface and provide a new overarching perspective or an updated reading of the text. Because of this, Nemirova's *Siegfried* is at heart an aesthetically rich and relatively effective traditional interpretation of the Wagnerian work, but one without any major conceptual addition to the Wagnerian text.

Based on the analysis of the company's aims and intended audience as articulated in the McKinsey report, and in light of the various analytical observations, it seems likely that *Siegfried* was celebrated by both Oper Frankfurt patrons and house employees for a combination of two reasons: firstly, the production offered no alternative conceptual reading that might controversially cast it as *Regietheater*, and, secondly, it overarchingly delivered a rich and theatrically convincing presentation of the music, narrative, and textual themes. Given the company's growing emphasis on 'quality' and 'emotion', two of the three descriptors emphasized in the McKinsey report, the 2011 staging seems to align with the company's present expectations of a mainstage production.

With this observation, it becomes clear that this analysis of the 2011 *Siegfried* produced at Oper Frankfurt has provided broader observations about the context

---

[19]   'Ein Transport von Themen kann nur dann funktionieren, wenn diese auf mehreren Ebenen verankert werden bzw. überhaupt verankerbar sind. Regietheater wird sofort und zwangsläufig platt, wenn Regisseure Thementransport mit Texttransport gleichsetzen.' Stephen Mösch, 'Störung, Verstörung, Zerstörung: Regietheater als Rezeptionsproblem', in Robert Sollich (ed.), *Angst vor der Zerstörung: Der Meister Künste zwischen Archiv und Erneuerung*, Theater der Zeit 52 (2008), p. 220. Translation is mine.

of this production than those that can be made via interpretive analysis alone. Furthermore, this discussion has begun to produce insights about the situation of the opera house itself, points that may ultimately offer the chance to study some of the greater developments in today's international operatic field.

By expanding scholarly discussion beyond the standard task of scrutinizing the artistic aspects of new readings, my work in this chapter has discussed individuals and events of the rehearsal period, even reaching into business matters of the company preparing the piece. And as the latter half of this chapter has demonstrated, to address the creative and business context of an operatic staging alongside the audience's perspective provides a more holistic understanding of the piece than would be available from interpretive analysis alone; such analysis not only offers deeper insights into the context and motivations of the production, but also prompts discussion of the field which brought it about. Of course, to expand the set of scholarly tasks in this way is a complex undertaking, and one that demands a great deal of access. Yet ultimately, the demonstration offered here has also shown the potential such work holds for better understanding of the nature of contemporary opera productions, and the import of what they present on today's stages.

Chapter 9

A *Ring* for People and Place: Creating Expectation and Fulfilling Demand

Jennifer Daniel

Introduction

Between 2011 and 2014, Opera North (the national opera company for the north of England) produced its first *Ring* cycle at home in Leeds, also touring to several northern venues. This chapter takes an ethnographic approach, observing some of the work done by the company in and around the production. Opera North prepared its audience for a *Ring* cycle, but also worked to create and enhance audience demand for a *Ring* in Leeds, and to ensure the production's success by setting appropriate audience expectations during the processes of audience preparation. These expectations would be fulfilled by the bespoke production. For a *Ring* spread over four years (with a full cycle also planned for 2016), this creation and fulfilment of expectation and demand essentially became a cyclical process. It should be noted at the outset that an audience for any production is made up of various demographics. There is a Wagner audience that will travel nationally and internationally for a reception experience, and Opera North is, of course, aware of this element. In a private interview, Head of Music Martin Pickard acknowledged to me an audience of 'Wagnerites'.[1] Opera North Technical Manager Peter Restall also anticipated an 'audience of aficionados'.[2] However, the Opera North *Ring* was heavily marketed to an audience of Wagner (and certainly *Ring* cycle) beginners. This may seem incongruous; however, as Pickard indicated to me, the seasoned Wagner followers will attend regardless of marketing focus or measures to familiarize audiences with Wagner's music. It remains sensible then for the company to cater, in terms of access and marketing, for those more locally that might otherwise not experience a *Ring*. When I asked Pickard why the focus on an audience new to the *Ring* was so important, his answer was largely geographical: because Opera North had not produced a *Ring*, its core audience had not been specifically provided with one and could not necessarily have been expected to see one elsewhere. Opera North has, in Leeds, a particularly loyal and

---

[1] Discussion with Opera North Head of Music Martin Pickard, 11 June 2012 (speech reported from notes).

[2] Informal conversation with Opera North Technical Director Peter Restall, 19 June 2013 (speech reported from notes).

fixed audience base.[3] These local operagoers reside hundreds of miles away from any other comparable company, thus it might be reasonable to assume their direct experience of live Wagner productions to be limited. The years approaching the bicentenary of Wagner's birth (2013) have produced a comparative spate of *Ring* productions, but prior to this there is a sense in which *Ring* cycles have been few and far between within the boundaries of our lifetimes and physical locations. For many audience members, taking into account issues of geography and finance, this *Ring* cycle could, in real terms, be a singular opportunity, and so, in this context, a *Ring* for beginners does not seem to be an unreasonable starting point.

With the loyal company audience in mind, and no full *Ring* cycle in Leeds since 1976,[4] Pickard described the concerns of the inexperienced audience member as the 'fear of the threshold into Wagner'. This fear can be understood as a preconception, or a set of preconceptions, derived from a number of factors. Perhaps most dramatically, Wagner was outspoken in his anti-Judaism, and his works have subsequently been presented as proto-Nazi propaganda, initially by Adorno and ever since in the popular press.[5] Other concerns for newcomers revolve around the scale of the works and the cultural importance with which they are imbued.[6]

---

[3]   For audience surveys conducted at a performance of *Das Rheingold* in Leeds Town Hall (2011), only 2 of 28 respondents had not been to any previous Opera North productions. But 19 of the 28 gave long lists of the productions attended, and replied that they had seen 'virtually everything' for a number of years. Some had subscribed for over twenty years, or even since the company was founded in 1978. More generally I have conducted audience questionnaires for a number of Opera North productions, and found this range of responses to be typical of Opera North audiences in Leeds.

[4]   English National Opera toured a *Ring* in English translation, from the London Coliseum to the Leeds Grand Theatre in 1975, under the baton of Sir Charles Groves. This production was then revived and returned to the Grand the following year under the musical direction of Nicholas Braithwaite, the cycle being again played out over the course of a week.

[5]   Theodor Adorno, *In Search of Wagner* (London, 1991) p. 23. In 2012, on a popular BBC television documentary programme, Howard Goodall sensationally presented Wagner as a forerunner of Hitler, his music as 'the most dangerous music ever written'. 'Howard Goodall's Story of Music: The Age of Tragedy', BBC 2, 16 February 2013. In 2013, Nicholas Baragwanath told a BBC Radio 3 Proms audience that he felt that 'there's a lot of guilt attached to Wagner'. 'Introduction to *Das Rheingold*', broadcast live on BBC Radio 3, 22 July 2013.

[6]   Again in 2013, on Radio 3, Proms presenter Sara Mohr-Pietsch shared with the audience 'a confession, which is that I've never listened all the way through to Wagner's *Ring* cycle and I've certainly never seen any of it or heard it live, [because] it's always felt like an absolutely huge undertaking that once it got to a certain point in my life and I hadn't done it I thought well how can I even begin now?' She also broadcast her concerns about the plot, which she described as 'daunting' and '*so* long and complicated'. 'Introduction to *Das Rheingold*', BBC Radio 3, 22 July 2013.

In light of this 'fear of the Wagner threshold', the preparation of a potential *Ring* audience by an opera company can become crucial to the perceived success of the production, particularly in the case of regional performances. For the first part of this chapter I used an ethnographic approach to track the preparation of audience by Opera North for the company's four-year *Ring* cycle. During this process it became apparent that the audience preparation involved an element of increasing musical understanding, but was in large part emotionally focused, aiming to tackle concerns around scale and difficulty. Regionality was a key tool in orientating audiences to an experience of the *Ring*; Opera North highlighted its local base in Leeds, and introduced key singers from its 'British cast'. There was also a specific focus on the production's home venue, Leeds Town Hall, with its architectural aesthetic integral to the mid- to late nineteenth century, in common with the aesthetic of Wagner's work (this is discussed later in the chapter). An emerging narrative, communicated by Opera North to its public, alluded to the concept of civic pride in Leeds, now in relation to Wagner's *Ring*.

With the application of Hans Robert Jauss's reception theory to opera production,[7] my final section outlines how the prior communication of all these elements (and of other aspects of the production that are essentially bespoke for this venue) inform a set of audience expectations which function as success criteria for judgement of the production. Expectation and demand are seen to be created by the company's own communication to the audience, and then fulfilled by the production. Because the work is a cycle, with one music drama performed per year, the very act of Opera North's annual production also created expectation and demand for the next instalment.

The Opera North *Ring*

Originally founded in Leeds in 1978 as a branch of English National Opera (ENO), Opera North became an independent company in 1981. In 2011, it began its first production of Wagner's *Ring* cycle. This 'four-year traversal'[8] was produced for the concert stage; primarily that of the great nineteenth-century monument to northern civic pride, Leeds Town Hall.[9] The production was described by designer Peter Mumford as a 'fully staged concert version';[10] there are no sets or props, costumes are enhanced concert dress, and the orchestra remains visible on stage behind the

---

[7]   Hans Robert Jauss, *Toward an Aesthetic of Reception* (Minneapolis, 1982).

[8]   Opera North website, <www.operanorth.co.uk/productions/gotterdammerung> (accessed 10 July 2014).

[9]   Leeds Town Hall has been described as a 'municipal palace'. Derek Linstrum, 'Broderick, Cuthbert', *Grove Art Online*, <www.oxfordartonline.com> (accessed 28 November 2012).

[10]   Peter Mumford speaking on 'Radio 3 Live in Concert: Wagner's *Die Walküre*', BBC Radio 3, 20 June 2012.

Figure 9.1   *Das Rheingold*, Leeds Town Hall. Photograph by Malcolm Johnson

singers, who act and sing 'out' to the audience, even when in conversation with one another. A triptych of giant screens displays abstract images, story text, and translated surtitles (Figure 9.1).[11]

It was decided by Opera North, in its staging and its preparation of audience, that this *Ring* cycle would be suitable for the Wagner beginner, with marketing and communications pitched accordingly, for the reasons previously outlined. The focus on a new audience was also a reaction to what Pickard referred to, primarily in Germany, as the 'cult of Wagner', and the typical 'top-end wealthy patrons' of Bayreuth. Indeed, *Ring* cycles recently produced at the Royal Opera House and the Metropolitan Opera, New York, also incurred huge production costs and ticket prices.[12] Opera North's response to this tradition of extravagant productions

---

[11]   In 2011, for *Das Rheingold*, there were separate smaller screens for the titles.

[12]   Ticket listings for the 2012 Royal Opera House *Ring* cycle ranged from £44 to £1,000. 'Royal Opera House prices hit new high for Ring cycle', *Intermezzo*, <http://intermezzo.typepad.com/intermezzo/2011/09/roh-ring-cycle-prices-revealed.html> (accessed 11 October 2012). The Metropolitan Opera, New York charged $300 to $2,650 for 2013 *Ring* cycle tickets. 'Met Opera Ring Cycles', *The Metropolitan Opera* <www.metoperafamily.org/metopera/season/subscriptions/new/reserve.aspx?PackageID=9988> (accessed 11 October 2012). Production costs reported in various press sources for the Met's 2012 *Ring* cycle range from $20 million to $40 million. Jerry Floyd, 'Going for the Gold', *wagneropera.net* <www.wagneropera.net/Articles/Metropolitan-Opera-Rheingold.htm> (accessed 24 October 2012).

and high ticket prices (which often restricts the audience to those who are able to afford it) was to play its *Ring* cycle to 'the widest possible audience', since Pickard asserted, practically as well as idealistically, that 'we who put on opera have no interest in limiting our audience'.[13] Consequently, he told me that Opera North had made the 'absolutely positive choice' to widen access to the work, attempting to address the 'fear of the threshold into Wagner' by coaxing its potential audience over this barrier.

Development of Audience

The focus of the company on the Wagner beginner, as explained by Pickard, is in accord with the words of Opera North's Music Director Richard Farnes, who in a public talk in 2010 described Opera North as 'more than an opera company' and elaborated on the company's mission to 'develop its artists, art-form and audience'.[14] In talking about the development of audience, Farnes referred to the preparation and development of audience members within an artistic and educational framework, as individuals and as a social group, as distinct from the concept of 'audience development' used in marketing to mean increased attendance and revenue.

In the focusing of Opera North's attention on an audience new to the *Ring* cycle, there arises the question of how the company might 'develop' its audience. This often falls within the remit of the Opera North Education department, but in the case of the *Ring* the 'Education' team did not have a role in preparing audience members for this work. The activities of this department are focused mainly on children. With *Das Rheingold* at over two and a half hours without interval, it is not difficult to imagine, on a practical level, why this might not be considered a beginner's piece.[15] The closest thing to a directly educational event was 'Sing ON: Wagner!', a public singing workshop devised and run by Chorus Master Timothy Burke. Access was not quite universal, but called 'for all singers who can read music'.[16] It was advertised as 'a unique opportunity to learn the piece from the inside'.[17] Burke had arranged *Das Rheingold* (which has no chorus) for mixed choir, and reduced the score to 30 minutes. The remaining tapestry of leitmotifs told the abridged story. Many of these motifs had originally been orchestral or belonged to particular characters, but were distributed by Burke through the chorus with suitably direct and descriptive English lyrics, so that each motif might

---

[13] Discussion with Martin Pickard, 11 June 2012 (from notes).

[14] Richard Farnes with Professor Stephen Pratt, 'Britten in Context' conference, Liverpool Hope University, 10 June 2010 (speech reported from the author's notes).

[15] John Deathridge warns that 'children are likely to be baffled'. *Wagner Beyond Good and Evil* (Berkeley, 2008), pp. 47–8.

[16] Opera North, Howard Assembly Room events leaflet, spring 2011.

[17] Ibid.

Example 9.1 *Das Rheingold*, arr. Timothy Burke (unpublished, 2011), bars 206–7

be clearly identified by the singing participants. This choral recreation gave a taste of Wagner's orchestral and dramatic technique. For example, occasional wordless permutations of what Ernest Newman termed the 'Ring motif'[18] were used to build tension, to hint at things to come, or sung under other conversations, revealing hidden motivations. These subtler variations were used only after the initial exposition of the leitmotif with lyrics, its meaning already explicitly established (Example 9.1).[19]

Opera North communicated its educational objectives like a manifesto: to 'enhance appreciation' in the participants, who would 'understand how [the piece is] put together and be introduced to all the leitmotifs through actually singing them'.[20] It was an idea born of an educational urge in Burke, who expressed his rationale to me during an interview:

> Either you're already a member of the Wagner audience, in which case you're like 'Ha ha well I'm fine!', or you're not. And you're just thinking 'where am I going to start?' […] We could have a really dry lecture […] But I just thought that […] it would bring the kind of people in who mainly already know [it] anyway, and so I thought 'why can't we analyse it practically? Why can't we sing bits of it to see how it's constructed?'[21]

To borrow a term from Pierre Bourdieu, Burke and Opera North could be described as widening the understanding of this work to those without the existing cultural capital that has traditionally been regarded as necessary for its reception.[22] The

---

[18] Ernest Newman, *Wagner Nights* (London, 1988) p. 479.
[19] Example 9.1 corresponds to bars 753–4 of Wagner's original, where the melody and harmony are heard on bassoons: *Das Rheingold*, 2 vols (Mainz, 1988) vol. 1, p. 97.
[20] Howard Assembly Room events leaflet, spring 2011.
[21] Interview with Opera North Chorus Master Timothy Burke, 1 September 2011 (speech recorded on Dictaphone).
[22] Bourdieu refers to 'cultural capital' as a form of value that is created by the cultural authorization of a set of specific tastes and consequent activities. *Distinction: A Social Critique of the Judgement of Taste*, trans. Richard Nice (London, 1984), pp. 11–18.

vehicle by which this is attempted is musical participation. Ideally, the knowledge gained ceases to be 'capital' as it is not acquired in order to be exchanged for future goods or position, but in order to be added to in the reception of a greater musical experience: the production. The concert nature of the *Rheingold* production makes this point particularly relevant; improving understanding of the musical content (rather than the work as a cultural phenomenon) was presented as a key motivator for the 'sing', which notably cost participants only £3 each. However, the primary motivation and outcome was musical enjoyment; in particular, many participants declared that they most appreciated the opportunity to sing with a professional opera chorus.[23] So the principle of public access went beyond access to Wagner's music, with participants able to access an experience of musical community with the company itself. Burke made the case that Wagner's music required this experience:

> It requires long, sustained lines, and real impact and forceful sound and big dynamic changes, and when you've got all of that it's really exciting to do it.[24]

Asked if the experience of joining in with a professional chorus was a confidence-building trick, he replied that the ultimate effect of participants' improved singing was real. This 'practical analysis', as Burke presented it, and the approach to Wagner via involvement in a singing community created educational engagement in an informal sense. Learning aims were communicated in advance, but in the event, as in the *Rheingold* production itself, elements of didacticism were present but concealed.

Burke's 'Sing ON: Wagner!' workshop is effectively an acknowledgement of, and response to, the concern of Carl Dahlhaus, who argues that for an emotionally immediate experience of the *Ring*, there must first be an intellectual, musical framework on which to reflect:

> The listener needs to be able to distinguish the musical motives [...], to recognize them when they recur, and to keep track of [...] their relationships and functions.[25]

The preparatory event introduced this structural, musical framework. However, 'Sing ON: Wagner!' was presented as an enjoyable afternoon's singing, and so it addressed simultaneously the issues of intellectual preparation and the emotional barrier, the audience's 'fear of the threshold into Wagner'.

---

[23]   'Sing ON: Wagner!' Opera North participant questionnaires.

[24]   Interview with Timothy Burke, 1 September 2011 (on Dictaphone).

[25]   Carl Dahlhaus, *Richard Wagner's Music Dramas*, trans. Mary Whittall (Cambridge, 1979) p. 82.

Emotional Preparation

Much of Opera North's work for and with its audience in preparation for *Das Rheingold* (and by extension the whole four-year *Ring* cycle) was not aimed at discounting perceptions of rigour, intensity, and difficulty in the reception experience of the *Ring*, but rather dismantling, examining, and rebuilding them. There was a strong sense of active audience inclusion in this process, and a drive to counter any sense of alienation that might be felt at the scale and relentless continuity of the work. Mention of the cultural and political issues and associations surrounding the reception of Wagner was strategically absent until 2013. But the public presentation of Opera North's ideas around its *Ring* began well before the *Rheingold* premiere in Leeds Town Hall on 18 June 2011. As well as press releases and previews, there was an interview about the production and its processes on BBC Radio 3, and numerous blogs, videos, and podcasts, featuring administrators and artists, broadcast by Opera North on its own web page. This material gave the appearance of intimate and direct communication by the company to its public. While such modes of outward communication served to promote the production, much of the content was informative, educating potential audience members about the piece and sharing the preconditions for the production. These communications gave an impression of the opening *Ring* opera as a very special and exciting event for the company, but did not allude to any heightened sense of 'cultural capital' in presenting this music as culturally superior, or authorizing the taste for this work over any other.

In an online company video, 'Richard Farnes introduces *Das Rheingold*', Farnes highlights the relationship between Opera North and its audience, making the case for a regional experience of the *Ring* that had previously been lacking.

> Well I think the interest about it [is], first of all [...] there hasn't been a *Ring* cycle up in this part of the country. We're always having people writing to us saying 'Why don't you perform the Wagner? It's such stirring music, it's so exciting!'[26]

This statement is in keeping with the projection of community values and audience involvement. It implies a company response to public demand and also serves to enhance the cultural value of this production by underlining the issue of scarcity in the locale. It is emotionally appealing; placing the 'specialness' of Leeds at the forefront, this message is a reminder of the city's achievement in hosting a national opera company capable of delivering a *Ring* cycle, and emphasizes the relationship of the public with that company. Farnes also refers to the excitement of the music, which is to be the central feature in the marketing and communication of this concert production. His assertion that 'there hasn't been a *Ring* cycle up in this part of the country' is not entirely accurate, and almost certainly verbal

---

[26] Opera North, 'Richard Farnes introduces *Das Rheingold*', <www.youtube.com/watch?v=Dqj9zZ3JNlg> (accessed 21 May 2014).

shorthand used for the purposes of a very brief web-video. Notably there was a full *Ring* cycle brought to Leeds in 1975 and 1976 by Opera North's parent company, ENO, just a couple of years before Opera North was 'born'.[27] Here Opera North's 'benign neglect of history',[28] as described by company biographer Kara McKechnie, effectively prioritizes the present, creating a sense of immediacy for this cycle and this audience. Later in the film, Farnes concedes that 'we've never done it here, and that's one of the reasons that makes it very special for us'. This approach serves to increase the experiential value or 'specialness', as it was presented, of a *Ring* cycle in Leeds and in the north. It is thus instrumental in building on existing concepts of civic pride.

Local journalist and archivist Geoffrey Mogridge notes that, in 1975 and 1976, ENO presented Leeds with a '"home grown" crop of world class Wagner singers'.[29] Similarly Opera North has highlighted the home nationality of singers in order to situate this *Ring* in local sentiment. Farnes declared:

> We also have a fantastically talented cast [...], mainly a British cast; some really exciting new singers coming up. I'm very excited about Michael Druiett, who's singing Wotan. He's a singer that I've known for quite a number of years, but he's never done anything as big as this before. [...] It would be great to think that we're finding new people to sing this repertoire who come from this country![30]

Here we are introduced to a new Wagner singer, a new 'find', and one of our own. We are encouraged to feel national ownership of Druiett as a talent. We might believe that he will develop in this role throughout his career. We, in the north of England, are here at the beginning.

---

27   Also, in 1911 and 1912–13, Austrian musician Ernst Denhof toured a *Ring* production from Edinburgh to the Grand Theatre, Leeds. *Leeds Grand Theatre, Herr Ernst Denhof's Operatic Festival Performance: The Ring of the Nibelung*, programme, 15 March 1911.
28   Kara McKechnie, 'Opera North: Knitting Together History from Ephemera', talk given 17 May 2013, University of Leeds. McKechnie later explains: 'the impression forms of a company that has always had to charge forward and whose members hardly ever have time to look back and reflect on Opera North's achievements. [...] the Company always needs to focus on what is ahead – reflecting and ordering its legacy would almost seem a luxury, generating neither artistic achievement nor income to fund such achievement.' *Opera North: Historical and Dramaturgical Perspectives on Opera Studies* (Bingley, 2014), pp. 5–6. .
29   Mogridge lists Rita Hunter, Alberto Remedios, Norman Bailey, Clifford Grant, and John Tomlinson. Geoffrey Mogridge, 'Towards a National Opera Company for the North, 1970s', *Discovering Leeds* <www.leodis.net/discovery/discovery.asp?pageno=&page=200 31110_356182278&topic=20031110_154781521&subsection=20031110_679348171&su bsubsection=20031110_889217556> (accessed 8 March 2012).
30   Opera North, 'Richard Farnes introduces *Das Rheingold*'. The claim for a British cast was made, in this case, for *Das Rheingold*, although the cast became less British as the cycle progressed.

The theme of this *Ring* production being 'special' and 'exciting' for the company and its very regionally based audience was presented extensively in the *Rheingold* pre-production web broadcasts and pre-show talks. Michael Druiett projected a sense of elation to be performing the role of Wotan, keen to share his excitement with the audience, contributing in large part to the 'Journey' web-video, another podcast, and writing two blog entries in 2011. In the video he draws together the experience of performers and audience, saying of the *Ring* cycle:

> Being involved in it is a special thing for a singer and a special thing for the audience. It's a journey we all go on through this.[31]

Echoing the sentiment expressed by Farnes, Druiett spoke at length about his experience as a developing Wagnerian, his relationship with Farnes and with Opera North, and the excitement of the music and the performance event:

> I'm sensing a real buzz within the company, an excitement about it.[...] It's such a special event; it's such special, life-changing music. It's something that just grabs you and takes you on a journey and you discover so much about it [...] It's just a love affair with it, that's all I can describe.[32]

His communications on behalf of Opera North continued similarly on his return to play the Wanderer in *Siegfried* in 2013.[33] Druiett presents the company and the music as central, viewed through a lens of child-like wonderment, or at the beginning of a life-long musical journey which we are all invited to commence. This atmosphere of musical revelation and personal discovery was also created more widely by Opera North. In '*Das Rheingold*: The Journey Begins', the company shares with the web audience the metaphorical journey of preparing the performance. Orchestra Director Dougie Scarfe tells us on 15 May 2011:

> [This] is a really exciting day in Opera North's history because we have our first rehearsals for the *Ring* cycle. The *Ring* is one of those great, almost monumental operas, and one of the pieces which every opera company has to perform. [...] So it's really quite an extraordinary day for members of the orchestra, particularly [those] who've been here for a number of years, because I think a lot of us thought we'd never get a chance to do the *Ring* cycle [...] It's a very exciting occasion.[34]

---

[31] Opera North, '*Das Rheingold:* The Journey Begins' <www.youtube.com/watch?v=oKcPlQeAW7E> (accessed 21 May 2014).

[32] '*Das Rheingold*: Richard Farnes and Michael Druiett in conversation with Ed Seckserson', originally linked to the Opera North website (2010) <http://html5-player.libsyn.com/embed/episode/id/1615685/height/100/width/360/autoplay/no/autonext/no/direction/forward/thumbnail/yes#.Ucl5uJpwbIU> (accessed 14 August 2013).

[33] Opera North, 'Siegfried', <www.operanorth.co.uk/productions/siegfried≥ (accessed 14 August 2013).

[34] Opera North, '*Das Rheingold*: The Journey Begins'.

Here, and in the Opera North broadcasts previously mentioned, the company is in the act of 'performing itself'. This is a performance of excitement, of scarcity and of fulfilling demand, sometimes of regional importance and often of friendly familiarity between company and audience. In his ethnographic account of Welsh National Opera, *Everyday Arias*, Paul Atkinson describes the social performance that an opera company gives of itself for the benefit of its audience, participants, and stakeholders.[35] Performers individually are in the act of performing themselves in the rehearsal studio and around the company. To document the widespread 'performance' of excitement around the Opera North *Ring* is not to doubt the validity of the emotion, but to acknowledge its enhancement, being homogenized, repeated, and projected into the public arena for a specific purpose. It should also be noted that the platforms of web broadcasts and blogs facilitate an extended opportunity for this performance of self, which is now capable of reaching a greater number of recipients.

The performance of familiarity of company (and audience) with the cast continued though the cycle. The idea of enhanced enjoyment of an event through acquaintance with the artists was raised in a private telephone interview I conducted with soprano Yvonne Howard, a regular Opera North artist, who sang Fricka in *Das Rheingold*. I asked her about the public masterclass in Leeds that she had undertaken with Anne Evans in June 2011, and what she felt the benefits might be for audience members attending such an event. After listing various aspects, such as a focus on working processes for different voices and the analysis of text, she also observed of the audience:

> It makes them feel more involved in it too, I think. […] If you go to see a performance of someone you know it's always more enjoyable than someone that's just a stranger because you feel more involved in it.[36]

The audience's emotional investment in the singers and consequent investment in the production are courted by Opera North, thus a sense of community is invoked and exploited. In 2012, soprano Alwyn Mellor (Sieglinde) repeated this claim of an enhanced relationship between stage and audience in the performance of *Die Walküre*, highlighting the importance that 'the audience feels connected with everybody involved'.[37] By the following year and the broadcast of *Siegfried*, the same idea was picked up by BBC Radio 3 presenter Adam Tomlinson, who borrowed the company's mantra of audience inclusion from previous years, describing a 'unique concert staging [that] gives the audience of Opera North the chance to be part of a complete *Ring* cycle'.[38]

---

[35]   Paul Atkinson, *Everyday Arias* (Oxford, 2006).

[36]   Private telephone interview with Yvonne Howard, 30 July 2011 (speech recorded, with permission, on Dictaphone).

[37]   Alwyn Mellor speaking on 'Radio 3 Live in Concert: Wagner's *Die Walküre*'.

[38]   Adam Tomlinson presenting 'Radio 3 Live in Concert: *Siegfried*', BBC Radio 3, 19 June 2013.

> The singers have a space in front of the orchestra very close to the front row of the audience, thus creating the feeling that we are all in this together.[39]

Through these examples we have seen how one crucial aspect in the preparation of the Opera North *Ring* audience is emotional. We are not told that we will love the production or the work, and we are not dissuaded that it might be 'hard work': many Opera North broadcasts refer to its epic scale, the need for stamina in its performers, the 'shock' of two and a half hours performing without a break, and a 'lifetime' spent learning the music. We are, however, persuaded that it is enjoyable for the performers, that we have been with them on a 'journey', and that elation might be experienced at this pinnacle of a long and arduous process. We are reminded that this event is special and scarce, and we engage in the almost operatic drama that this might not have happened here in Leeds, but that it did, and that the company is in a state of contagious excitement. Above all we, the audience, are included and involved.

The Importance of Venue

The preconditions for this *Ring* production and the history of its inception were shared and repeated in broadcasts, print, and public talks, perhaps most thoroughly in a pre-*Rheingold* podcast on the company website in April 2011. Here Richard Farnes gave his account of the reasons for the concert staging to interviewer Edward Seckerson. Farnes began with a practicality regarding Opera North's home, Leeds Grand Theatre, saying 'we simply cannot fit an orchestra of this size into our pit'.[40] There followed an account of the concert performances of opera mounted in 2005, while the Grand was being developed, with Farnes effectively extolling the virtues of Opera North as a local employer, and also promoting its developing relationships with great, northern concert halls:

> We were absolutely determined that nobody was going to lose their jobs, that there were going to be no lay-offs [...]. And during this potentially very difficult period we actually mounted some [...] concert performances. [...] And we began to develop a very good relationship with a number of different places, particularly the Sage concert hall in Gateshead.[41]

Finally, artistic and technical benefits emerged as Farnes detailed the favourable acoustics of the concert halls, the visibility of the orchestra as 'the most important character in the entire cycle', the 'physical sight of six harpists' and the 'fascinating

---

[39]   Ibid.

[40]   '*Das Rheingold*: Richard Farnes and Michael Druiett in conversation with Ed Seckerson'.

[41]   Ibid.

instruments' that Wagner created for this work.[42] This account was repeated in various media around *Das Rheingold*, sometimes including detail about Peter Mumford's lighting design, screens, and titling, which are presented as a novel, artistic use of technology, and as a tool for clarity of storytelling.[43]

The home venue for this *Ring* cycle, Leeds Town Hall, and the concert halls to which the work toured, are presented in various media around *Das Rheingold* as the very *raison d'être* for this production: venues are key characters in an unfolding dramatic narrative that is played out regarding the preconditions for this *Ring*. '*Das Rheingold*: The Journey Begins' displays shots of ornate, Victorian ceilings and imposing neoclassical statues, signifying, perhaps for some, a degree of nineteenth-century resonance with the work itself. Orchestra leader David Greed remarks that 'this piece seems to me to be absolutely built for this wonderful hall, Leeds Town Hall'.[44] Although this sentence seems slightly confused, it was retained; a reminder that Opera North's *Ring* productions were indeed created for this great symbol of civic pride, the Town Hall.

Musically, the degree of resonance in Leeds Town Hall's central space, the Victoria Hall, was perfectly complementary to the repertoire itself: dynamic levels and tempi were refined by Farnes accordingly. Elaborating on the words of David Greed, Farnes said in a Radio 3 broadcast:

> Leeds Town Hall is a spectacularly good venue for not only this composer but also this cycle of work. I think Wagner works better in here than almost any other composer. Also I think if you're actually in this building looking at the architecture, it's almost contemporary with the writing of the *Ring* anyway. It has that slightly sort of Valhalla visual experience to it.[45]

As Farnes hinted here, this Valhalla aesthetic is no coincidence. Contemporary fashions for classical antiquity in the nineteenth century mean there are visual references to Greco-Roman gods and myth in the architecture of Leeds Town Hall,

---

[42]   By 2013, with *Siegfried*, the message was more explicit. Musical Director Richard Farnes clarified: 'I'd be the first to admit that by making the orchestra such an important visual element in the performance, we're going completely contrary to Wagner's intentions, which was to keep the orchestra well out of sight. [...] We have made a virtue of the visibility of the orchestra' 'Radio 3 Live in Concert: *Siegfried*', broadcast live on BBC Radio 3, 19 June 2013.

[43]   Mumford's input was described at greater length during the run of *Die Walküre* in 2012, after small changes had been made to the format of the surtitling to increase clarity and ease of viewing. See 'Radio 3 Live in Concert: Wagner's *Die Walküre*'. While the use of projections is not particularly novel in a theatrical context, this hybrid between a staged and concert *Ring* cycle, presented in a town hall with such encompassing screen projections throughout, is certainly out of the ordinary.

[44]   Opera North, '*Das Rheingold*: The Journey Begins'.

[45]   Richard Farnes speaking on 'Radio 3 Live in Concert: Wagner's *Die Walküre*'.

Figure 9.2   Archway over the main entrance to Leeds Town Hall, by kind
              permission of Leeds Library and Information Services <www.
              leodis.net>

while Wagner's aesthetic was informed by his idea of the theatre of Aeschylus.[46]
Wagner's characters, the Norse gods of pagan myth, are the very counterparts of
those that, as audience members, we see around and above us in sculpted plaster
(Figure 9.2).

More powerfully still in Leeds Town Hall (itself a symbol of industry, wealth,
and local 'boom'), the nineteenth-century ideology of a transcendent experience
of art merges visibly with the grounded humility of the working-classes upon
whose labour this hall was built. Marble statues of contemporary activists and
philanthropists of the region grace the opening vestibule.[47] Symbols of Yorkshire
and of Leeds, of its faith and industry, are omnipresent: the owl (an emblem for
Leeds, as for Athens), the weavers' fleece, the white Yorkshire rose. Biblical and
secular aphorisms are inscribed in elevated archways on all sides of the central
concert hall, intended to be uplifting and improving.[48] The drive of the nineteenth-

---

[46]   Michael Ewans, *Wagner and Aeschylus: The 'Ring' and the 'Oresteia'* (London,
1982), traces the influence of this particular work on the *Ring*.

[47]   Statues include benevolent Leeds MP Edward Baines (1774–1848) and humanitarian
lawyer Robert Hall (1801–1857).

[48]   Aphorisms include: 'In union is strength'; 'Honesty the best policy'; 'Auspicium
Melioris Aevi'; 'Deo, Regi, Patriae'; 'God in the highest'; 'Weave truth with trust'; 'Virtue

century social reformers to 'improve' the condition of the workers is evident in this architecture, as the onus of moral and social instruction was expanded from the auspices of the established church to industrial leaders and civic life. A great, municipal concert hall facilitated quality musical experiences for the masses which might transcend the struggles of their everyday lives. While the detail of political motivations may be quite different, there is nonetheless a common, international zeitgeist for social or moral improvement via the arts, and a connection between Wagner's ideal of *Kunstreligion*, where art becomes or replaces a religious experience, and the 'religious' experience of this civil architecture in Leeds.[49] Indeed, this connection is made tangible by the *Ring* production, as indicated by Farnes' description of the 'Valhalla visual experience'. Connections can also be drawn between Wagner's festival concept for the *Ring* in Bayreuth and the festivals held in Leeds Town Hall from its opening,[50] and between Wagner's desire to remove financial obstacles to the reception of his work and similar aims at the opening of Leeds Town Hall by the city council for the working people of Leeds.[51] In short, the history of Leeds Town Hall, its inception and the politics

---

the only nobility'; 'Except the Lord build the house, they labour in vain that build it'; 'Except the Lord keepeth the city, the watchman waketh but in vain'.

[49] While the *Kunstreligion* concept is attributed to Hegel (originally applied to the function of art in ancient Greek society), Deathridge and Dahlhaus argue that, in Wagner, religion was no longer manifested in art, but art itself as a 'transcendent' and altering experience occupied the role formerly played by religion. John Deathridge and Carl Dahlhaus, *The New Grove Wagner* (London, 1984), p. 95. In 'Religion und Kunst' (1880), Wagner postulated: 'Where religion becomes artificial it is reserved for art to save the spirit of religion by recognizing the figurative value of the mythic symbols […] and revealing their deep and hidden truth through an ideal presentation'. Richard Wagner, 'Religion und Kunst', in *Richard Wagner's Prose Works*, trans. William Ashton Ellis (New York, 1966), Vol. 6, pp. 211–85 (p. 213, pp. 223–4).

[50] The immediate forerunner of Wagner's festival was the German music festival tradition. According to Glenn Stanley, this is a more direct example of *Kunstreligion* in practice than Wagner's romanticized version of the Greek festival ideal, which he claimed as his inspiration. Stanley cites 'cultural nationalism and religious aesthetics' as common factors between the German festival and Wagner's Bayreuth. Glenn Stanley, '*Parsifal*: Redemption and *Kunstreligion*', in Thomas S. Grey (ed.), *The Cambridge Companion to Wagner* (Cambridge, 2008), pp. 151–75 (p. 154). Parallel to the German festival and similar in aesthetic and ethos, also being built on the traditions of choral music and oratorio, was the English music festival, expanding in the nineteenth century from the cathedrals to the town halls of newly industrialized towns. The Leeds Music Festival was conceived with the opening of Leeds Town Hall in 1858. The building subsequently became home to the Leeds Triennial Festival, which began in earnest in 1874.

[51] Nicholas Vazsonyi provides a thorough account of Wagner's struggles between idealism and practicality in funding his great venture. Wagner is quoted from a letter to the editor of *Amerikanischen Revue* in June 1874: 'My intention was to offer the public free performances supported only by individual contributions'. Nicholas Vazsonyi, 'Selling the *Ring*' in John DiGaetani (ed.), *Inside The Ring: Essays on Wagner's Opera Cycle*

of those who built it serve as background to an integrated aesthetic experience of venue and work, and the way in which the *Ring* appeared, to David Greed, to be made for this space. In that the working people of Leeds were so integral to the building design, the *Ring*, if it appears to be made for this space, might also appear to be made for them. For Opera North's production, created for this space, Leeds audience members are linked to their nineteenth-century predecessors by the experience of this great civic building as a concert venue, complete with its visible, political ideology.[52]

Audience members were prepared emotionally for the reception of *Das Rheingold* and the *Ring* by Opera North's endeavours. This preparation included a strong sense of location, the idea of a very special geographic place in the world that is host to this 'exciting' musical work. Opera North as a company presented itself as humbled and excited by the facility to perform this work, and projected these emotions onto us, the audience, by virtue of our access to it. A sense of familiarity and community is invoked by allowing us to 'know' the artists involved, and allowing us to access, via the company's own produced narrative, the 'journey' towards the *Ring*. The excitement we are encouraged to feel is at the music and the musical experience, not at any tradition of cultural cachet afforded by Wagner or the background of German Romantic philosophy and art. This is a local experience, in the main a Leeds Town Hall experience, and it is to be had at Town Hall prices, which in 2011 ranged from £17 to £45.[53] Cultural power, visible but largely unmentioned by Opera North, emanates from the intersection between the performance reception and the architectural aesthetic and political history of Leeds Town Hall. The experience of Leeds Town Hall, a venue so integrated into the performance and the production values, effectively embedded the audience within a democratic history of concert-going in Leeds, whereby Wagnerian values might be subconsciously conflated with those of Leeds concert-attendance, or else replaced by the cultural power of this locale.

(Jefferson, NC, 2006), pp. 51–68 (p. 53). In her doctoral thesis, '*A New Impetus to the Love of Music': The Role of the Town Hall in Nineteenth Century English Musical Culture*, Rachel Milestone asserts that 'the Leeds public were able to hear brand new repertoire in their Town Hall, often for free'. 'Penny Concerts' are also mentioned, whereby 'a portion of the hall was reserved purely for the working classes who gained entry for a penny each' (PhD diss., University of Leeds, 2009) pp. 190–96.

[52]   One respondent to my audience questionnaires noted, in 2013, that 'the civic feel of the building in some way taps into some of Wagner's aspirations', and another noted that the venue was 'perfect' for the work.

[53]   'Opera North brings Wagner's *Das Rheingold* to Leeds Town Hall', *Leeds International Concert Season* <http://leedsconcertseason.com/MODULES/NEWS/LICS_ NEWSmoduleASP/NEWSMOD_newsitem.asp?type=&itemid=6267≥ (accessed 14 August 2013).

Werktreue, Expectations and Success Criteria

Lydia Goehr, in *The Imaginary Museum of Musical Works*, has written about the nineteenth-century *Werktreue* concept, by which performers exhibit fidelity to the wishes of the composer.[54] In conflict with this is the 'event' paradigm, whereby we might value and analyse the experience of an event for its own sake, rather than the accuracy by which past events and works are recreated. Wagner himself was imbued with the 'work' model, making, according to Deathridge and Dahlhaus:

> a strict distinction between the authentic version of the work, that in which it should survive as part of the 'museum of the imagination', and unavoidable accommodations to local circumstances in actual productions [...], which he [...] regarded as incidental.[55]

Performance today in the classical and opera spheres, and by extension its reception by audiences, is often tied to the *Werktreue* ideal. However, this concept works in direct conflict with the *Regietheater* model of contemporary stage production, where it is the prerogative of the director to update, reinterpret, and resignify visually on the stage.[56] Consequently, two conflicting ideals are often in play in opera production today: fidelity to the composer's intentions in musical terms, and reinterpretation according to the director visually. It is therefore not surprising that audiences' reception of opera can suffer from the conflation of these two contradictory paradigms and is fraught with contradictions and strong opinions of how works ought (or ought not) to be produced. This debate is amplified in the case of Wagner, whose intentions were set out for his music, his stage, and the very architecture in which the work would be received to be firmly under his own control in the all-encompassing *Gesamtkunstwerk*.[57]

In *Toward an Aesthetic of Reception*, Jauss introduces the concept of the 'horizon of expectations' regarding a work, referring to the criteria that readers use to judge literary texts at any given time.[58] Jauss's 'horizons' are altered with the changing criteria of those receiving the work in successive time periods, so are

---

[54] Lydia Goehr, *The Imaginary Museum of Musical Works: An Essay in the Philosophy of Music* (Oxford, 1992).

[55] Deathridge and Dahlhaus, *The New Grove Wagner*, p. 106.

[56] This is, of course, a simplification of these terms and the arguments behind them for the sake of brevity. It is worth noting that *Regietheater* is a term used to describe a movement in directing that was primarily German, and is now a label often imposed by critics elsewhere.

[57] It could also be argued that it was the *Ring* that, in 1951, gave birth to *Regietheater*, with Wieland Wagner's 1951 *Ring* production for the post-war reopening of Bayreuth. This was a visual attempt, in a country emerging from Nazi rule and wartime defeat, to expunge the German gods and to remove all traces of nationalism. Steven Cerf, 'Wagner's *Ring* and German Culture', in DiGaetani (ed.), *Inside The Ring*, pp. 133–49.

[58] Jauss, *Toward an Aesthetic of Reception*, p. 22.

fluid when applied to a work through time; its meaning is not set by the author but made also by the receiver.

> A literary work is not an object that stands by itself and that offers the same view to each reader in each period. It is not a monument that monolithically reveals its timeless essence.[59]

Jauss's theory becomes more relevant still when applied to the 'live' arts of music and the stage. Indeed, Jauss goes on to say (of the literary work):

> [It] is much more like an orchestration that strikes ever new resonances among its readers and that frees the text from the material of the words and brings it to a contemporary existence.[60]

With the arguable exception of recordings, music and theatre cannot be a 'monument' but must rather be lived, interpreted, performed, heard, and experienced in 'real' time. However, in terms of the musical and theatrical experience (as opposed to Jauss's experience of a literary text) the relationship between composer and audience is not a direct one; in this case the opera company must come in between, mediating the work, communicating with audience and setting expectations of the production. Music drama does not only change its 'face' (as Jauss would have it) for each time-period of reception, but also for its socio-geographical place, with each company that might reinterpret it, and with each audience that might receive it.

We have seen how Opera North began to communicate the priorities and values of its own *Ring* production more prominently than those of Wagner. The act of bespoke creation affords a production a higher likelihood of success in terms of the unique group of criteria the creators have set themselves, so long as these criteria (or, as Jauss described it, the 'horizon of expectations') have been adequately shared with the audience in advance of reception. As a company identifies and suggests back to the audience a set of expectations, it is able to articulate and fulfil its own success criteria. In a *Ring* cycle drawn out over four years, these expectations can be identified, refined, and reiterated over time, so that subtle alterations can be achieved within the horizon of expectation; unpredicted elements of success can be highlighted in advance of the next instalment. This is evident in the subtle changes in focus promoted by Opera North over its four-year cycle. The year 2011 saw a spotlight on musical preparation for the audience, involving familiarization with Wagner's orchestral forces and leitmotifs. There was also an introduction to the company's relationships: with the cast and with home and touring venues.[61] In 2012, the concept was developed of an 'austerity

---

[59]   Ibid., p. 21.
[60]   Ibid.
[61]   Opera North's *Ring* operas toured from Leeds Town Hall to the Sage, Gateshead, as well as Symphony Hall, Birmingham and the Lowry, Salford.

Ring';[62] a production made affordable for audience and taxpayers, a consideration thath had been previously mentioned only briefly and in passing.[63] In 2013, it was made explicit that this production, with its images, titles, and story text on large screens, was akin to a 'filmic' experience; one could 'walk in off the street' without preparation and understand it.[64]

Consolidating the emerging concept of civic pride in a *Ring* cycle, *Götterdämmerung* in 2014 was advertised as a part of the Yorkshire Festival. Tellingly, comments from the audience mirrored the expectations given by Opera North each year.[65] In another example of communicating success criteria direct to audience, Richard Farnes declared in 2013 that 'We're going completely contrary to Wagner's intention, which was to keep the orchestra well out of sight'.[66] This statement came after much marketing and communication in 2011 and 2012, about the benefits of the orchestra being visually present and prominent on stage.[67]

Opera North has asserted success criteria that accord with the ideal of *Werktreue*, in relation to fidelity in musical performance but also to what the company presented on stage visually. While Wagner had attempted to make his claim over all aspects of the staged production, opera audiences hold fast to *Werktreue*, mainly in musical terms.[68] Visual reduction or adaptation is judged far more leniently, although opera audiences in Leeds (as elsewhere in the UK) are by their nature conservative, and this production, while presented as novel in technical terms, was far from the heavy modifications of *Regietheater*.[69] By reducing staging and creating relatively simple and slow-moving visuals on screen, this *Ring* was seen as a beginners'

---

[62]   Alfred Hickling, 'Opera North Tackles Wagner's Ring Cycle', *The Guardian*, 12 June 2012, <www.theguardian.com/music/2012/jun/12/wagner-ring-cycle-opera-north> (accessed 18 July 2014).

[63]   Interviewing Richard Farnes, broadcaster Edward Seckerson assumed an economic motivation for a 'concert' staging; this went undiscussed by Farnes. '*Das Rheingold*: Richard Farnes and Michael Druiett in conversation with Ed Seckerson'. In a pre-show talk in September 2011, Dougie Scarfe mentioned the potential of a *Ring* cycle production to bankrupt a company.

[64]   Richard Farnes explained the thought behind the *Siegfried* production: 'The idea being that somebody could come in off the street, like they would going to the cinema and not really knowing what on earth this piece was about'. 'Radio 3 Live in Concert: *Siegfried*'. Artistic consultant John Tomlinson used almost identical terms: 'You could literally walk in from the street, sit down and enjoy this performance'. Opera North, '*Siegfried* teaser trailer', <www.operanorth.co.uk/productions/siegfried#video_introduction> (accessed 25 June 2013).

[65]   This was evident in various broadcast 'vox pops' but also in my audience questionnaires of 2011–13.

[66]   'Radio 3 Live in Concert: *Siegfried*'.

[67]   '*Das Rheingold*: Richard Farnes and Michael Druiett in conversation with Ed Seckerson'; 'Richard Farnes introduces *Das Rheingold*'.

[68]   This was evidenced consistently in my own audience questionnaires.

[69]   *Regietheater* examples of the *Ring* cycle include Wieland Wagner's revolutionary post-war *Ring*, and Patrice Chéreau's 'Centenary *Ring*' of 1976 in Bayreuth.

production for those who required visual clarity. For aficionados, the music was perceived as prominent. By the judgement of a concert-going public and those committed to the music of Wagner, this production was a triumph of authenticity and *Werktreue*, free from heavy-handed stage direction, or as Orchestra Director Dougie Scarfe termed it, 'unencumbered by a director's vision'.[70]

Conclusion

Opera North addressed its audience's perceived 'fear of the threshold into Wagner' by processes of familiarization, in various ways. These processes also involved strengthening company ties with audience members, with venues, and with the region, while promoting access to the *Ring* cycle and to the experience of being a Wagner audience. By accustoming audiences to the Opera North *Ring*, the company set expectations by which audiences and critics might judge the *Ring* opera productions.

Anticipated audience concerns regarding the epic and unknown music were addressed, primarily in 2011, by events introducing leitmotifs and structure.[71] Musical learning was presented as participatory and entertaining, and thus regarded as being more 'fun' than challenging or rigorous by those involved.[72] Further emotional familiarization occurred with communications about the performers initially presented as 'mainly British', the company's journey and its relationship with venues, and, in 2014, with Yorkshire. A sense of excitement was performed around the productions and a 'special event' character was created by citing a scarcity of *Ring* productions in the north of England. The importance of the *Ring* in the region was thus enhanced by Opera North, while encouraging and strengthening audiences' sense of place. This was done with regard to the north in general, but also with particular relevance to the home venue, Leeds Town Hall. By mobilizing a sense of civic pride around its *Ring* production, Opera North as the national opera company for the north of England, brought to the fore a key element of its own enduring popularity. In highlighting the region's operatic importance (i.e. the existence of the company) and the rarity of a regional *Ring* production, public demand is seen to be created, in order to be fulfilled over four years.

In the process of setting audience expectation, Opera North initially foregrounded music, thus playing into existing criteria of musical *Werktreue*. However, the company overcame such sensibilities in the visual arena, where expectations of the productions themselves were communicated in preference to

---

[70]   Dougie Scarfe in conversation with Stuart Leeks in a pre-show talk at the Sage, Gateshead, 23 June 2012 (taken from notes by Kara McKechnie).

[71]   In addition to Burke's 'Sing ON: Wagner!', Martin Pickard hosted a demonstration, with singers, of leitmotifs and music. 'Inside Opera Special: *Das Rheingold*', Leeds Town Hall, 1 July 2011.

[72]   'Sing ON: Wagner!' questionnaires.

the original wishes of the composer. This is important for judgements made of the productions, since well-communicated company priorities for productions act as a benchmark 'success criteria' for audiences and critics, in a far more immediate way than the priorities of a nineteenth-century composer, particularly in an extra-musical context.

More immediate still, the essential spirit of this cycle in reception, and the engendered excitement of its audience, was encapsulated in the inclusion of *Götterdämmerung* in the Yorkshire Festival of 2014. Here is the finale of epic, regional, operatic expectation, created and fulfilled.

Chapter 10

Strategic Nationalism Towards the Imagined Community: The Rise and Success Story of Finnish Opera

Liisamaija Hautsalo

We are no longer Swedes; we cannot become Russians; we must be Finns.[1]

During its 400-year existence, opera has spread all over the world and, in addition to journeying beyond national boundaries, has taken on 'nationalist' qualities. The connections between nationalism and music have been investigated since the beginning of the twenty-first century, and, according to musicologist Philip V. Bohlman, 'much of the attention [...] has been devoted to art music, especially traditions of national opera'.[2] Finland currently enjoys a flourishing opera culture rich in first performances, yet this art form arrived there relatively late. Between 1852 and 1907, only six operas were composed, five of them to Swedish texts and one to a German libretto.[3] The first Finnish-language opera was composed

---

[1] This is a famous statement known as the 'Finland Concept', generally believed to be an adaptation (*c.* 1810) of Adolf Ivar Arwidsson's words aimed at gaining Swedish speakers' support for a Finnish national identity that was neither Swedish nor Russian. See, for example, Osmo Jussila, Seppo Hentilä, and Jukka Nevakivi (eds), *From Grand Duchy to a Modern State*, trans. David and Eva Arter (London, 1999), p. 24.

[2] Philip V. Bohlman, *Focus: Music, Nationalism, and the Making of the New Europe* [2004], 2nd edn (New York, 2011), p. xxiv. See also Richard Taruskin, 'Nationalism', *Oxford Music Online*, <www.oxfordmusiconline.com> (accessed 17 January 2014); William A. Everett, 'Opera and National Identity in Nineteenth-Century Croatian and Czech Lands', *International Review of the Aesthetics and Sociology of Music* 35/1 (2004): pp. 63–9; Krisztina Lajosi, 'National Opera and Nineteenth-Century Nation Building in East-Central Europe', in Lotte Eilskov Jensen, Joseph Theodoor Leerssen, and Marita Mathijsen (eds), *Free Access to the Past: Romanticism, Cultural Heritage and the Nation* (Leiden, 2010), pp. 227–46.

[3] In the nineteenth century, opera in Finland was performed mainly by foreign touring groups, and there were only a few productions by Finnish amateurs, such as *Il barbiere di Siviglia* in 1849 and *Lucia di Lammermoor* in 1850. Foreign touring groups performed several operas during each of their visits, and it was not until 1873 that the first more permanent Finnish group, the Finnish Opera Company, was founded. After its closure in 1879, opera in Finland was again dependent on foreign visitors, mainly Italian groups.

at the dawn of the twentieth century. In a country caught between West and East, and without any court traditions or luxurious ecclesiastical practices, opera (as well as other arts) was used in the process of creating a nation that did not yet exist. At the end of the nineteenth century, the creation of authentic 'Finnishness' and Finnish identity was part of what was called 'national enlightenment'.[4] The driving forces in this enlightenment process were the Finnish nationalists – that is, the Fennomans[5] – who were a small group of defenders of Finnish language and culture in a Swedish-speaking country. It is significant that it was the Fennomans who started, in addition to several other Finnish-language cultural activities,[6] the first operatic enterprise in the country in the 1870s, and later took part in many other activities to create national operatic institutions and a vernacular opera repertoire in Finland. Thus, the rise of Finnish opera written by Finnish or Finnish-based composers and the concurrent Fennoman movement can be seen as tightly interwoven.

Considering the modest and relatively late start of operatic activities in Finland in general, the current flourishing of opera culture is worth exploring. 'The opera boom',[7] as the phenomenon of large-scale production of new operatic works

---

At the beginning of the twentieth century, Finns produced some Wagner, but permanent operatic activity effectively started only when the Domestic Opera – now the Finnish National Opera – was founded in 1911. See Pekka Hako, *Finnish Opera*, trans. Jaakko Mäntyjärvi (Helsinki, 2002), pp. 10–14.

[4]   Many historians have used the term 'national awakening': for example, Päiviö Tommila in *Herää Suomi: Suomalaisuusliikkeen historia* (Kuopio, 1989). His book even bears the verb 'awaken' (*herää*) in its title. In musicology, in the Finnish context, the term has often been connected to Jean Sibelius, as in Glenda Dawn Goss, *Sibelius: A Composer's Life and the Awakening of Finland* (Chicago, 2009).

[5]   There was not a single unified group of the Fennomans. Instead, there were several different tendencies among the nationalists, regarding language, social issues, and the Russian connection. The connecting issue for them all was to create and support Finnish culture. In that sense, some of the Swedish-speaking Finns were also Fennomans. See Tommila, *Herää Suomi*; Jussila et al., *From Grand Duchy*, pp. 57–8; and Vesa Vares, *Varpuset ja pääskyset: Nuorsuomalaisuus ja Nuorsuomalainen puolue 1870-luvulta vuoteen 1918* (Helsinki, 2000).

[6]   At present, Finland has two official languages: Finnish and Swedish. However, until 1919, Swedish was the only official language even though Finnish could be used, for example, in administration from 1863 on. See Jason Lavery, *History of Finland* (Westport, CT, 2006), pp. 60–61. As a consequence of the language fights between the Finnish and Swedish speakers that erupted again in the 1870s, the cultural field was also divided, and both language groups had for a while their own theatres and opera companies: the opera company of the Swedish Theatre and the Finnish Opera Company. Both companies were closed in 1879; see Pentti Paavolainen, 'Two Opera or One – or None', in Anne Sivuoja et al. (eds), *Opera on the Move in the Nordic Countries* (Helsinki, 2012), pp. 125–55.

[7]   The expression 'opera boom' was introduced by the Finnish musicologist Mikko Heiniö in 1999. Heiniö uses the term to refer to the exceptional popularity of contemporary tonal operas with rural topics in Finland from the 1970s onwards, which were successful

in Finland has been called, began in the 1970s, and there seems to be no end in sight. According to my statistics, there are approximately 350 operas in the whole operatic corpus in Finland, composed between 1852 and 2013.[8] However, recent statistics show that approximately 293 of these were composed between 1975 and 2013 – in other words, during the 'opera boom'.[9] This number is even more impressive when one considers that Finland has had only one permanent opera house and three summer opera festivals. The boom peaked in 2011, when altogether 23 new works by Finnish composers were premiered; during 2012 and 2013, there were at least 26 operatic premieres.[10] A comparison might be made with the UK, where during 1970–2010 British opera houses and companies produced around 71 works by British or British-based composers[11] – only a third of Finland's 244-work output during the same years.

Opera is an expensive and overwhelming art form, still affected by prejudice. Hence, in times of economic difficulty, which have often included radical budget cuts and reductions in European cultural activity, the persistent opera boom in Finland deserves to be investigated. Instead of exploring this phenomenon directly through the lens of economics, this chapter examines the rise and success story of Finnish opera, and relates the continuing opera boom to the ideological, political, and cultural tendencies in late-nineteenth-century Finland that are still evident in Finnish society today. Although there has been some general research on music and nationalism in Finland, the connection of opera promotion to nationalism has not been explored.[12]

---

among the general public as well as in the media. See Heiniö, *Karvalakki kansakunnan kaapin päällä: kansalliset attribuutit Joonas Kokkosen ja Aulis Sallisen julkisuuskuvassa* (Helsinki, 1999), pp. 10, 15–32. See, also, Liisamaija Hautsalo, 'The New Finnish Opera Boom', *Finnish Music Quarterly* 1 (2000): pp. 39–42; Hautsalo, 'Vuosi 2000 tuo Suomeen oopperabuumin', *Keskisuomalainen* (9 February 2000): p. 16; Hako, *The Finnish Opera*; Elke Albrecht, *Der finnische Opernboom: Hintergründe und Meilensteine der finnischen Operngeschichte* (Saarbrücken, 2009); Hautsalo, 'A Century of Opera', *Finnish Music Quarterly* 2 (2012): pp. 32–7.

[8]   These statistics are partially based on listings given by Pekka Hako (up to 2002; see Hako, *The Finnish Opera*, pp. 211–56) and by Elke Albrecht (up 2008; see Albrecht, *Der finnische Opernboom*, pp. 162–72). However, the years between 2009 and 2013 are based on my statistics only. Moreover, I have counted only performed works while the others included manuscripts.

[9]   Liisamaija Hautsalo and Sidsel Karlsen, *Articulations of Identity in Finnish Opera* (forthcoming).

[10]   Hautsalo and Karlsen, *Articulations of Identity*. It is possible that some more operas will be found, thus the numbers are not absolutely exact. However, these figures show the scope of the phenomenon.

[11]   Mario Ferraro Jr., *Contemporary Opera in Britain, 1970–2010*, Ph.D. diss. (London, 2011), pp. 51, 55, 169–75.

[12]   See, however, Liisamaija Hautsalo, 'Fennomania, Suomi-neito ja Oskar Merikannon oopperoiden naishahmot', *Musiikki* 3–4 (2013): pp. 29–69; Ulla-Britta Broman-Kananen,

Theoretical Context

When discussing vernacular opera promoted by a nationalist movement, it is necessary, despite the ambiguity of the topic, to touch upon the meaning of nationalism and the concept of a nation.[13] Nationalism as such has been recognized as one of the major political and cultural factors in European history after the eighteenth century. In this study, I will limit my exploration to just one interpretation of a nation, Benedict Anderson's idea of a nation as 'imagined community',[14] which is used here to refer to a collective unit – the culturally united Finland with a homogeneous and unified people, *the Finns*, holding the shared idea of Finnishness and Finnish identity.[15] Secondly, I will use the concept of *strategic nationalism* as an application of 'strategic essentialism'[16] after Gayatri Chakravorty Spivak. Since the early 1990s, Spivak's concept has been applied in several contexts, including feminism, queer theory, and post-colonialism. In this study, it is applied in a manner close to its original meaning when analysing ethnic groups or minorities and their processes in order to create a collective, unified identity that achieves political goals. The goals are achieved, according to Spivak, by 'the strategic use of positivist essentialism in a scrupulously visible political interest'.[17] More specifically, I understand strategic nationalism to be implemented by a minority, namely the originally Swedish-speaking Fennoman elite and later the second generation of Fennomans who spoke Finnish. In this context the two

---

'Operasångerskan Emmy Achté som ikon för den finska-nationella rörelsen', *Musiikki* 3–4 (2013): pp. 5–28.

[13]   There has been much research on nationalism since 1980. A comprehensive summary on the subject is given in Umut Özkirimli, *Theories of Nationalism: A Critical Introduction*, foreword by Fred Halliday (Basingstoke, 2000).

[14]   Benedict Anderson, *Imagined Communities: Reflections on the Origin and Spread of Nationalism* [1983], revised edn (London, 2006), pp. 5–7.

[15]   Hanna Suutela has applied the concept of 'imagined community' in the context of Finnish theatre history. Hanna Suutela, 'An Instrument for Changing Nationalist Strategies: The Finnish Theatre Company', in Helka Mäkinen, S.E. Wilmer and W.B. Worthen (eds), *Theatre, History, and National Identity* (Helsinki, 2006), pp. 76, 84. My interpretation coincides with that of Derek Fewster who, in *Nationalism and the Construction of the Early Finnish History* (Saarbrücken, 2009), analyses Finnish identity construction process by way of a 'Finnish Antique' in the nineteenth century.

[16]   In the context of nationalism, according to Graig J. Calhoun, essentialism refers to 'a reduction of the diversity in a population to some single criterion held to constitute its defining "essence" and most crucial character'. Calhoun quoted in Özkirimli, *Theories of Nationalism*, p. 215. Thus, the essence can refer to the group identity, for instance the Finns. Even though all the Finns are not the same, for certain purposes, the group identity, 'the Finns', can be utilized.

[17]   Gayatri Chakravorty Spivak, 'Subaltern Studies: Deconstructing Historiography', in Donna Landry and Gerald McLean (eds), *Spivak Reader: Selected Works of Gayatri Chakravorty Spivak* (New York, 1985), pp. 203–35.

concepts, the imagined community and strategic nationalism, refer to 'the strategic interest' of the Fennomans in their aim to construct Finnishness as an imagined community representing a homogeneous, Lutheran, Finnish-speaking nation against Russia, the backward 'Other' and the threatening enemy. My maxim in this study is, as Nicholas Till has put it, 'to study opera we have to study more than opera'.[18] Hence, my theoretical framework draws from opera studies, Finnish opera history, political history, and nationalism studies.

I will first argue that there are parallels between the Finnish-language opera of the early twentieth century and the recent Finnish opera boom starting from the 1970s. Secondly, I will argue that the explicit strategic nationalism of the Fennomans towards an imagined community of a culturally united Finland with collective and unified Finnish identity established the starting point for early Finnish opera, and that the significance opera achieved in its early years in this cultural–political context can also be identified as the backdrop of the current success story of Finnish opera. Moreover, not only is the legacy of the late-nineteenth-century Fennomania present in the today's operatic field in Finland, but the same discursive construction towards the imagined community of the Fennomans can also be identified in many operatic practices. To support my arguments I will proceed chronologically by exploring the operatic key moments in the history of Finnish opera through the lenses of the early Fennomania and its later legacy. I will also map the periods when the vernacular works in the programming of opera institutions have appeared in Finland. This exploration will be made on the basis of my previous research data on Finnish opera (spanning the years 1852–2013), articles in newspapers (1904–11, 1993, and 2011–12),[19] and previous literature on the history of opera in Finland.

Finnish Nationalism: Fennomania

It is obvious that Fennomania and several other nineteenth-century national movements in Europe – whether philosophical, cultural or political – were adaptations of German nationalism.[20] The Fennomans used nationalism strategically by selecting suitable theories to support their political objectives 'when constructing Finnish nationalism and a national identity for the Finns'.[21] In particular, in the 1840s the early Fennomans followed Herder's

---

[18] Nicholas Till (ed.), *The Cambridge Companion to Opera Studies* (Cambridge, 2012), p. 2.

[19] These articles are kept in the Archive of the Finnish National Opera.

[20] Naturally, Finland was not the only country starting to create a national identity on the basis on European models. See for example Lajosi, 'National Opera', pp. 51–9, and Everett, 'Opera and National Identity', pp. 63–9.

[21] Pertti Karkama, *Kansakunnan asialla: Elias Lönnrot ja ajan aatteet* (Helsinki, 2001), p. 5. Unless otherwise stated, all translations are my own.

idea on language.[22] However, it was Hegel's philosophy on the nation that was adopted primarily, and the philosopher J.V. Snellman (1806–1881) developed and systematized an explicit programme for the Finnish nation in the same vein. In Snellman's programme, the Swedish-speaking elite had immediately to change their language into Finnish, the vernacular, and all levels of education had to be conducted in Finnish, since only a coherent and culturally strong Finnish nation could survive in difficult times as a Grand Duchy of Russia.[23] For Snellman, the essential means to educate people had to be by literature written in Finnish.[24] Since literature in the vernacular did not exist, the Fennomans under the leadership of Snellman founded in 1831 the Finnish Literature Society in order to create and further develop literature in Finnish. The Society's greatest accomplishment was the publication of the national epic *The Kalevala*, a collection of folk poetry[25] that has been described as 'arguably the most important symbolic event with respect to the development of Finnish national identity in the nineteenth century',[26] even though the epic with its ancient heroes was to some extent invented.[27] The central organization in charge of implementing 'national enlightenment' and spreading Fennoman ideology throughout the country was the Kansanvalistusseura (Society for the Advancement of Public Education), founded in 1874.[28]

The Fennomans and the Pre-History of Finnish Opera

The first known reference to an opera house in Finland is in the 1810s, at the beginning of Russian rule, in the architectural plans for the new capital city of Helsinki. In these plans, opera was seen as a patriotic enterprise, although not yet a national one in a traditional, nationalistic sense.[29] One of the bureaucrats wrote that the opera house was planned for 'a precious seedbed of the goddesses of the

---

[22]   For instance, Zacharias Topelius, the librettist of the first opera composed in Finland, belonged to this group. See for example Fewster, *Nationalism*, p. 133.

[23]   Tommila, *Herää Suomi*, pp. 60–63; Fewster, *Nationalism*, pp. 120–22.

[24]   Karkama, *Kansakunnan asialla*, pp. 240–327.

[25]   *The Kalvela* was compiled by the folklorist Elias Lönnrot. The first edition was published in 1835 and the second 1849. See Karkama, *Kansakunnan asialla*, pp. 240–327.

[26]   Matti Huttunen, 'The National Composer and the Idea of Finnishness: Sibelius and the Formation of Finnish Musical Style', in Daniel M. Grimley (ed.), *The Cambridge Companion to Sibelius* (Cambridge, 2004), p. 9.

[27]   Fewster, *Nationalism*, pp. 12–13. See also Hautsalo, 'Fennomania', p. 32.

[28]   Jussila et al., *From Grand Duchy*, p. 59.

[29]   The concepts of patriotism and nationalism have changed during the centuries, and the relationship between patriotism (Gr. *patris*) and nationalism is complex; it has intrigued a multiplicity of scholars. Patriotism is often defined as love for a country, and nationalism is often connected to power and a need to differentiate oneself from 'the Others'. See Maurizio Viroli, *For Love of Country: An Essay on Patriotism and Nationalism* (Oxford, 1995).

patriotic song'.[30] This plan was not realized, and in 1827 a theatre for visiting groups was built in Helsinki, naturally by the Swedish theatre-enthusiasts; only in 1866 was the first permanent Swedish theatre company founded,[31] and finally, in the 1870s, the first institution for Finnish-language theatre. There were no permanent opera activities prior to these institutional establishments. Beyond the occasionally touring theatre companies that sometimes performed opera, the operatic scene was, with a few sparse exceptions, empty. The most important of these exceptions was the first opera composed in Finland – *Kung Karls jakt* (King Charles's Hunt) of 1852 – written by the German-born Fredrik Pacius with a libretto in Swedish by the Finnish journalist and professor of history Zacharias Topelius.[32] The basic elements of Finnishness were already included in this opera about one of the Swedish kings visiting Åland,[33] but its general mood can be described as patriotic and pre-Snellmanian;[34] it relates also to German Romantic opera as well as folk opera, such as *Alt-Wiener Volkskomödie*.[35] Its amateur production was a unique case among the various activities of the University of Helsinki. Thus, I would argue that Pacius' *Kung Karls jakt* and his two other operas represent the *pre-history* of Finnish opera.

Finnish Operatic Enterprise as Strategic Nationalism

Along with the rise of the Fennoman movement in the 1870s, a Finnish theatre appeared on the agenda of the Fennomans because it was regarded as unfair that Swedish speakers had a permanent theatre company in Helsinki, but not the Finnish speakers. A vernacular theatre, actors, and repertoire were demanded, without rejecting the best foreign repertoire, if performed in Finnish.[36] The future director of the Finnish Theatre, Kaarlo Bergbom, justified the need for a vernacular theatre in a groundbreaking article, published in March 1872:

---

[30]   This was declared by J.A. Ehrenström, who was the designer of Helsinki's city plan. Ehrenström's statement was quoted several times because of the opening of the new house for the Finnish National Opera, for instance by Heikki Tuomi-Nikula in 'Sadan vuoden unelma', *Lapin Kansa* (1 December 1993).
[31]   According to the Swedish Theatre (Svenska Theatern), 1866 was the official founding year of the theatre even though there had been earlier Swedish theatre activities. See <www.svenskateatern.fi/fi/teatteri/historia_fi> (accessed 7 June 2014).
[32]   The premiere was on 24 March 1852 in Helsinki. See <http://digi.lib.helsinki.fi/sanomalehti/binding/503776> (accessed 7 June 2014).
[33]   Juhani Koivisto, *Kansa, ooppera ja Kaarle-kuningas: Kun Suomi loi oopperaa ja ooppera Suomea* (Helsinki, 2006), pp. 15–16.
[34]   This is the term the Finnish historian Vesa Vares uses to refer to Fennomania in the 1840–50s; *Varpuset ja pääskyset*, p. 22.
[35]   Liisamaija Hautsalo, 'Toiset oopperassa *Kaarle-kuninkaan metsästys*: Postkolonialistinen analyysi markkinakohtauksen juutalaisrepresentaatiosta', *Musiikki* 3–4 (2012): pp. 48–87 (pp. 64–7).
[36]   Eliel Aspelin-Haapkylä, *Suomalaisen teatterin historia I* (Helsinki, 1906), p. 267.

If theatre is luxury, the state funding [that cannot be shared between the theatres of the language groups] does not belong to the Swedish theatre either. It would be cruel to spend money on luxury when people are living in poverty, and children are starving, as during the crop failures. If theatre is understood as an educative, enlightening institution that endows love for everything beautiful, for good behaviour, and refined manners which make life bright and feelings high-minded [...], why are we, the Finnish-speaking people, excluded from this spring of educational and civilizing elevation; why is this clear light sullied for us?[37]

Kaarlo Bergbom became the director of the first Finnish Theatre Company,[38] founded by enthusiastic Fennomans in 1872. A year later, under its auspices arose the Finnish Opera Company, founded by the same Fennomans. It was a small touring group without a permanent theatre, and during its short existence from 1873 to 1879 it performed 24 full operas in 450 nights, all of them taken from existing European repertoire.[39]

Theatre was understood to be an important means of education and national enlightenment. As the Finnish theatre historian Hanna Suutela has demonstrated, the Finnish Theatre Company was founded as a tool for educating people to adopt Fennoman values,[40] and, according to her, 'in the theatre rhetoric of the 1880s the Finnish people become a unified concept'.[41] The goal of the Finnish Opera Company was to educate, but it was also an essential forum for the Fennomans to socialize in. It was thought particularly suitable for the young female members of the community.[42] According to another theatre historian, Timo Tiusanen, 'the Finnish Opera Company served as a propaganda headquarters of the Finnish-Fennoman Party, which, on the basis of music, assured the presentability of the Finnish language and Finnish culture'.[43] What differentiated the Finnish Opera Company was its language: all performances were, at least in principle, to be sung in Finnish.[44]

Politics were closely tied to cultural development in the end of the nineteenth century in Finland. The same leading Fennomans that took part in political life

[37]   Kaarlo Bergbom, quoted in Hannu-Ilari Lampila, *Suomalaisen oopperan historia* (Helsinki, 1997), pp. 54–5.
[38]   Today it is known as the Finnish National Theatre.
[39]   Suutela, 'An Instrument for Changing Nationalist Strategies', p. 81.
[40]   Hanna Suutela, *Impyet: Näyttelijättäret Suomalaisen Teatterin palveluksessa* (Helsinki, 2005), p. 17.
[41]   Suutela, 'An Instrument for Changing Nationalist Strategies', p. 90.
[42]   Suutela, *Impyet*, pp. 53–8.
[43]   Timo Tiusanen, *Teatterimme hahmottuu: Näyttämötaiteemme kehitystie kansanrunoudesta itsenäisyyden ajan alkuun* (Helsinki, 1969), p. 104.
[44]   Even though the principle of the leaders of the Finnish Opera Company was to hire only Finnish singers, it was not always possible. Several singers from Sweden and Germany were performing at the Finnish Opera Company without adequate skills in Finnish, see e.g. Ulla-Brita Broman-Kananen, 'Staging a National Language: Opera in Christiania and Helsinki in 1870s', in Sivuoja, *Opera on the Move*, pp. 156–91 (pp. 166–70).

also attended cultural activities and were active in the construction of a Finnish cultural identity. Indeed, as indicated above, the leaders of the Fennoman party were also the founders of the Finnish Theatre and its opera.[45] Consequently, in his article on soprano Emmy Achté, Snellman (a key figure among the Fennomans) saw this prima donna of the Finnish Opera Company as a symbol of the Finnish opera and implicitly also of Fennomania:

> Maybe she [Emmy Achté] would have been more successful on foreign stages, and won greater benefits abroad. Her faithfulness to the Finnish language might seem a sacrifice. But what is sure is that she has become what she is by the love of the Finns, even as she has been brought up by them. Here [in Finland] her name shall live forever in the history of Finnish art.[46]

This passage by Snellman, an eminent statesman, was one of the starting points of the Finns' 'imagined community', in which the contemporary appreciation of Finnish opera was manifested.

The Opera Competition of the Finnish Literary Society

After the Singing Department of the Finnish Theatre closed in 1879, there were no permanent opera companies left; furthermore, Finland still lacked an original Finnish-language repertoire. Thus, the next step in the Fennomans' strategy was to create a vernacular opera repertoire. In the 1890s, the Finnish Literary Society announced two competitions for composing operas with a Finnish libretto in order to establish a vernacular operatic tradition. The Society's call for the competition emphasized that 'with respect to [the opera's] content, [it should] encompass mythological or historical matter'.[47] This call echoes European models for cultural nationalism – that is, 'the urgent need for an early history'[48] – here transformed for Finnish aims. The first competition announced in 1891 did not attract attention from any artists, but the second, in 1898, received one score before the deadline. This was the score to Oskar Merikanto's opera *The Maiden of the North* (*Pohjan*

---

[45]   Swedish-speaking Kaarlo Bergbom, the leader of the Finnish Theatre, was also a Fennoman. He wrote in both Finnish and Swedish, and thus can be described as a personification of Fennoman politics.

[46]   Snellman 1877, quoted in Aspelin-Haapkylä, *Suomalaisen teatterin historia II* (Helsinki, 1907), p. 305.

[47]   This is how Johan Daniel Stenberg, the initiator and sponsor of the opera competition formulated the aim of the contest in his will in 1880. Quoted in Erkki Salmenhaara, *Suomen musiikin historia 2* (Helsinki, 1996), p. 355. See also Hannele Ketomäki, *Oskar Merikannon kansalliset aatteet: Merikannon musiikkijuhlatoiminta sekä ooppera Pohjan neiti ja kuorolaulut venäläistämiskauden laulu- ja soittojuhlien ohjelmassa*, PhD diss. (Sibelius Academy, Helsinki, 2012), pp. 150, 153.

[48]   Fewster, *Nationalism*, p. 11.

neiti), which, being based on the *Kalevala*, adhered to the instructions of the Finnish Literary Society in the competition announcement.

During the first decades of the nineteenth century, the ruling Russian authorities had supported the development of national culture in order to separate Finland from its Western (Swedish) connections. Until the end of the 1890s, the situation between Russia and its Finnish Grand Duchy was relatively peaceful. However, the political situation in Finland changed at the end of the nineteenth century. Owing to Russia's integration policy, implemented by Emperor Nicholas II, Finland began to lose its privileges, and Russian oppression – that is, 'Russification' – was implemented twice in Finland: 1899–1905 and 1908–1917. Therefore, despite the constant 'language fights' between Swedish- and Finnish-speaking Finns, the shared aim for all Finland's political groups was separation from Russia, which was culturally, ethnically, linguistically, and religiously unfamiliar.

The two Russification periods were the crucial culmination for the Fennoman's culture-based nationalism. Strategic work was done, in addition to that by the political elite, by several renowned Fennoman intellectuals. The latter included writers, journalists, painters, and musicians, among whom was the composer Jean Sibelius. Fewster called them the representatives of 'the machinery of nationalism',[49] despite their individual accomplishments in arts. The Fennomans understood Finnish culture – literature, folk poetry, design, architecture, and both folk and art music, including opera – to be the most powerful means of passive resistance to Russification. As the Finnish historian Seppo Knuuttila has recognized, there was the underlying belief that Finland 'is everything that has been said, written, painted, composed, and acted'.[50]

Before continuing, there are several key moments in the history of Finnish opera that I would like to single out as particularly meaningful in the context of nationalism. For instance, in 1899, the first performance of Sibelius's *Finlandia*, written for the protest festivities against the so-called first Russification period, can be seen as a nationally important event *par excellence*. Furthermore, the premiere of Merikanto's *The Maiden of the North* is another important example of resistance to Russification. When Merikanto was composing his opera, the political situation in Finland was relatively peaceful, but had changed radically by the time of its premiere. On 2 June 1908, Emperor Nicholas II began a second Russification process in Finland, and the premiere of *The Maiden of the North* was given some days later in Viipuri, on 18 June. Organized by the Fennoman Society for the Advancement of Public Education, the premiere manifested Fennoman ideology and was a significant event in many ways. For instance, when considering the context of oppression, the performance, ending with the national hymn, was a powerful manifestation of passive, cultural resistance against Russia.

[49] Ibid., p. 15.
[50] Seppo Knuuttila, 'Paikan synty suomalaisen ilmiönä', in Pertti Alasuutari and Petri Ruuska (eds), *Elävänä Euroopassa: Muuttuva suomalainen identiteetti* (Tampere, 1998), p. 197.

Or, to put it in Spivakian terms, the Fennomans used the premiere of the opera strategically to underline nationalistic goals via a significant cultural event – to celebrate Finnishness through the opera performance.

Early Opera Institutions: The Domestic Opera and the Savonlinna Opera Festival

As Russification made rapid progress, the political situation in Finland in the beginning of the twentieth century became more tense. By 1911, the street signs in Helsinki were written in three languages: Swedish, Finnish, and Russian. Despite the political instability, there was an intensified public discussion about the possibility of establishing a national opera institution in Finland;[51] it was understood as a symbol of a proper nation. In 1909 the cultural magazine *Nuori Suomi* (*Young Finland*) published an issue concentrating on the question: Is there a need for a national institution for opera in Finland? One of the writers stated: 'A Finnish opera is not impossible – it must be brought to life by national enthusiasm'.[52]

Finally, the predecessor of the Finnish National Opera, the Domestic Opera[53] was founded in June 1911 by a handful of opera-enthusiastic Fennomans.[54] One of the key figures was the internationally renowned soprano Aino Ackté,[55] daughter of earlier mentioned Emmy Achté[56] and the artistic leader of the company.[57] In October that same year, the Domestic Opera gave its first premiere, and, in line with its bilingual-language politics, one work was performed in Finnish (Massenet's

---

[51] The first article demanding a national opera was published in 1904 in the newspaper *Helsingin kaiku*.

[52] Alku Siikaniemi, quoted in Lampila, *Suomalaisen oopperan historia*, p. 112.

[53] The official name included both Finnish (Kotimainen Ooppera) and Swedish (Inhemska Operan) versions.

[54] Aino Ackté wrote in her letters and memoirs that it was she who gave the final initiative to the founding of the national opera. However, as Juhani Koivisto has pointed out, many preparations had been done before Ackté came back to Finland and started her campaign to advocate the opera plans; see Juhani Koivisto, *Suurten tunteiden talo: Kohtauksia Kansallisoopperan vuosisadalta* (Helsinki, 2011), p. 12.

[55] Aino Ackté even acquired her first name from one of the female protagonists in the *Kalevala*.

[56] The whole Achté family was Fennoman: father, N. Achté, was a conductor at the Finnish Opera Company, and the sister of Aino Ackté, mezzosoprano Irma Tervani, was also a 'passionate Fennoman' as described by Seppo Heikinheimo. Furthermore, Oskar Merikanto, the Fennoman composer and pianist, accompanied Aino Achté in her domestic tours, and worked as a first conductor of the Domestic Opera. Thus, the circle of the Fennoman musicians was small and tight. See Seppo Heikinheimo, *Oskar Merikanto ja hänen aikansa* (Helsinki, 1995), p. 225.

[57] The original name for the family was Achté. Aino Ackté changed the spelling of her name when she was in Paris.

La Navarraise) and one in Swedish (Leoncavallo's *Pagliacci*).[58] Since the company did not have an opera house of its own, it undertook tours in the countryside. Its visit to Tampere in 1917 led one journalist to write: 'those of us for whom the Finnish-national cultural enlightenment is precious must rejoice at our own national opera and what it is doing'.[59] Since the basic repertoire at the Domestic Opera was international, there were demands for vernacular opera. It was stated in several newspapers before the openings of the Domestic Opera in 1911 that the national stage, or the 'lyrical scene' as it was sometimes called in the press, was understood as a forum for 'operas particularly by Finnish composers'.[60]

After Finnish independence in 1917 the most significant operatic event in the young republic of Finland was the opening of the first permanent house of the Finnish Opera in 1919. Members of the cultural and political elite of the republic as well as foreign diplomatic corps were present during the opening ceremony, where after several speeches the national hymn was sung, followed by a performance of Verdi's *Aïda*.[61] The opening of the opera house was a nationally significant event, as one newspaper confirms: 'The celebration day is not only owed to the opera, but also belongs to national music and its friends.'[62] Again the operatic event was strategically harnessed to the goals of the nation and nationalism.

Another important operatic venture initiated at this time was the Savonlinna Opera Festival in 1912. One year following her efforts to establish the Domestic Opera, Aino Ackté founded this festival at a medieval castle in eastern Finland. This summer event was also intended to be part of the national opera scene. Ackté had the special objective of 'promoting the Finnish performing and creative arts' throughout her career.[63] In January 1912 she wrote a letter to persuade the Savonlinna town leaders to accept her opera festival idea:

> It is very important for the small and isolated nation [Finland] that all the Finns can take part in cultural activities. Especially in times when its existence as a nation is threatened, our responsibility to educate people is clearer than ever before.[64]

---

[58]   The Russians had a theatre of their own, the Alexander Theatre, which was inherited by the Finnish Opera after independence.

[59]   *Aamulehti*, 23 May 1917.

[60]   This demand was mentioned at least in two articles written just before the openings of the Domestic Opera in October 1911, which can be found in the earliest scrapbook of the Finnish Opera, which includes articles from the beginning of the year 1911. The names of the newspapers or the exact dates of the articles are not given. One of the articles is in Finnish (p. 1) and the other is in Swedish (p. 2) .The scrapbook is preserved in the archive of the Finnish National Opera.

[61]   See Lampila, *Suomalaisen oopperan historia*, pp. 156–7.

[62]   19 February 1919. There is no mention of the name of the newspaper that published this article even though the date is included in the earliest scrapbook of the Finnish National Opera, p. 88.

[63]   Hako, *Finnish Opera*, p. 18.

[64]   Aino Ackté, *Aino Ackté: Elämänkaari kirjeiden valossa* (Helsinki, 2002), p. 331.

Ackté used nationalist discourse to justify her enterprise, and effectively so; the town leaders approved her plan within the same year. Although the festival did not run for more than five seasons (1912, 1913, 1914, 1916, and 1930) before it was suspended, those five seasons laid the foundation for subsequent national operatic activities in Finland – for the most part, only vernacular repertoire was to be programmed.[65] In this way, the three most prominent institutions for opera in Finland – the Finnish Opera Company, the Domestic Opera, and the Savonlinna Opera Festival – were founded on Fennoman ideology, which held that wider cultural and political goals should be intertwined with Finnish cultural activities.

The Legacy of Early Fennomans in the 1920s–1970s

As mentioned earlier, the Finnish Opera Company and the Domestic Opera had performed an international repertoire, such as Italian *bel canto* and French *grand opéra*, although in Finnish. Alongside this repertoire, however, vernacular works with Finnish topics were already being demanded regularly in the 1890s. The main priority during the Domestic Opera's early years, according to Finnish musicologist Erkki Salmenhaara, was 'to build up a national opera repertoire in the vernacular'.[66] As previously mentioned, the Savonlinna Opera Festival was the first to perform operas composed by Finnish composers and in Finnish; the first vernacular works at the Domestic Opera were performed in the 1910s.[67]

When exploring the corpus of Finnish opera as a whole, one sees an astonishing number of operas relating to myth, history, and rural life.[68] These themes were introduced first, as indicated earlier, in the Opera Competition call organized by the Finnish Literature Society,[69] and first applied by Oskar Merikanto in his three operas.[70] Other Finnish operas written during the first decades of the twentieth

---

[65]   In 1916, however, Gounod's *Faust* was in the programme. See <www.operafestival. fi/fi/footer/Historia/Teosluettelo> (accessed 7 June 2014).

[66]   Salmenhaara, *Suomen musiikin historia 2*, pp. 355–66.

[67]   These works were composed by Armas Launis, who used *The Seven Brothers*, one of the first novels written in Finnish, and the national epic *Kalevala* in his librettos. Thus, Launis also followed the quest of Finnishness.

[68]   Hautsalo and Karlsen, *Articulations of Identity*.

[69]   The musicologist Robert Canon has found that three categories of themes of the nationalist Russian composers in the nineteenth century are analogous to those in the Finnish opera; see Robert Cannon, *Opera: Cambridge Introductions to Music* (Cambridge, 2012), pp. 219. Although Russian influences, as such, were (are) repelled in Finland, one can say that the mechanism of nationalism in European cultures operated in more or less the same manner when developing a nation and national imagery. According to Krisztina Lajosi, in 'National Opera', pp. 227–46, this kind of thematic material can also be found in Central and Eastern European countries.

[70]   Hautsalo, 'Fennomania', pp. 40–41.

century were mainly based on the same topics.[71] The quest for Finnishness had been taken seriously.

The most crucial opera premiere of the Finnish Opera in the 1920s, as understood by contemporaries, was Leevi Madetoja's *Pohjalaisia* (*The Ostrobothnians*) in 1924. Madetoja's opera was based on the contradiction between the right-minded, independent peasants and an arbitrary Russian chief of police in the mid-nineteenth century. This opera was hailed as a 'national opera',[72] and to this day it is the most frequently performed Finnish opera.[73] At the time of the premiere it was understood as a glorious mark of identification: the Ostrobothnian peasant heroes become a signifier for all Finns.

In the 1920s, even though the shared enemy feared by all Finns, Russia, was no longer an explicit threat, the young nation still faced critical times, struggling against economical difficulties and deeply divided after the civil war. Thus, in some ways, Fennoman values had become outdated. In the 1930s, the Finnish National Opera programmed many foreign operettas, and during the following decades the bulk of the performed repertoire continued to include mainly international works. One could say, however, that some of the cultural values of the early Fennomans gradually spread and started to exert wider influence. These values were later articulated, for instance, in the programming of the Finnish National Opera and the festivals.

The Quest for Finnishness in the 1970s

After the Second World War, the Finnish Opera was converted into a foundation and, in 1956, renamed the Finnish National Opera. There had been decades of performances of operetta and international repertoire, but in 1970 it was strongly suggested once more that Finnish repertoire should be emphasized. The starting shot for the 'Finnish opera boom', according to Heiniö, was in 1975, when *Ratsumies* (*The Horseman*) by Finnish composer Aulis Sallinen was premiered at the Savonlinna Opera Festival.[74] The same autumn another key work, Joonas Kokkonen's new *The Last Temptations*, was performed at the Finnish National Opera. In these operas the archaic, glorious past of the Finns was articulated again, in the same way as in the 1920s. Heiniö, when launching the concept of the opera boom, mapped in the backdrops for the phenomenon during the 1960s and the early 1970s. According to him, they were: the founding of the orchestra for the National Opera; a first performance of Aarre Merikanto's nationalistic but musically radical

---

71   Hautsalo and Karlsen, *Articulations of Identity*.
72   See Koivisto, *Suurten tunteiden talo*, p. 48.
73   Juhani Koivisto, 'The First Hundred Years: History of the Finnish National Opera', <www.opera.fi/en/about_us/fno_history> (accessed 7 June 2014).
74   Concurrently, in the background, the Festival held a competition for opera composers in order to select a work to celebrate the 500th centenary of Olavinlinna Castle; Heiniö, *Karvalakki kansakunnan kaapin päällä*, pp. 25–9.

Juha, which was abandoned by the Domestic Opera in the 1920s; the revival of the Savonlinna Opera Festival; the new leadership at the Finnish National Opera; the foundation of regional operas; and the incorporation of Brechtian ideas in the direction of musical theatre.[75] The musical pluralism and new tonal style in the 1970s, after decades of modernism, was also welcomed.[76] An 'easy' music with domestic, rural topics was found tempting by audiences.[77]

The Finnish National Opera took the task of Finnishness seriously, commissioning and programming operas with national themes. The General Manager Juhani Raiskinen declared that he wished to produce opera 'for all people'.[78] During his leadership several operas with national themes were commissioned and performed. At the societal level in the 1960s and 1970s, Finland went through several big changes, including large-scale migration from the countryside to housing estates in the cities. In tandem with these societal changes, several summer festivals were founded in the countryside, becoming extremely popular. This phenomenon could be interpreted as an urban nostalgia towards the lost pastoral-like past in country.

The Savonlinna Opera Festival restarted in 1967, and when the international basso-star Martti Talvela became an artistic director in 1972, he shared Aino Ackté's vision for the festival 'to place Savonlinna on an artistic par with the great European festivals while presenting the world with Finnish opera at its very best'.[79] Although the Savonlinna Opera Festival has lately taken large-scale international works into its programme, it shows it values Finnish works by commissioning a new opera approximately every two years.[80] In 2012 there were in fact two first performances: one by a Finnish composer and another, an experimental work *par excellence*, by an international online group of participants supervised by a professional composer.[81] Another festival, the Ilmajoki Music Festival (founded in 1975 and still continuing), also concentrates on opera, and emphasizes national themes involving myth, history, or peasant life.

After incorporating down-to-earth topics, opera as an art form became popular in the 1970s among larger and more diverse audiences. According to Lampila, this

---

[75]   Ibid., pp. 16–23.
[76]   Ibid., p. 23.
[77]   Ibid., pp. 23–4.
[78]   See 'Kansan pelihimo koitui oopperan pelastukseksi', *Turun Sanomat*, 29 January 2011. Raiskinen worked at the National Opera during 1973–84. See 'Uuden Kansallisoopperan talo toimii', Kimmo Korhonen, *Classica*, 3 (1998), p. 4.
[79]   See <www.operafestival.fi/fi/footer/Historia> (accessed 7 June 2014).
[80]   All together there have been 12 first performances of a Finnish opera at the Savonlinna Opera Festivals. See <www.operafestival.fi/en/footer/History> (accessed 7 June 2014).
[81]   The first is *La Fenice* by Kimmo Hakola, see <www.operafestival.fi/en/footer/History> (accessed 7 June 2014). The second is *Free Will* (Opera by You); see Heidi Partti and Heidi Westerlund, 'Envisioning Collaborative Composing in Music Education: Learning and Negotiation of Meaning in operabyyou.com', *British Journal of Music Education* 30/2 (2013): pp. 207–22.

new, easier kind of programming practice enacted at the Finnish National Opera led to a substantial increase in 'the popularity of opera' and helped it to shed 'its elitist label'.[82] In the 1980s there were also continuous demands for vernacular opera as a contrast for the new modernist wave. It is noteworthy that during the 1980s there were fewer national themes in the opera than ever before. To improve the situation, the former General Manager of the Finnish National Opera, Jorma Hynninen, stated in the opening of the 1988–89 season: 'The composing of new and high-quality works must be constantly and vigorously supported. The great triumph of Finnish opera must not be allowed to break.'[83] By 'great triumph' he was referring to the international tours of the Finnish National Opera in the 1980s, justifying his demands for the vernacular repertoire by those tours and the opera boom in general.[84]

The Legacy of the Fennomans in the 1990s: A New Building for the Finnish National Opera

The biggest enterprise in the history of Finnish opera was the building of the new theatre house for the Finnish National Opera at the end of the 1980s and in the early 1990s. Since 1919, the company had performed in a temporary theatre with fewer than 800 seats and outdated technical stage equipment; there was no proper space for rehearsals, and only a few dressing rooms. The process of building the new opera house was a huge project that took over two decades – from the first plans in the 1970s to the inauguration in 1993 – and its construction continued despite the general economic depression in Finland in the early 1990s. Even though there were several critical comments in the media, mainly by anonymous writers submitting letters to newspapers,[85] the majority of the journalists wrote in a neutral or positive manner – and repeated Fennoman slogans. A headline in 1990, for example, declared: 'An Opera house is one of the basic elements of an enlightened nation'.[86] Assurance was also given in the speeches of the 'topping out ceremony'[87] in April 1990 that the new building would not be 'an institution for an elite'; instead, it would 'give something to every Finn'.[88] In 1993, some months

---

[82] Lampila, *Suomalaisen oopperan historia*, p. 707.

[83] *Itä-Savo*, 13 August 1988.

[84] See Heiniö, *Karvalakki kansakunnan kaapin päällä*, pp. 27–31.

[85] For some examples of 'letters to the editor', see T. Lehtinen, 'Jokainen joutuu maksamaan oopperatalosta', *Helsingin Sanomat*, 15 November 1987; Laihialainen veronmaksaja, 'Turha oopperatalo', *Ilkka*, 15 November 1988; and Oopperavoileipä, 'Oopperavouhotuksesta', *Alueuutiset/Helsinki Pohjoinen*, 27 August 1989.

[86] *Lapin Kansa*, 4 April 1990.

[87] 'Topping out' ('harjannostajaiset' in Finnish) is a ceremony for the workers held by the developer at a certain stage of a building project. It is a widely known convention in Finland and Scandinavia.

[88] See 'Oopperatalon hillitty charmi näkyy', *Uusi Suomi*, 4 April 1990.

before the inauguration festivities, it was repeated in several newspapers that 'the new opera house is the house of all the Finns',[89] and when the new building was introduced to the press in March 1993, the then General Manager of the National Opera, Walton Grönroos, announced: 'The [new] house is built by the Finns and also meant for the Finns'.[90] A journalist, Heikki Tuomi-Nikula, justified the building of the house by repeating another slogan: 'Finland has above all played and sung itself into a nation.[91]

The inauguration ceremony received glowing comments: the audience was enthusiastic and, according to the press, the top brass and the cultural elite of the nation were present.[92] The minister of culture, Tytti Isohookana-Asunmaa, declared in the inauguration ceremony that 'as an international art form, opera in Finland is also connected to the cultural practices elevated by the national spirit'.[93] Surprisingly, this statement not only relates to the ideas of the national philosopher Snellman, but also connects directly to Hegelian thought. The inauguration ceremony for the new building was notably solemn, with an appropriate cantata and speeches,[94] and it ended with the national hymn – as did the premiere of Merikanto's first opera in 1908 and the opening of the Domestic Opera in 1919. Before the ceremony, the Lutheran bishop of Helsinki blessed the building.[95] In this context it is also significant that the inauguration ceremony was broadcast nationwide.[96]

The new theatre house of the Finnish National Opera pushed operatic life in Finland onto a larger scale. For instance, a new regional opera was founded in 1993 in Vantaa. *Kaleva* wrote in May 1993, referring to the new company: 'The National Opera has moved. But opera in Finland does not live only in Helsinki.'[97] Particularly, it fired the enthusiasm of composers to write new works, whether commissioned or not. According my statistics, during the years 1990–99 there were 54 first performances of Finnish operas; during the years 2000–2009 there were 120, and the year 2000 represented a peak, with 17 first performances. It can even be suggested that the 'second phase of the opera boom' arose at the turn of the twentieth and twenty-first centuries. The first phase of the boom involved the condensation of nationalist topics in 1970s; the second phase stood for an expansion of heterogeneous themes and unconventional forums for performances.

---

[89] 'Suomalaisen oopperan kokoinen oopperatalo', *Kristityn vastuu*, 15 May 1993; 'Uusi oopperatalomme kaunis valkoinen ja ylevä', *Helsinki*, May 1993.

[90] *Uusimaa*, 23 March 1993.

[91] 'Sadan vuoden unelma', *Lapin Kansa*, 1 December 1993.

[92] See *Aamulehti, Etelä-Suomen Sanomat, Helsingin Sanomat, Itä-Savo, Keskisuomalainen*, 1 December 1993.

[93] *Aamulehti, Etelä-Suomen Sanomat, Helsingin Sanomat, Itä-Savo, Keskisuomalainen*, 1 December 1993; *Kalajokilaakso*, 2 December 1993.

[94] *Helsingin Sanomat, Keskisuomalainen, Aamulehti, Itä-Savo*, 1 December 1993.

[95] *Aamulehti*, 20 August 1993.

[96] *Kalajokilaakso*, 2 December 1993.

[97] 'Uusi oopperayhdistys', *Kaleva*, 29 May 1993.

Expanding the Operatic Genre into the Twenty-First Century

In 2011, the Finnish National Opera celebrated its hundredth anniversary. Compared to a hundred years before, the conditions were luxurious. There were many events in the festivities, such as the company's tours all over Finland, TV and radio broadcasts and live 'streamings' over the Internet, exhibitions, the publication of a history of the National Opera, workshops for children, a jubilee concert, and a winter ball outside the house, under the open sky. It was planned that two new Finnish operas were to be commissioned for the anniversary; the first was, surprisingly, targeted at teenage boys,[98] and the other was special in another sense: it was about the life of soprano Aino Ackté.[99] One of the wealthiest private supporters of arts in Finland, the Finnish Cultural Foundation, participated in the celebration with a considerable investment, and brought almost seven thousand pupils of upper-secondary schools from all over the country to see opera performances.[100] The informal character of visiting the performance was also emphasized in the press, with some headlines inviting the public to 'come and celebrate in jeans'.[101] Attempts were made to diversify the audience for opera more than ever. One columnist commented on a performance of *The Magic Flute*, for which children made up half of the audience: 'It is difficult to even think of anything more demotic than that event with its extremely colourful and informal clothing, checks glowing red, and shining eyes'.[102] For him, opera was at its best in this situation. Although the Finnish National Opera's field of activity has expanded since its birth, the jubilee concert was not at all 'modern' or up-to-date, and the concert ended not with the national hymn, but *Finlandia* by Sibelius.[103]

The history of Finnish opera can easily seem to parallel the history of the Finnish National Opera; yet, despite the fact that the Finnish National Opera is the only permanent opera stage in Finland, there are currently several other forums for opera. It is evident that the building of the new house for the National Opera not only further expanded the vernacular repertoire, but also generally encouraged new interests in operatic endeavours. Two examples illustrate these two effects. In 1975, the recognized starting point of the opera boom, the number of organizations producing operas was small. According to my statistics, there

---

[98]   This work was Robin Hood by Jukka Linkola; *Annual Report of the Finnish National Opera* (2011), p. 5.

[99]   This commission was cancelled because the libretto of the opera did not attain the necessary high level; see 'Ackté-oopperan libretto ei kelpaa Kansallisoopperalle', *Helsingin Sanomat*, 21 January 2011.

[100]   This was naturally organized in cooperation with the National Opera. See *Annual Report of the Finnish National Opera*, p. 9; and 'Tuhannet koululaiset oopperaan', *Ilkka*, 27 February 2011.

[101]   *Länsi-Suomi*, 8 January 2011.

[102]   Tuomas Rousi, 'Tuuli alkaa jo kääntyä', *Ilkka*, 19 January 2011.

[103]   'Suomalainen oopperalaulu näytti voimansa', *Helsingin Sanomat*, 31 January 2011.

were five Finnish opera premieres: one production by the Finnish National Opera, and four productions by an established festival, a regional opera, and the Sibelius Academy. It is also noteworthy that three out of these five works were based on Finnish peasant life and the mythological history of Finland. Thus, to give this as a percentage: 60 per cent of the operas composed in 1975 were based on national topics.

Comparing this with first performances in the year 2000, or in the peak year 2011, the operatic scene has expanded and, in addition to the established stages, there are multiple other stages and forums from the fell area in Lapland to Åland archipelago, from cowshed to mine, from ice stadium to castle forecourt, to malls and churches, and even to a municipal assembly hall. Productions have been organized by independent groups with minimal budgets, volunteers, students as a part of their postgraduate studies, and individual enthusiasts. New sub-genres have been created, the boundaries of the art form have been tested, and new media, such as mobile applications and the Internet with its many possibilities, have been exploited. There have been pop-up operas, online operas, mobile-phone operas, and improvised operas. Among other things, operas have focused on environmental issues, global politics, human trafficking, pornography, alienation, and homosexuality. Some of the most extraordinary works worthy of mention are *Kuntaliitosooppera* (*Municipal Merger Opera*, 2011), which was about the fight to prevent smaller municipalities from being merged into larger administrative units, and was performed in the municipal assembly hall in Lohja town, one of the municipalities in question; *Putkiremonttiooppera* (*Plumbing Opera*, 2011), which concerned the struggles against bad renovation companies repairing the plumbing in older buildings; and *Makuukamariooppera* (*Bed Chamber Opera*, 2010), which dealt with a one-night stand by two strangers. Even the most extreme experimental projects in the operatic field have been made possible, such as *Sulkapallo-ooppera* (*The Badminton Opera*, 2005), in which the naked players played one set in real time, and meatballs cooked from the blood of the artistic director during the performance were also served in real time to the audience. This has all been possible – despite the fact that opera in general has often been accused of being pointless, expensive, and elitist – because the genre has found an audience.

Despite their topical heterogeneity, operas with national topics accounted for 30 per cent of the output of 2011, as they did for 2013. When looking at the years between 1975 and 2013 as a whole, the percentage of national topics is even bigger: 40 per cent of the entire output of 294 works used national topics. Thus, national topics have not at any time disappeared, and the legacy of the Fennomans remains clearly visible in Finnish opera. Consequently, the Finnish opera boom can, in fact, be divided into three phases. In spite of the national features that have been preserved in the whole Finnish operatic output from 1975 to 2013, each phase has a characteristic of its own. During the second phase of the opera boom, starting in 2000, topics expanded and performances found their way into extraordinary locations. My observations lead me to identify a third phase commencing during the first decade of the twenty-first century with the new experimental techniques, media, and formats that have been brought into the genre. It is interesting to anticipate what the future might hold in store for a fourth phase.

Conclusion

In this chapter, I have examined Finnish opera through the lens of the late-nineteenth century Fennomania and demonstrated how the Fennomans constructed the Finnish identity through cultural activities such as opera. The Fennomans, a minority among the Finns, created an idea of the Finnish people, an imagined Finnishness that was supposed to be shared by all the Finns. They appealed to this imagined, shared Finnishness in discourse that justified and celebrated work for national operatic institutions and repertoire.

Political power and opera have always been connected and, as I have tried to demonstrate, they have been closely intertwined since the birth of Finnish vernacular opera. Even though the early Fennomania had already lost its significance before the 1930s, one can see that the legacy, an appreciation of the arts and especially opera that was inherited from the early Fennomans, is still evident. It is visible in operatic activities in general, in the overwhelming expansion into subjects referencing contemporary societal issues, and especially in the great number of new operas that have nationalist, mythical, and rural themes. Hence, against the analysis demonstrated here, it was not surprising to read an advance notice about the Ilmajoki Music Festival in June 2014, which announced that a new opera had been commissioned, the subject of which was Oskar Merikanto, the composer who created the first Finnish-language opera.

Bibliography

Abbate, Carolyn, 'Music: Drastic or Gnostic?' *Critical Inquiry* 30/3 (2004): pp. 505–36.

Abbing, Hans, *Why are Artists Poor? The Exceptional Economy of the Arts* (Amsterdam: Amsterdam University Press, 2002).

Ackermann, Peter, 'Musikgeschichte und historische Aufführungspraxis: Paul Hindemiths Versuch einer Rekonstruktion der ersten Aufführung von Monteverdis Orfeo', *Hindemith Jahrbuch* 23 (1994): pp. 61–81.

Ackté, Aino, *Aino Ackté: Elämänkaari kirjeiden valossa* (Helsinki: WSOY, 2002).

Adorno, Theodor, *In Search of Wagner*, trans. Rodney Livingstone (London: Verso, 1991).

Agid, Philippe and Jean-Claude Tarondeau, *L'Opéra de Paris: gouverner une grande institution culturelle* (Paris: Vuibert, 2006).

—, *The Management of Opera: An International Comparative Study* (Basingstoke: Palgrave Macmillan, 2010).

Albrecht, Elke, *Der finnische Opernboom: Hintergründe und Meilensteine der finnischen Operngeschichte* (Saarbrücken: VDM Verlag Dr Müller, 2009).

Anderson, Benedict, *Imagined Communities: Reflections on the Origin and Spread of Nationalism* [1983], revised edn (London: Verso, 2006), pp. 5–7.

Annual Report of the Finnish National Opera (2011).

Anon., 'Table Talk', *Musical Standard* 6 (1867): p. 156.

—, 'An Interview with Cerberus', *Musical World* 57 (1879): pp. 811–12.

—, 'What the Incorporated Society of Musicians Might Do', *Magazine of Music* 10 (1893): p. 17.

—, 'Trade Unionism Again', *Musical Standard* 5 (1896): p. 244.

—, 'Comments and Opinions', *Musical Standard* 12 (1899): p. 243.

—, 'Musicians Under Control', *Musical Herald* 831 (1917): p. 171.

—, 'Music To-Day', *Musical Mirror* 10 (1930): p. 309.

Aspelin-Haapkylä, Eliel, *Suomalaisen teatterin historia I–IV* (Helsinki: WSOY, 1906–1910).

Atkinson, Paul, *Everyday Arias* (Oxford: Altamira, 2006).

Auvinen, Tuomas, *Unmanageable Opera? The Artistic-Economic Dichotomy and its Manifestations in the Organisational Structures of Five Opera Organisations* (PhD diss., City University, London, 2000).

Balme, Christopher, 'Werktreue: Aufstieg und Niedergang eines fundamentalistischen Begriffs', in Ortrud Gutjahr (ed.), *Regietheater: Wie sich über Inszenierungen streiten lässt*, Theater und Universität im Gespräch 6 (Würzburg: Königshausen and Neumann, 2008), pp. 43–52.

Bargainnier, Earl F., 'W.S. Gilbert and American Musical Theatre', in Timothy E. Scheurer (ed.), *American Popular Music Vol. 1: The Nineteenth Century: Tin Pan Alley* (Bowling Green, OH: Bowling Green State University Popular Press, 1989), pp. 120–33.

Barker, Paul, *Composing for Voice* (London: Routledge, 2004).

Barrett, Estelle and Barbara Bolt, *Practice as Research: Approaches to Creative Arts Enquiry* (London: I.B. Tauris, 2007).

Bartholomäi, Paul, *Das Frankfurter Museumsorchester* (Frankfurt am Main: C.F. Peters, 2002).

Baumol, William and William Bowen, *Performing Arts, The Economic Dilemma: A Study of Problems Common to Theater, Opera, Music, and Dance* (New York: The Twentieth Century Fund, 1966)

BBC Four, *Castrato*, <www.bbc.co.uk/programmes/b0074spg>.

—, *The Voice*, <www.bbc.co.uk/programmes/b008s99k>.

Beckman, Katrin, *The Tromsø World Opera Project*, a documentary, 2011. <http://vimeo.com/35689367>.

Behne, Klaus-Ernst and Clemens Wöllner, 'Seeing or Hearing the Pianists? A Synopsis of an Early Audiovisual Perception Experiment and a Replication', *Musicae Scientiae* 15/3 (2011): pp. 324–42.

Bendikas, Kristina, *The Opera Theatre of Jean-Pierre Ponelle*, Studies in the History and Interpretation of Music 105 (Lewiston, NY: Edwin Mellen Press, 2004).

Bereson, Ruth, *The Operatic State: Cultural Policy and the Opera House* (London: Routledge, 2002).

Bevir, Mark, *A Theory of Governance* (Berkeley: University of California Press, 2013).

'Beyond black tie and bubbly: recuing opera from stereotypes', OBERTO Conference <http://obertobrookes.com/conference-2014>.

Bianconi, Lorenzo and Giorgio Pestelli, eds, *Opera Production and Its Resources. The History of Italian Opera, Part II: Systems*, trans. Lydia G. Cochrane (Chicago: University of Chicago Press, 1998).

Bien, Fabian, *Oper im Schaufenster: Die Berliner Opernbühnen in den 1950er Jahren als Orte nationaler kultureller Repräsentation* (Munich: Oldenbourg, 2011).

Bohlman, Philip V., *Focus: Music, Nationalism, and the Making of the New Europe* [2004], 2nd edn (New York: Routledge, 2011).

Born, Georgina, *Rationalizing Culture: IRCAM, Boulez, and the Institutionalization of the Musical Avant-garde* (Berkeley: University of California Press, 1995).

Bourdieu, Pierre, *Distinction: A Social Critique of the Judgement of Taste*, trans. Richard Nice (London: Routledge, 1984).

—, *Language and Symbolic Power* (Cambridge: Cambridge University Press, 2003).

Bovier-Lapierre, Bernhard, 'Die Opernhäuser im 20. Jahrhundert', in Arnold Jacobshagen and Frieder Reininghaus (eds), *Musik und Kulturbetriebe,*

Medien, Märkte, Institutionen. Handbuch der Musik im 20. Jahrhundert (Laaber: Laaber-Verlag, 2006), pp. 231–56.

Bowan, Kate, 'R.G. Collingwood, Historical Reenactment and the Early Music Revival', in Iain McCalman and Paul A. Pickering (eds), *Historical Reenactment: From Realism to the Affective Turn* (New York: Palgrave Macmillan, 2010), pp. 134–58.

Bradley, Christopher H.J., *Mrs. Thatcher's Cultural Policy: A Comparative Study of the Globalized Cultural Systems* (New York: Columbia University Press, 1998).

Briner, Andres, 'Paul Hindemiths "Versuch einer Rekonstruktion der ersten Aufführung des Orfeo"', in Attila Csampai and Dieter Holland (eds), *Claudio Monteverdi, Orfeo / Christoph Willibald Gluck, Orpheus und Eurydike: Texte, Materialien, Kommentare* (Reinbek: Rowohlt, 1988), pp. 162–4.

Broman-Kananen, Ulla-Brita, 'Staging a National Language: Opera in Christiania and Helsinki in 1870s', in Anne Sivuoja *et al.* (eds), *Opera on the Move in the Nordic Countries*, Docmus Research Publications 4 (Helsinki: Sibelius Academy, 2012), pp. 156–91.

—, 'Operasångerskan Emmy Achté som ikon för den finska-nationella rörelsen', *Musiikki* 3–4 (2013): pp. 5–28.

Brown, Ismene, 'Technology's New Fields of Dreams in Dance', <www.theartsdesk.com/dance/technologys-new-fields-dreams-dance>.

Brown, Mark and Mark Tran, 'ENO forced to tighten the reins while 58 groups lose all funding from Arts Council', *The Guardian*, 2 July 2014, p. 11.

Brug, Manuel, 'Richard Löwenherz: nur echt mir der Goldkante', *Die Welt*, 23 February 2014, <www.welt.de/kultur/buehne-konzert/article125120877/Richard-Loewenherz-nur-echt-mit-der-Goldkante.html>.

Busch, Max W., *Jean-Pierre Ponelle 1932–1988* (Berlin: Henschel Verlag, 2002).

Butt, John, *Playing with History: The Historical Approach to Musical Performance* (Cambridge: Cambridge University Press, 2002).

Cáceres, Juan-Pablo and Chris Chafe, 'JackTrip: Under the Hood of an Engine for Network Audio', *Journal of New Music Research* 39/3 (2010): pp. 183–7.

Canning, Hugh, 'It's not all roses', *The Sunday Times: Culture*, 25 May 2014, pp. 22–3.

—, 'Opera as West End show', *The Sunday Times: Culture*, 15 June 2014, p. 30.

Cannon, Robert, *Opera: Cambridge Introductions to Music* (Cambridge: Cambridge University Press, 2012).

Cardiff University, 'Opera at Cardiff: CIRO', <www.cardiff.ac.uk/music/research/ciro>.

Cerf, Steven, 'Wagner's *Ring* and German Culture', in John DiGaetani (ed.), *Inside The Ring: Essays on Wagner's Opera Cycle* (Jefferson, NC: McFarland, 2006), pp. 133–4.

Chafe, Chris, Juan-Pablo Cáceres and Michael Gurevich, 'Effect of Temporal Separation on the Synchronization in Rhythmic Performance', *Perception* 39 (2010): pp. 982–92, <https://ccrma.stanford.edu/~cc/pub/pdf/temporalSep.pdf>.

Charlet, Gerard, *L'Opéra de la Bastille: Genèse et Réalisation* (Paris: Electa Moniteur, 1989).

Chartrand, Harry Hillman and Claire Mc Caughey, 'The Arm's Length Principle and the Arts: An International Perspective – Past, Present, and Future', in Milton C. Cummings and J. Mark Davidson Schuster (eds), *Who's to Pay for the Arts? The International Search for Models of Support* (New York: American Council for the Arts Books, 1989).

Co-Opera Co, 'Co-Opera Co', <www.co-opera-co.org>.

Collingwood, Robin George, 'Outlines of a Philosophy of History', in Jan van der Dussen (ed.), *The Idea of History with Lectures 1926–1928* (Oxford: Oxford University Press, 1994), pp. 438–95.

Cone, Edward, *The Composer's Voice* (Berkeley: University of California Press, 1974).

Cooperstock, Jeremy, 'Multimodal Telepresence Systems', *IEEE Signal Processing Magazine* 77 (January 2011): pp. 77–86.

Cooperstock, Jeremy, J. Roston and W. Woszczyk, 'Ultra-Videoconferencing Work at McGill', SURA/ViDe 6th Annual Digital Video Workshop, Indiana University-Purdue University, Indianapolis, Indiana, 22–5 March 2004.

CreST Network, 'The Creative Speech Technology Network', <http://crestnetwork.org.uk>.

CROMT (Centre for Research in Opera and Music Theatre), 'Opera and the Media of the Future', <www.sussex.ac.uk/cromt/projects/operamediafuture>.

Crosten, William L., *French Grand Opera: An Art and a Business* [1948] (New York: Da Capo, 1972).

Culture Lab, 'Newcastle University: Culture Lab', <http://di.ncl.ac.uk>.

Dahlhaus, Carl, *Richard Wagner's Music Dramas*, trans. Mary Whittall (Cambridge: Cambridge University Press, 1979).

Dancedigital, 'Dance Digital', <www.dancedigital.org.uk/dancedigitaldev>.

'*Das Rheingold*: Richard Farnes and Michael Druiett in conversation with Ed Seckserson', <http://html5-player.libsyn.com/embed/episode/id/1615685/height/100/width/360/autoplay/no/autonext/no/direction/forward/thumbnail/yes#.Ucl5uJpwbIU≥>.

DCMS, 'Department for Culture Media and Sport: Creative Industries', <www.culture.gov.uk/what_we_do/Creative_industries>.

de Frantz, Monika, *Capital City Cultures: Reconstructing Contemporary Europe in Vienna and Berlin* (Brussels: Peter Lang, 2011).

De Montford University, Leicester, 'Digital Opera Research Group. DORG', <www.ioct.dmu.ac.uk/dorg/index.html>.

Deathridge, John, *Wagner Beyond Good and Evil* (Berkeley: University of California Press, 2008).

Deathridge, John and Carl Dahlhaus, *The New Grove Wagner* (London: Macmillan, 1984).

Desblache, Lucile, 'Music to My Ears, but Words to My Eyes? Text, Opera and Their Audiences', *Linguistica Antverpiensia* 6 (2007): pp. 155–75.

Devlin, Graham, *Beggars 'Opera* (London: Calouste Gulbenkian Foundation, 1992).

DHA Communications for the Musicians' Union, *The Working Musician* (Musicians' Union, 2012), <www.musiciansunion.org.uk/wp-content/uploads/2012/12/The-Working-Musician-report.pdf>.

DiGaetani, John, ed., *Inside The Ring: Essays on Wagner's Opera Cycle* (Jefferson, NC: McFarland, 2006).

Dixon, Steve, *Digital Performance: A History of New Media in Theater, Dance, Performance Art, and Installation* (Cambridge, MA: The MIT Press, 2007).

Dray, William, *History as Re-enactment: R.G. Collingwood's Idea of History* (Oxford: Clarendon Press, 1995).

Edwards, Alistair and Christopher Newell, 'Creative Speech Technology: Editorial Introduction to this Special Issue', *Logopedics, Phoniatrics, Vocology* 38/3 (2013): 91–5.

Eggert, Mara and Hans-Klaus Jungheinrich, *Die Oper Frankfurt: Durchbrüche* (Berlin: Ullstein Quadriga Verlag, 1991).

EPSRC, 'Sandpits', <www.epsrc.ac.uk/funding/howtoapply/routes/network/ideas/whatisasandpit>.

ERC, 'European Research Council', <http://erc.europa.eu>.

European Commission, 'Research and Innovation', <http://ec.europa.eu/research/index.cfm>.

Everett, William A. 'Opera and National Identity in Nineteenth-Century Croatian and Czech Lands', *International Review of the Aesthetics and Sociology of Music* 35/1 (2004): pp. 63–9.

Ewans, Michael, *Wagner and Aeschylus: The 'Ring' and the 'Oresteia'* (London: Faber and Faber, 1982).

Fabian, Imre, *Imre Fabian im Gespräch mit Jean-Pierre Ponelle* (Zurich, Schwäbisch Hall: Orell Füssli, 1983).

Ferraro Jr., Mario, *Contemporary Opera in Britain, 1970–2010*, PhD diss. (City University, London 2011).

Fewster, Derek, *Nationalism and the Construction of Early Finnish History* (Saarbrücken: VDM Verlag Dr Müller, 2009).

Finkle, David. 'Elaine Stritch in the Stephen Sondheim Stretch', <http://www.huffingtonpost.com/david-finkle/elaine-stritch-in-the-ste_b_416508.html>.

Fischer, Christine, 'Vorwort', in Christine Fischer (ed.), *Oper als 'Gesamtkunstwerk': Zum Verhältnis der Künste im barocken Musiktheater*, Basler Jahrbuch für historische Musikpraxis 33 (Winterthur: Amadeus, 2009), pp. vii–xix.

Fischer, Christine, Johannes Keller and Francesco Pedrini, 'Wissenschaft und Aufführung: Zur Inszenierungsarbeit an *Penelope la casta* (Alessandro Scarlatti / Matteo Noris, Napoli 1696)', in Christine Fischer (ed.), *Oper als 'Gesamtkunstwerk': Zum Verhältnis der Künste im barocken Musiktheater*, Basler Jahrbuch für historische Musikpraxis 33 (Winterthur: Amadeus, 2012), pp. 267–87.

Fischer-Lichte, Erika, 'Die Wiederholung als Ereignis: Reenactment als Aneignung von Geschichte', in Jens Roselt and Ulf Otto (eds), *Theater als*

Zeitmaschine: Zur performativen Praxis des Reenactments. Theater- und kulturwissenschaftliche Perspektiven, Theater 45 (Bielefeld: Transcript Verlag, 2012), pp. 13–52.

Flierl, Thomas, *Perspektiven durch Kultur* (25 June 2003) <www.kultur-in-berlin. com/archiv/reden/thomas_flierl.pdf>.

Floyd, Jerry, 'Going for the Gold', wagneropera.net <http://www.wagneropera. net/Articles/Metropolitan-Opera-Rheingold.htm>.

Fortune, Nigel, 'The Rediscovery of Orfeo', in John Whenham (ed.), *Claudio Monteverdi: Orfeo* (Cambridge: Cambridge University Press, 1986), pp. 78–118.

Frey, Ulrich, 'Was wird gespielt? Eine Bestandsaufnahme', in Isolde Schmid-Reiter and Dominique Meyer (eds), *Oper im 17. und 18. Jahrhundert: L'Europe Baroque*, Schriften der Europäischen Musiktheater-Akademie (Regensburg: ConBrio, 2010), pp. 19–42.

Fricke, George R., James Andrew Deaville, and Evan Baker (eds), *Wagner in Rehearsal 1875–1876: The Diaries of Richard Fricke*, No. 7 (New York: Pendragon Press, 1998).

Galloway, Kit and Sherrie Rabinowitz, 'Hole-In-Space, 1980', *The Electronic Café*. <www.ecafe.com/getty/table.html>.

Genschel, Philipp and Bernhard Zangl, *Die Zerfaserung von Staatlichkeit und die Zentralität des Staates*. TranState Working Papers No. 62 (Bremen: University of Bremen, 2007).

—, *Transformations of the State: From Monopolist to Manager of Political Authority*. TranState Working Papers No. 76 (Bremen: University of Bremen, 2008).

Gerhard, Anselm, *Die Verstädterung der Oper: Paris und das Musiktheater des 19. Jahrhunderts* (Stuttgart: Carl Ernst Poeschel Verlag, 1992); English trans. Mary Whittall, *The Urbanization of Opera* (Chicago: University of Chicago Press, 1998).

—, 'Was ist Werktreue? Ein Phantombegriff und die Sehnsucht nach "Authentischem"', in Gerhard Brunner and Sarah Zalfen (eds), *Werktreue: Was ist Werk, was Treue?*, Die Gesellschaft der Oper: Musikkultur europäischer Metropolen im 19. und 20. Jahrhundert 8 (Berlin: Oldenbourg, 2011), pp. 17–23.

Glixon, Beth L. and Jonathan E. Glixon, *Inventing the Business of Opera: The Impresario and His World in Seventeenth-Century Venice* (New York: Oxford University Press, 2006).

Goehr, Lydia, *The Imaginary Museum of Musical Works: An Essay in the Philosophy of Music* (Oxford: Clarendon Press, 1992).

Goodall, Howard, *Howard Goodall's Story of Music: The Age of Tragedy*, BBC 2, 16 Feb. 2013.

Goss, Glenda Dawn, *Sibelius: A Composer's Life and the Awakening of Finland* (Chicago: University of Chicago Press, 2009).

Gossett, Philip, 'From Score to Stage', in *Divas & Scholars: Performing Italian Opera* (Chicago: University of Chicago Press, 2006), 443–86.

Grange, Henry-Louis de la, *Mahler*, 4 vols. (London: Victor Gollancz, 1974).

Green, David. 'Beyond Participatory Video: Supporting User-Generated Video Content Production through Documentary', unpublished article, Newcastle University, Newcastle upon Tyne, UK.

H2020 Work programme 2 FET <http://ec.europa.eu/research/participants/data/ ref/h2020/wp/2014_2015/main/h2020-wp1415-fet_en.pdf>.

Hagen, Oskar, 'Die Bearbeitung der Händelschen Rodelinde und ihre Uraufführung', *Zeitschrift für Musikwissenschaft* 2 (1920): pp. 725–32.

Haider, Hilde, 'Regietheater', in Isolde Schmid-Reiter (ed.), *Opera Staging: Erzählweisen*, Schriften der europäischen Musiktheater Akademie 9 (Regensburg: ConBrio, 2014), pp. 35–62.

Hako, Pekka. *The Finnish Opera*, trans. Jaakko Mäntyjärvi (Helsinki: Finnish Music Information Centre, 2002).

Handley, Ellenor and Kinna, Martin, *Royal Opera House Covent Garden: A History from 1732* (West Wickham: Fourlance Books, 1978).

Haskell, Harry, *The Early Music Revival: A History* (London: Thames and Hudson, 1988).

Hautsalo, Liisamaija, 'The New Finnish Opera Boom', *Finnish Music Quarterly* 1 (2000): pp. 39–42.

—, 'Vuosi 2000 tuo Suomeen oopperabuumin', *Keskisuomalainen* (9 February 2000): p. 16.

—, 'A Century of Opera', *Finnish Music Quarterly* 2 (2012): pp. 32–.

—, 'Toiset oopperassa *Kaarle-kuninkaan metsästys*: Postkolonialistinen analyysi markkinakohtauksen juutalaisrepresentaatiosta', *Musiikki* 3–4 (2012): pp. 48–87.

—, 'Fennomania, Suomi-neito ja Oskar Merikannon oopperoiden naishahmot', *Musiikki* 3–4 (2013): pp. 29–69.

Hautsalo, Liisamaija and Sidsel Karlsen, *Articulations of Identity in Finnish Opera* (forthcoming).

Haynes, Bruce, *The End of Early Music: A Period Performer's History of Music for the Twenty-First Century* (New York: Oxford University Press, 2007).

Heikinheimo, Seppo, *Oskar Merikanto ja hänen aikansa* (Helsinki: Otava, 1995).

Heiniö, Mikko, *Karvalakki kansakunnan kaapin päällä: kansalliset attribuutit Joonas Kokkosen ja Aulis Sallisen julkisuuskuvassa* (Helsinki: WSOY, 1999).

Helms, Dietrich, 'Westöstlicher Händel: Die "Opernrenaissance" in den beiden deutschen Staaten', in Ulrich Tadday (ed.), *Händel unter Deutschen*, Musik-Konzepte, N.F. 131 (Munich: Text + Kritik, 2006), pp. 87–106.

Hickling, Alfred, 'Opera North tackles Wagner's Ring cycle' *The Guardian*, 12 Jun. 2012, <http://www.theguardian.com/music/2012/jun/12/wagner-ring-cycle-opera-north>.

Higgins, Charlotte, 'Arts Council considers opera shakeup', *The Guardian*, 16 January 2013 <www.theguardian.com/music/2013/jan/16/arts-council-opera-eno-loss>.

'History of Spatially Distributed Performance: aka Milestones in Real-Time Networked Media'. <http://srl.mcgill.ca/projects/rtnm/history.html>.

HM Revenue and Customs, Staff Manuals ESM4140 and 4121, <www.hmrc.gov. uk/manuals/esmmanual/ESM4140.htm> and <www.hmrc.gov.uk/manuals/ esmmanual/ESM4121.htm>

Huttunen, Matti, 'The National Composer and the Idea of Finnishness: Sibelius and the Formation of Finnish Musical Style', in Daniel M. Grimley (ed.), *The Cambridge Companion to Sibelius* (Cambridge: Cambridge University Press, 2004), pp. 7–21.

'Introduction to *Das Rheingold*', BBC Radio 3, 22 July 2013.

Jack Documentation: 'The Jack Audio Connection Kit', <http://jackaudio.org/ documentation>.

Jacobs, René, speaking with Silke Leopold, *Ich will Musik neu erzählen* (Kassel: Bärenreiter; Leipzig: Henschel, 2013).

Jauss, Hans Robert, *Toward an Aesthetic of Reception*, trans. Timothy Bahti (Minneapolis: University of Minnesota Press, 1982).

Jays, David, 'Will it be unmissable?' *The Sunday Times: Culture*, 11 May 2014, pp. 6–7.

Jourdaa, Fréderique, *À l'opéra aujourd'hui: de Garnier à Bastille* (Paris: Hachette Littératures, 2004).

Jussila, Osmo, Seppo Hentilä, and Jukka Nevakivi (eds), *From Grand Duchy to a Modern State*, trans. David and Eva Arter (London: Hurst, 1999).

Karkama, Pertti, *Kansakunnan asialla: Elias Lönnrot ja ajan aatteet* (Helsinki: WSOY, 2001)

Kenyon, Nicholas (ed.), *Authenticity and Early Music* [1988] (New York: Oxford University Press, 2002).

Ketomäki, Hannele, *Oskar Merikannon kansalliset aatteet: Merikannon musiikkijuhlatoiminta sekä ooppera Pohjan neiti ja kuorolaulut venäläistämiskauden laulu- ja soittojuhlien ohjelmassa* (PhD diss., Sibelius Academy, Helsinki, 2012).

King's College London. 'The Opera Group', <http://www.kcl.ac.uk/artshums/ depts/music/research/operagroup.aspx>.

Kivy, Peter, *Authenticities: Philosophical Reflections on Musical Performance* (Ithaca, NY: Cornell University Press, 1995).

Knuuttila, Seppo, 'Paikan synty suomalaisen ilmiönä', in Pertti Alasuutari and Petri Ruuska (eds), *Elävänä Euroopassa: Muuttuva suomalainen identiteetti* (Tampere: Vastapaino, 1998).

Koivisto, Juhani, 'The First Hundred Years: History of the Finnish National Opera', <www.opera.fi/en/about_us/fno_history>.

Koivisto, Juhani, *Kansa, ooppera ja Kaarle-kuningas: Kun Suomi loi oopperaa ja ooppera Suomea* (Helsinki: Kirja kerrallaan, 2006).

Koivisto, Juhani, *Suurten tunteiden talo: Kohtauksia Kansallisoopperan vuosisadalta* (Helsinki: WSOY, 2011).Korhonen, Kimmo, 'Uuden Kansallisoopperan talo toimii', *Classica*, 3 (1998): pp. 4–5.

Lajosi, Krisztina, 'National Opera and Nineteenth-Century Nation Building in East-Central Europe', in Lotte Eilskov Jensen, Joseph Theodoor Leerssen, and Marita Mathijsen (eds), *Free Access to the Past: Romanticism, Cultural Heritage and the Nation* (Leiden: Brill, 2010), pp. 227–46.

Lampila, Hannu-Ilari, *Suomalaisen oopperan historia* (Helsinki: WSOY, 1997).

Lavery, Jason, *History of Finland* (Westport, CT: Greenwood Press, 2006).

le Huray, Peter and James Day, *Music and Aesthetics in the Eighteenth and Early Nineteenth Centuries*, abridged edn (Cambridge: Cambridge University Press, 1988).

Lebrecht, Norman, *Covent Garden: The Untold Story* (London: Simon and Schuster, 2000).

Leeds Grand Theatre, Herr Ernst Denhof's Operatic Festival Performance: *The Ring of the Nibelung*, theatre programme, 15 Mar. 1911.

Leong, Tuck Wah and Peter Wright. 'Proceedings of the 25th Australian Computer-Human Interaction Conference on Augmentation, Application, Innovation, Collaboration – OzCHI '13; Understanding "Tingle" in Opera Performances'. 2013, <http://vbn.aau.dk/files/173308065/OzCHI_2013_Proceedings_preface_.pdf>.

Lessing, Doris, *The Marriages Between Zones Three, Four and Five* (London: Jonathan Cape, 1980).

Levin, David, 'Reading a Staging/Staging a Reading', *Cambridge Opera Journal*, 9 (1997): 47–71.

—, *Unsettling Opera: Staging Mozart, Verdi, Wagner, and Zemlinsky* (Chicago: University of Chicago Press, 2008).

Linstrum, Derek, 'Broderick, Cuthbert', *Grove Art Online*, <www.oxfordartonline.com>.

Lorentz, Iny [Iny Klocke, Elmar Wohlrath], *Die Wanderhure* (Munich: Knaur, 2004).

McClintock, Pamela, 'Met Opera Standoff Threatens $60 Million Theater Business', *The Hollywood Reporter*, 15 August 2014, <www.hollywoodreporter.com/news/met-opera-standoff-threatens-60–723614>.

McGilchrist, Iain, *The Master and his Emissary* (New Haven, CT: Yale University Press, 2010).

Machover, Tod. 'MIT Media Lab: Opera of the Future', <https://www.media.mit.edu/research/groups/opera-future>.

McKechnie, Kara, 'Opera North: Knitting Together History from Ephemera' (unpublished), talk given 17 May 2013, University of Leeds.

—, *Opera North: Historical and Dramaturgical Perspectives on Opera Studies* (Bingley: Emerald Group Publishing, 2014).

McLuhan, Marshall, *The Gutenberg Galaxy* (Toronto: University of Toronto Press, 1962).

Martorella, Rosanne, *The Sociology of Opera* (South Hadley, MA: J.F. Bergin, 1982).

Marvin, Carolyn, *When Old Technologies Were New: Thinking about Electric Communication in the Late Nineteenth Century* (New York: Oxford University Press, 1988).

The Metropolitan Opera, *'Met Opera Ring Cycles'*, <www.metoperafamily.org/
metopera/season/subscriptions/new/reserve.aspx?PackageID=9988>.

Midgley, Mary, *Heart and Mind* (London: Routledge, 2003).

Milestone, Rachel, *'A New Impetus to the Love of Music': The Role of the Town
Hall in Nineteenth Century English Musical Culture* (PhD diss., University of
Leeds, 2009).

Mogridge, Geoffrey, 'Towards a National Opera Company for the North, 1970s',
Discovering Leeds <www.leodis.net/discovery/discovery.asp?pageno=&page
=20031110_356182278&topic=20031110_154781521&subsection=2003111
0_679348171&subsubsection=20031110_889217556>.

Mösch, Stephen, 'Störung, Verstörung, Zerstörung: Regietheater als
Rezeptionsproblem', in Robert Sollich (ed.), *Angst vor der Zerstörung: Der
Meister Künste zwischen Archiv und Erneuerung*, Theater der Zeit 52 (2008):
pp. 216–32.

Mulder, Catherine P., *Unions and Class Transformation: The Case of the Broadway
Musicians* (New York: Routledge, 2009).

Müller, Kai Hinrich, *Wiederentdeckung und Protest: Alte Musik im kulturellen
Gedächtnis*, Musik – Kultur – Geschichte 1 (Würzburg: Verlag Königshausen
and Neumann, 2013).

Müller, Sven Oliver and Toelle, Jutta (eds), *Bühnen der Politik: Die Oper
in europäischen Gesellschaften im 19. und 20. Jahrhundert* (Munich:
Oldenbourg, 2008).

Müntzenberger, Isabelle, '"Händel-Renaissance(n)": Aspekte der Händel-
Rezeption der 1920er Jahre und der Zeit des Nationalsozialismus', in Ulrich
Tadday (ed.), *Händel unter Deutschen*, Musik-Konzepte, N.F. 131 (Munich:
Text + Kritik, 2006), pp. 67–86.

Napier, John, *Hands* (New York: Knopf Doubleday Publishing, 1980).

Naugle, Lisa M., 'Distributed Choreography: A Video-Conferencing Environment',
PAJ: A Journal of Performance and Art 24/2 (2002): pp. 56–62.

Nelson, Fraser, 'Our tantric Chancellor doesn't realise he's winning the debate',
The Telegraph, 28 June 2013.

Newell, Christopher and Paul Barker, 'Can a Computer-Generated Voice Be
Sincere? A Case Study Combining Music and Synthetic Speech', *Logopedics
Phoniatrics Vocology (Informa Healthcare)* 38/3–4 (2013): pp. 126–34.

Newes, Virginia, 'Baroque Re-enactment at its very best: BEMF's "Acis and
Galatea"', *The Boston Musical Intelligencer: A virtual journal and essential
blog of the classical music scene in greater Boston*, 29 November 2009 <www.
classical-scene.com/2009/11/29/baroque-re-enactment-at-its-very-best-
bemfs-"acis-and-galatea">.

Newman, Ernest, *Wagner Nights* (London: Bodley Head, 1988).

Ntuli, Pitika, *Storms of the Heart: An Anthology of Black Arts and Culture*, ed.
K. Owusu (London: Comedia, 1988).

O'Dea, Jane, *Virtue or Virtuosity? Explorations in the Ethics of Musical
Performance* (Westport, CT: Praeger, 2000).

Oliveros, Pauline, *et al.*, 'Telematic Music: Six Perspectives', *Leonardo Music Journal* 19 (2009): pp. 95–6. <https://ccrma.stanford.edu/groups/soundwire/publications/papers/chafeLMJ19-2009.pdf>.

Olmos, Adriana, *et al.*, 'Exploring the Role of Latency and Orchestra Placement on the Networked Performance of a Distributed Opera', 12th Annual International Workshop on Presence, Los Angeles, 2009, <http://astro.temple.edu/~tuc16417/papers/Olmos_et_al.pdf>.

'Opera North brings Wagner's *Das Rheingold* to Leeds Town Hall', *Leeds International Concert Season*, <http://leedsconcertseason.com/MODULES/NEWS/LICS_NEWSmoduleASP/NEWSMOD_newsitem.asp?type=&itemid=6267>.

Opera North, 'DARE Sandpits', <www.dareyou.org.uk/projects/lectures-conferences-debates-and-discussions/dare-think-tank>.

Opera North, '*Das Rheingold*: The Journey Begins', <www.youtube.com/watch?v=oKcPlQeAW7E>.

Opera North, 'Richard Farnes introduces *Das Rheingold*', <www.youtube.com/watch?v=Dqj9zZ3JNlg>.

Opera North, '*Siegfried* teaser trailer', <www.operanorth.co.uk/productions/siegfried#video_introduction>.

Opera North, '*Siegfried*, the vocal and mental challenges of Wotan', <www.operanorth.co.uk/productions/Siegfried>.

Opera North, Howard Assembly Room events leaflet, Spring 2011.

Opera North and the University of Leeds, 'DARE', <www.dareyou.org.uk>.

Özkirimli, Umut, *Theories of Nationalism: A Critical Introduction*, foreword by Fred Halliday (Basingstoke: Palgrave Macmillan, 2000).

Paavolainen, Pentti, 'Two Operas or One – or None', in Anne Sivuoja *et al.* (eds), *Opera on the Move in the Nordic Countries*, Docmus Research Publications 4 (Helsinki: Sibelius Academy, 2012), pp. 125–55.

Partti, Heidi and Heidi Westerlund, 'Envisioning Collaborative Composing in Music Education: Learning and Negotiation of Meaning in operabyyou.com', *British Journal of Music Education* 30/2 (2013): pp. 207–22.

Patureau, Frédérique, 'L'Opéra de Paris ou les ambiguïtés de l'enjeu culturel', in Raymonde Moulin (ed.), *Sociologie de l'art: colloque international, Marseille 13.–14. 6. 1985* (Paris: La Documentation Française, 1986), pp. 83–93.

Perkin, Harold, *The Origins of Modern English Society 1780–1880* (London: Routledge and Kegan Paul, 1969).

'Point 25: An Event within the Connected Performance Spaces Project', 18 June 2004. First report, September 2004 <www.r1.kth.se/point25/point25.pdf>.

Pountney, David, Letter to *The Spectator*, 13 February 1999.

—, 'The Future Of Opera', speech given on Saturday, 13 February 2000, at The Royal Over-Seas League, London, UK. Available on Opernhaus Zürich website <www.rodoni.ch/OPERNHAUS/novembre/intervistapountney.html>.

—, Response to Kate Molleson's article for *The Guardian*, <www.wno.org.uk/news/response-david-pountney>.

Preston, Katherine K., *Opera on the Road: Traveling Opera Troupes in the United States, 1825–60* (Urbana-Champaign: University of Illinois Press, 1993).

Prout, Ebenezer, 'The Amalgamated Musicians' Union', *Monthly Music Record* 23 (1893): pp. 145–7.

Radio 3 Live in Concert, Wagner's *Die Walküre*, BBC Radio 3, 20 June 2012.

—, *Siegfried*, BBC Radio 3, 19 June 2013.

Ranan, David, *In Search of a Magic Flute: The Public Funding of Opera* (Bern: Peter Lang, 2003).

Rätzer, Manfred, *Szenische Aufführungen von Werken Georg Friedrich Händels vom 18. bis 20. Jahrhundert: Eine Dokumentation* (Halle an der Saale: Händel-Haus, 2000).

Rau, Milo (ed.), *Die letzten Tage der Ceaucescus: Materialien, Dokumente, Theorie* (Berlin: Verbrecher-Verlag, 2010).

—, *Hate Radio: Materialien, Dokumente, Theorie* (Berlin: Verbrecher-Verlag, 2014).

RCUK, 'Research Councils UK: Pathways to Impact', <www.rcuk.ac.uk/ke/ impacts>.

RCUK, 'What Do Research Councils Mean by "Impact"?' <www.rcuk.ac.uk/ke/ impacts/meanbyimpact>.

Rebelo, Pedro, 'Dramaturgy in the Network', *Contemporary Music Review* 28/4–5 (2009): pp. 387–93.

Reidemeister, Peter, *Historische Aufführungspraxis: Eine Einführung* (Darmstadt: Wissenschaftliche Buchgesellschaft, 1988).

Research Excellence Framework, 'Main Panel D Criteria', <www.ref.ac.uk/ media/ref/content/pub/panelcriteriaandworkingmethods/01_12_2D.pdf>.

Ridley, Frederick F., 'Tradition, Change and Crisis in Great Britain', in Milton C. Cumming and Richard S. Katz (eds), *The Patron State: Government and the Art in Europe, North America, and Japan* (New York: Oxford University Press, 1987).

Risi, Clemens, 'Shedding Light on the Audience: Hans Neuenfels & Peter Konwitschny Stage Verdi (and Verdians)', *Cambridge Opera Journal* 14 (2002): pp. 201–10.

Roberts, Caroline, 'Is Stephen Hawking's Voice Music to the Ears?', *The Guardian*, 16 January, 2012, <www.theguardian.com/education/2012/jan/16/ research-operatic-singers-speech-generating-technology>.

Robinson, Ken, *Out of Our Minds: Learning to Be Creative* (Chichester: Capstone, 2001).

Rodenburg, Patsy, *The Need for Words* (London: Methuen Drama, Bloomsbury Publishing, 1993).

Rohr, Deborah, *The Careers of British Musicians, 1750–1850: A Profession of Artisans* (Cambridge: Cambridge University Press, 2001).

Roselt, Jens and Ulf Otto, 'Nicht hier, nicht jetzt: Einleitung', in Jens Roselt and Ulf Otto (eds), *Theater als Zeitmaschine: Zur performativen Praxis des Reenactments. Theater- und kulturwissenschaftliche Perspektiven*, Theater 45 (Bielefeld: Transcript, 2012), pp. 7–12.

Rosselli, John, *The Opera Industry in Italy from Cimarosa to Verdi: The Role of the Impresario* (Cambridge: Cambridge University Press, 1984).

The Royal Opera House Covent Garden, 'The Science of Opera', YouTube, <www. youtube.com/watch?v=0tvNbwZzuaM>.

'Royal Opera House prices hit new high for Ring cycle', *Intermezzo*, <http://intermezzo.typepad.com/intermezzo/2011/09/roh-ring-cycle-prices-revealed. html>.

Salmenhaara, Erkki, *Suomen musiikin historia 2* (Helsinki: WSOY, 1996).

Schmidt, Michael, '"Possente spirto" Monteverdi, Hindemith und die Historische Interpretationspraxis', in Hans-Martin Linde and Regula Rapp (eds), *Provokation und Tradition: Erfahrungen mit der Alten Musik* (Stuttgart: J.B. Metzler, 2000), pp. 365–76.

Schulze, Gerhard, *Die Erlebnisgesellschaft: Kultursoziologie der Gegenwart* (Frankfurt: Campus, 2005).

Schümer, Dirk, 'Das muss man gesehen haben', *Frankfurter Allgemeine Zeitung*, 5 March 2014, <www.faz.net/aktuell/feuilleton/buehne-und-konzert/karlsruher-haendel-festspiele-12831618.html>.

Sermon, Paul, 'Telematic Dreaming: Statement', and linked pages. <http://creativetechnology.salford.ac.uk/paulsermon/dream>.

Service, Tom, 'Barrie Kosky: "When I first saw The Magic Flute, I didn't get it and I didn't like it"', *The Guardian*, 13 July 2015. < http://www.theguardian. com/music/2015/jul/13/barrie-kosky-the-magic-flute-i-was-like-euggh>.

Silsbury, Elizabeth, *State of Opera: An Intimate New History of the State Opera of South Australia 1957–2000* (Adelaide: Wakefield Press, 2001).

Sivuoja, Anne, *et al.* (eds), *Opera on the Move in the Nordic Countries*, Docmus Research Publications 4 (Helsinki: Sibelius Academy, 2012).

Southgate, T.L., 'Questionable Orchestral Associations', *Musical News* 5 (1893): pp. 395–6.

—, 'The First Step in Musical Trades-Unionism', *Musical News* 6 (1894): p. 57.

Spivak, Gayatri Chakravorty, 'Subaltern Studies: Deconstructing Historiography', in Donna Landry and Gerald McLean (eds), *Spivak Reader: Selected Works of Gayatri Chakravorty Spivak* (New York: Routledge, 1985), pp. 203–35.

Spohr, Matthias, 'Barockoper zwischen Repertoire- und Stagionesystem: Zu den unterschiedlichen Traditionen im deutschen und romanischen Sprachgebiet', in Isolde Schmid-Reiter and Dominique Meyer (eds), *Oper im 17. und 18. Jahrhundert: L'Europe Baroque*, Schriften der Europäischen Musiktheater-Akademie (Regensburg: ConBrio, 2010), pp. 43–64.

Stanley, Glenn, '*Parsifal*: Redemption and *Kunstreligion*', in Thomas S. Grey (ed.), *The Cambridge Companion to Wagner* (Cambridge: Cambridge University Press, 2008), pp. 151–75.

Steglich, Rudolf, 'Händels Oper Rodelinde und ihre neue Göttinger Bühnenfassung', *Zeitschrift für Musikwissenschaft* 3 (1920/21): pp. 518–34.

—, 'Die neue Händel-Opernbewegung', *Händel-Jahrbuch* 1 (1928): pp. 71–158.

Storey, John, 'The Social Life of Opera', *European Journal of Cultural Studies* 6/1 (2003): pp. 5–35.

Suutela, Hanna, *Impyet: Näyttelijättäret Suomalaisen Teatterin palveluksessa* (Helsinki: Like, 2005).

——, 'An Instrument for Changing Nationalist Strategies: The Finnish Theatre Company', in Helka Mäkinen, S.E. Wilmer and W.B. Worthen (eds), *Theatre, History, and National Identity* (Helsinki: Helsinki University Press, 2006).

Taruskin, Richard, 'The Authenticity Movement Can Become a Positivistic Purgatory, Literalistic and Dehumanizing', *Early Music* 12/1 (1984): pp. 3–12.

——, 'Nationalism', *Oxford Music Online*, <www.oxfordmusiconline.com>.

——, *Text and Act: Essays on Music and Performance* (New York: Oxford University Press, 1995).

Thompson, Abbey E., *Revival, Revision, Rebirth: Handel Opera in Germany, 1920–1930* (PhD diss., Chapel Hill: University of North Carolina, 2006).

Till, Nicholas (ed.), *The Cambridge Companion to Opera Studies* (Cambridge: Cambridge University Press, 2012).

Tiusanen, Timo, *Teatterimme hahmottuu: Näyttämötaiteemme kehitystie kansanrunoudesta itsenäisyyden ajan alkuun* (Helsinki: Kirjayhtymä, 1969).

Tommila, Päiviö, *Herää Suomi: Suomalaisuusliikkeen historia* (Kuopio: Kustannuskiila, 1989).

Tuck Wah Leong and Peter Wright, 'Proceedings of the 25th Australian Computer-Human Interaction Conference on Augmentation, Application, Innovation, Collaboration – OzCHI '13; Understanding "Tingle" in Opera Performances', 2013, <http://vbn.aau.dk/files/173308065/OzCHI_2013_Proceedings_preface_.pdf>.

Tuomi-Nikula, Heikki, 'Sadan vuoden unelma', *Lapin Kansa* (1 December 1993).

Umathum, Sandra, 'Seven Easy Pieces, oder von der Kunst, die Geschichte der Performance Art zu schreiben', in Jens Roselt and Ulf Otto (eds), *Theater als Zeitmaschine: Zur performativen Praxis des Reenactments. Theater- und kulturwissenschaftliche Perspektiven*, Theater 45 (Bielefeld: Transcript, 2012), pp. 101–24.

University of Sussex. 'The Centre for Research in Opera and Music Theatre: CROMT', <www.sussex.ac.uk/cromt>.

Vares, Vesa, *Varpuset ja pääskyset: Nuorsuomalaisuus ja Nuorsuomalainen puolue 1870-luvulta vuoteen 1918* (Helsinki: SKS, 2000).

Vazsonyi, Nicholas, 'Selling the *Ring*', in John DiGaetani (ed.), *Inside The Ring: Essays on Wagner's Opera Cycle* (Jefferson, NC: McFarland, 2006), pp. 51–68.

Vincent, Andrew, *Theories of the State* (Oxford: Blackwell, 1987).

Viroli, Maurizio, *For Love of Country: An Essay on Patriotism and Nationalism* (Oxford: Clarendon Press, 1995).

Vogt-Schneider, Sabine, *'Staatsoper Unter den Linden' oder 'Deutsche Staatsoper': Auseinandersetzungen um Kulturpolitik und Spielbetrieb in den Jahren zwischen 1945 und 1955* (Berlin: Kuhn, 1998).

Volpe, Michael, 'Reassessing audiences and the "not for us debate"', <http://volpeversion.blogspot.co.uk/2014/09/oberto-conference-paper.html>.

—, 'Why opera really isn't just for toffs', *The Sunday Times, Culture* supplement, 1 June 2014, pp. 6–7.

Wagner, Richard, *Siegfried*, Klavierauszug mit Text von Felix Mottl (Leipzig: C.F. Peters, 1914).

—, 'Religion und Kunst', in *Richard Wagner's Prose Works*, trans. William Ashton Ellis (New York: Broude Brothers, 1966), Vol. 6, pp. 211–85.

—, *Das Rheingold* (Mainz: Schott, 1988).

—, *Das Rheingold*, arr. Timothy Burke (unpublished, 2011).

Wald, Chelsea. 'Revived Echoes Opera Augments Research Results', *New Scientist* <www.newscientist.com/blogs/culturelab/2011/10/revived-echoes-augment-research-results.html>.

Wellcome Trust, <www.wellcome.ac.uk/index.htm>.

Wiegelmann, Lucas, 'Wanderhuren aus dem finsteren Zeitalter der Oper', *Die Welt*, 4 March 2014, <www.welt.de/kultur/buehne-konzert/article125422750/Wanderhuren-aus-dem-finsteren-Zeitalter-der-Oper.html>.

Wiesel, Jörg, 'Re-enactment: Zur Dramaturgie kulturhistorischen Wissens bei Rimini Protokoll und Friedrich Dürrenmatt', in Flavia Caviezel, Beate Florenz, Melanie Franke and Jörg Wiesel (eds), *Forschungsskizzen: Einblicke in Forschungspraktiken an der Hochschule für Gestaltung und Kunst FHNW* (Zurich: Scheidegger and Spiess, 2013), pp. 107–13.

Wilson, Alexandra and Barbara Eichner, 'OBERTO: The Opera Research Unit', <http://arts.brookes.ac.uk/research/oberto>.

Wilson, Stephen, *Information Arts: Intersection of Art, Science, and Technology* (Cambridge, MA: The MIT Press, 2002).

Wintour, Patrick, 'State-backed arts must reach out to public – Harman', *The Guardian*, 6 June 2014, p. 5.

Woodfield, Ian, *Opera and Drama in Eighteenth-Century London: The King's Theatre, Garrick and the Business of Performance* (Cambridge: Cambridge University Press, 2004).

Worldopera, <www.theworldopera.org/wordpress>.

Wright, Matt, 'The Open Sound Control 1.0 Specification, 2002', <http://opensoundcontrol.org/spec-1_0>.

Zalfen, Sarah, *Staats-Opern? Der Wandel von Staatlichkeit und die Opernkrisen in Berlin, London und Paris am Ende des 20. Jahrhunderts* (Vienna: Böhlau, 2011).

—, 'Sera un opéra moderne et populaire', in Deutsch-Französisches Institut (ed.), *Frankreich Jahrbuch 2011: Kulturnation Frankreich? Die kulturelle Dimension des gesellschaftlichen Wandels* (Wiesbaden: VS Verlag für Sozialwissenschaften, 2012), pp. 99–116.

Zalfen, Sarah and Sven Oliver Müller, 'An Interesting Eastern Potentate? Staatsaufführungen für den Schah von Persien in Berlin 1873 und 1967', in

Sven Oliver Müller, Philipp Ther, Jutta Toelle and Gesa zur Nieden (eds), *Die Oper im Wandel der Gesellschaft* (Munich: Oldenbourg, 2010), pp. 277–300.

Zietz, Karyl Lynn, *Opera Companies and Houses of Western Europe, Canada, Australia and New Zealand: A Comprehensive Illustrated Reference* (Jefferson, NC: McFarland, 1999).

Zürn, Michael et al. (eds), *Staatlichkeit im Wandel – Transformations of the State?* TranState Working Papers No. 1 (Bremen: University of Bremen, 2004) <http://econstor.eu/bitstream/10419/28252/1/497808811.PDF>.

Internet

The following websites are useful to the business of opera researcher.

Database of opera performances, opera houses and companies, performers and agents: <http://operabase.com/>.

List of opera companies on the web: <www.fsz.bme.hu/opera/companies.html>.

Search tool (for performances, artists, managers, companies) and statistics database (1996–present): <http://operabase.com/top.cgi?lang=en>.

The National Opera Center, America: <www.operaamerica.org/content/research/quick1011.aspx>.

Index

For Product Safety Concerns and Information please contact our EU
representative GPSR@taylorandfrancis.com
Taylor & Francis Verlag GmbH, Kaufingerstraße 24, 80331 München, Germany

www.ingramcontent.com/pod-product-compliance
Ingram Content Group UK Ltd.
Pitfield, Milton Keynes, MK11 3LW, UK
UKHW021000180425
457613UK00019B/763